20TH-CENTURY COMPOSERS

Maurice Ravel

Maurice Ravel

by Gerald Larner

Φ

to Lynne – for her understanding

Phaidon Press Limited
Regent's Wharf
All Saints Street
London N1 9PA

First published 1996
© 1996 Phaidon Press Limited

ISBN 0 7148 3270 7

A CIP catalogue record for this book is
available from the British Library

Printed in Singapore

Frontispiece, always the
dandy, Maurice Ravel
elegantly portrayed at the
age of eleven by the
Montmartre artist Léon Tanzi

Contents

Preface

Ravel's *Boléro* is one of the most popular pieces of music ever written. His *Pavane pour une Infante défunte* is familiar to millions who might not know its title or the name of its composer. In one form or another his *Daphnis et Chloé* is performed more often in the concert hall than most ballet music, while *La Valse,* the Piano Concerto in G and the orchestral versions of *Ma Mère l'Oye* and *Le Tombeau de Couperin* are essential items in the repertoire. No twentieth-century string quartet is heard more often than Ravel's in F major and few works for mixed chamber ensemble more often than his *Introduction and Allegro.* His *Gaspard de la nuit* is celebrated everywhere as one of the all-time masterpieces of piano writing and *L'Enfant et les Sortilèges* as one of the most delightful of modern operas. His orchestral version of Mussorgsky's *Pictures at an Exhibition* is so well known that the original is in danger of sounding like a piano arrangement.

There are other high-quality Ravel works in all these categories, some of them as good as their more favoured companions, some of them even better. There are also dozens of vocal works with piano, chamber-ensemble or orchestral accompaniment. Although only *Shéhérazade* has transcended the language barrier so successfully as to be as welcome outside France as in it, many of Ravel's songs must be included among the most inspired of their kind. It is one of the aims of this book, while shedding fresh light on the more familiar scores, to demonstrate the interest and the attractions of the others. Every one of them, with the exception of academic exercises and competition entries, is discussed not only in chronological order but also in the context of the composer's personal development.

The advantage of a closely integrated approach to Ravel's life and work is that the two elements are mutually illuminating. At first sight, and even after a long experience of his music, Ravel might strike one as potentially the least rewarding subject for this kind of examination: the works seem to reveal so little of the personality. But that in itself is an important observation and, once it is accepted that one of Ravel's

basic characteristics is his reserve, you are well on the way to understanding him. To hear in his music the sort of man he was, to
discover the sensitivity and vulnerability and compassion in music
where irony is often the more obvious quality, you just have to listen
more carefully.

But you have to know what to listen for. And that is where the
life comes in. The composer's state of mind at a given time, the state
of his health, what he was reading, what he was hearing, how he was
influenced by colleagues and collaborators, such generalities as the
characteristics he inherited or derived from his social background,
the image he cultivated, his religion, his politics, his sexuality … all
these things offer important clues to the motivation and interpretation
of his music. The problem is that Ravel – whose exterior was often
self-defensively cool to those who did not know him and sometimes
even to those who did – was not predisposed to reveal very much of
himself, least of all his sexuality. Fortunately, more and more of his
letters, some of them surprisingly confiding, have become available in
recent years. I have drawn on them extensively and with particularly
frequent recourse to the original French version of the collection
edited by the American Ravel scholar Arbie Orenstein (all the translations are my own). But there are limits to what can be learned about
him even here. And that is where the music comes in.

One of the most revealing statements Ravel ever made – characteristically presented as a paradox – was his answer to the accusation
that his art was artificial: 'Doesn't it ever occur to these people that
I can be "artificial" by nature?' Tracing the development of Ravel's
life and music, in both of which there is so much artifice, is a process
of getting to know a man and a composer for whom sincerity
and integrity were unquestionable and inviolable absolutes. It is a
refreshing – and paradoxical – experience.

Gerald Larner
Alderley Edge, 1996

I

Maurice Ravel on the
harbour wall at St-Jean-de-
Luz with his birthplace in
Ciboure – the tallest of the
houses on the other side of
the Nivelle – in the
background behind him

Look, they say I'm dry at heart. That's wrong.
And you know it. I am Basque. Basques feel
things violently but they say little about it and
only to a few.

Maurice Ravel

Heredity 1875

'The sea bordered with acacias ... and those gentle green hills with little round-trimmed oak trees tumbling down them from top to bottom ... and, above all of this, the Pyrenees with their enchanting mauve colour ... and then the light, which isn't the fierce sunshine of other parts of the South but a more subtle kind of brilliance.' The Basque country in the far southwest corner of France was for Maurice Ravel 'one of the most beautiful places of all'. It was, he liked to say, 'my country'.

It is certainly true that Ravel was born in the Basque country – in Ciboure, a fishing village just across the Nivelle from St-Jean-de-Luz – and that he often returned there. But his attachment to the region was actually more sentimental than instinctive, more acquired in later life than developed through roots set down in childhood. He was under four months old when he was taken to Paris and, holidays and concert tours apart, that is where he stayed. The house where he spent the last sixteen years of his life, a modest building surmounted by a quaint Basque-style conical tower, is actually outside Paris, in Montfort l'Amaury in the Ile-de-France. But it was scarcely more than an hour away from the capital by train and he always kept a pied-à-terre, a hotel room or a studio apartment, near his friends on the edge of Montmartre or close to his brother in Levallois-Perret. He had friends in or near Montfort too, including the writer Colette, who wrote the libretto for one of his operas, and the violinist Hélène Jourdan-Morhange, to whom he was as close as to anyone outside his immediate family. There was also an artistic community, though a not entirely sympathetic one, in St-Jean-de-Luz, which was well placed in a comparatively sheltered inlet in the Bay of Biscay to attract writers and painters and musicians as residents or as regular summer visitors. The centre of his professional life, however – and, at least until the death of his mother in 1917, the centre of his personal life too – was Paris.

Ravel's mother, he said with some pride, was a descendant of 'an old Basque family'. She too was born in Ciboure, in a little house near the parish church of St Vincent in rue Pocalette. This was in 1840, according to most authorities (and according to the Ravel family tombstone), although the age of twenty-eight attributed to her in the document registering the birth of her first son in 1875 seems more likely than thirty-five, particularly since she was to give birth to a second son three years later. Another interesting aspect of the register, where she is identified as 'Marie Delouart, wife of Pierre-Joseph Ravel', is that she is described as 'temporarily resident' at Ciboure – which supports the theory that, following local custom, she had returned to her native village so that her first child would also be born a Basque.

Certainly there were friends and relations in Ciboure to help her, the most prominent among them being Gracieuse Billac who – in the apparent absence of the child's father, and with a tax collector and schoolteacher as witnesses – went to register the birth at the Town Hall. Described as a 'fish merchant, aged 50' in the registration document Gracieuse Billac is generally recognized as Marie's maternal aunt. That is just about all we know about Marie's family background: of her father, apart from a vague hint dropped by the composer that he was a seaman of some kind, a Basque or perhaps a Spaniard, and apart from a local understanding that he was not married to her mother, we know nothing. Anyway, Marie's first son was born at ten in the evening on 7 March 1875 on the third floor of 12 rue du Quai (now 27 quai Maurice Ravel) and six days later he was baptized Joseph-Maurice in the parish church in rue Pocalette, just behind the house on the Quai.

Marie Delouart had married Pierre-Joseph Ravel in Paris in 1873, although they had first met in Spain (in Aranjuez according to most biographers, in Madrid according to Maurice Ravel). Joseph was working as an engineer on the extension of the railway from Madrid to Irún. Marie was in Spain at this particular time as the representative of a Parisian modiste with connections in St-Jean-de-Luz. But, as a photograph taken by a Spanish photographer in about 1870 seems to confirm, she must have been there before. Certainly, she had spent long enough in that country – mainly in Madrid – not only to learn excellent Castilian but also to get to know the popular music of the time, as Manuel de Falla later testified. In fact, it was only when that

severely Spanish composer met Mme Ravel that he was able to
understand what he called the 'subtly authentic Spanishness' of his
French colleague's music. 'Ravel's Spain,' he said,

> *was a Spain experienced through the ideal medium of his mother,*
> *whose exquisite conversation, always in excellent Spanish, so delighted me*
> *when she recalled the years she had spent in Madrid as a girl … Then*
> *I understood how fascinating it must have been for him to listen to*
> *her nostalgic evocations which were intensified, no doubt, by the power*
> *invested in every memory by a song or dance tune inseparably linked*
> *with it.*

There are other reasons why Ravel had such a passionate interest
in Spanish music and why he was so much at ease in alluding to its
idioms in a whole series of works from *Sérénade grotesque*, his earliest
acknowledged work, to *Don Quichotte à Dulcinée*, the very last. But
his mother, to whom he was more than ordinarily devoted – she was
'a veritable cult', said Hélène Jourdan-Morhange with just a hint of
exasperation – must have been the major formative influence in this
respect. It was also at least partly because of its associations with her
that he had such an affection for the Basque country and its culture.
Her recollections of life in and around Ciboure surely had no less an
evocative repertoire of songs to go with them than her memories of
Madrid. 'When I was a baby,' Ravel is reported as saying, 'my mother
used to send me to sleep with Basque and Spanish songs.' He must
have got to know something of the Basque language through her too,
since he had a good understanding of it, if no real fluency in it, and
when he was staying in what he was pleased to call Ziburu (Ciboure)
or Donibane-Lohizune (St-Jean-de-Luz) he enjoyed sending Euskarian
greetings to his friends in Paris.

Looking at the handsome pastel portrait of Marie, which was
executed by her brother-in-law Edouard Ravel in 1885 and which still
hangs on the wall by the composer's piano in the carefully preserved
house at Montfort l'Amaury, it is possible to see how he takes after
her. There is something in the set of the mouth, the prominent nose,
the piercing dark eyes beneath the strongly defined eyebrows … but
the likeness is not immediately obvious. He certainly inherited many
characteristics from her, including her scepticism in matters of religion

The composer's mother, Marie Ravel, from a pastel executed by her brother-in-law, Edouard Ravel, in 1885. It occupied pride of place on the wall nearest the piano in Ravel's studio in Le Belvédère (where it is still to be seen).

– Ravel admiringly quotes her as saying that 'she would rather be in hell with her loved ones than all alone in paradise' – and his friends frequently referred to his typically Basque appearance. It wasn't just the pointed little beard which, among many other facial-hair styles, he sported at one time but also his 'small stature, his wiry build, his agile movements, his alert eye, his firm chin, his elongated cranium.' Some of this you can see in a photograph of him taken in 1902, without beard but with luxuriant moustache and sideburns, sitting elegantly on a rock by the River Nivelle in his Basque beret and incongruously metropolitan white shoes.

There were also those who saw in him a pronounced likeness to the other side of the family, not least in the 'elongated cranium' which is such a striking feature of the portrait of the composer's father painted by Marcellin Desboutin in 1892 and now also on view (and wrongly

After their departure to Paris, the Ravel family did not return to the Basque country until (at the latest) 1902 – when the composer was photographed on the bank of the River Nivelle, half-acclimatized in Basque beret and Parisian shoes.

dated) in Le Belvédère at Montfort l'Amaury. And there was nothing remotely Basque about Pierre-Joseph Ravel. He came from Versoix on Lake Geneva in Switzerland – which, of course, is the origin of Stravinsky's characteristically pithy but not entirely helpful description of Maurice Ravel as 'the most perfect of Swiss watchmakers'. Pierre-Joseph's own father was born not in Switzerland but in Collonges-sous-Salève (in what is now the French département of Haute-Savoie) and was naturalized Swiss only in 1834, fourteen years after he settled in Versoix and two years after the birth of the first of his five children. Pierre-Joseph's mother, on the other hand, was authentic Swiss and it was she who, presumably by inheritance, brought a grocery business into the Ravel family in Versoix. There is an attractive story that while the oldest of their children, Pierre-Joseph, applied himself to inventing a machine to simplify the making of paper bags for the shop, the youngest, Jean-Edouard, amused himself by decorating the walls with portraits of its most important customers. Whatever the truth of that, Joseph Ravel did go on to become a distinguished engineer and Edouard a successful portrait painter.

Although Edouard stayed in Switzerland – he died in Geneva in 1920 – Joseph clearly felt that there was no future for him there. He obtained visas to travel to France as an engineer in 1857 and 1859 and to Spain in 1861. He must have settled in Paris some time before 1868 because that was the year in which he patented in that city his great invention, 'a steam generator heated by mineral oils and applicable to locomotion on ordinary roads.' He created, in fact, an early form of automobile based on the same principle as the contemporary railway engine except that the water was heated by burning oil rather than coal. Unfortunately, although the internal-combustion engine seemed a non-starter at that time, Joseph Ravel had backed the wrong kind of horse-power.

Worse still, Joseph Ravel housed his motor-driven carriage just outside the city wall at Saint-Ouen, the fortifications of which naturally became a focus of attention for the Prussian gunners during the siege of Paris in 1870. Destroyed by an enemy shell, apparently, the historic vehicle disappeared without trace. With it disappeared the inventor's fortune, or so it is reasonable to assume from his immediate departure to work on the extension of the railway in Spain. It is also reasonable to assume that what brought him back to Paris in 1873, with Marie Delouart as his fiancée, was a legacy from his father, who had died in Versoix a few months earlier.

Joseph Ravel's enthusiasm for the automobile was not diminished by his early misfortunes. He created a really useful two-stroke internal-combustion engine and a spectacular though rather less useful circus-act called the Whirlwind of Death, which featured a car rolling at speed off the end of a steep ramp and turning a complete somersault before landing on its wheels again. The Whirlwind of Death was seen at the Casino de Paris and at Barnum & Bailey's when Joseph and his younger son Edouard took it to the USA in 1903. According to American sources, the act went disastrously wrong on one occasion, killing the unfortunate driver. However that may be, Joseph Ravel was successful enough to set up a manufacturing business in the industrial suburb of Levallois-Perret where, after a bewildering series of house-moves in and out of the Montmartre area, he finally installed himself and his family in 1905.

If Edouard, who worked with his father and carried on in the same line of business at Levallois after his death, was Joseph's favourite son – while Maurice had closer bonds with his mother – this does not mean that the Ravel family was anything but lovingly united and mutually supportive. Nor does it mean that Joseph Ravel was unsympathetic to his older son's musical aspirations: on the contrary, he had studied music as a boy and, as the composer himself observed, 'being far more expert in the art than most amateurs, he was able to develop

my taste and stimulate my enthusiasm from an early age.' Maurice
Ravel took a reciprocal interest in the world of manufacturing represented by his father. He was thrilled by fine craftsmanship, fascinated
by machines, inspired by the activity of a factory at work, awed by the
grandeur of the industrial landscape. The terminology of motoring he
absorbed into his own vocabulary.

He could be as lyrical about the beauty of Switzerland, moreover,
as about that of the Basque country, if not with the same proprietary
sentiment. Writing to his friend and pupil Maurice Delage from
Hermance on Lake Geneva, where he had taken his father to recuperate after a stroke in 1906, he said,

*Here I am, installed in Switzerland, and I must say I no longer miss
the sea so much. It's not quite the same here but it's no worse for that.
The lake sometimes astonishes me by reminding me of the Mediterranean,
although the shores are not so grey. The colours are intense and paradoxical with illusory shadings. And then the boats with their shining
sails and ancient shapes. And above all the surprisingly pure and
gentle climate.*

The Desboutin portrait of Joseph Ravel is interesting not only
for its subject's 'elongated cranium' but also for the Old Testament
prophet the artist seems to have seen in him. In fact, there was a
theory at one time put about in American newspapers that Ravel was
of Jewish descent – partly on the ground that Ravel is not unknown as
a Jewish name (deriving from *Rabbele* or 'little Rabbi') and partly on
the ground that he arranged three Jewish songs, including *Kaddisch*,
which is the one religious text he set to music. It is true that he had
many Jewish friends, some of them very close to him. It is also true
that he was noted for his kindness to the Jewish refugee musicians
who came his way from Germany in the early years of the Hitler
regime. The fact is, however, that the family name in Collonges-sous-
Salève in the eighteenth century could be written as Ravex or Ravet
or Ravez (all pronounced in the same way) and that it subsequently
became Ravel through misunderstandings in official documents.
The composer's own comment was that, although he would be happy
to be associated in this way with Mendelssohn, one of his favourite
composers, 'not one of my ancestors was in fact Jewish.' A few months

The composer's father, Joseph Ravel, from a painting exhibited by Marcellin Desboutin in 1892. It occupied a prominent position in the studio in Le Belvédère (where it is still to be seen).

before his death a similar disclaimer was made on his behalf by his publisher who, fearing perhaps that his music would be banned in Nazi Germany, insisted on having Ravel's name removed from a racist directory of Jewish musicians, *Judentum und Musik*, published in Munich in 1936.

The question of racial identity was important to Ravel not because he had any objection to being Jewish or Swiss or Savoyard but because he was determined to be Basque. Logically perhaps, he should have inclined towards Switzerland. The landscape round Lake Geneva, where the Ravel family regularly took their holidays, would have been more familiar in his formative years than any in the Basque country. He had more relations in and around Versoix than in Ciboure or St-Jean-de-Luz, at least as far as he was aware, and he certainly had more in common with them: he was fascinated to find, for example, that he had a Swiss cousin in the watch-making business who also played violin in a theatre in Geneva. Much of his character, including important aspects of his creative personality, he clearly inherited from his Swiss-French father – above all the pride in precision craftsmanship but also the inventor's delight in producing something totally new and unexpected, even the need to test his technique in high-risk situations: Maurice Ravel's *Boléro* is the composer's spectacular equivalent to Joseph Ravel's Whirlwind of Death.

Even so, in spite of all the affection he had for his father and all he owed him, the composer insisted on being Basque. One of the major virtues regularly cited by his friends, which was his complete honesty, he attributed to the Basque in him. One of his major problems, as others saw it, which was his apparent emotional coldness, he explained in the same way: 'Look,' he confided to Jacques de Zogheb, a neighbour and good friend at Montfort l'Amaury, 'they say I'm dry at heart. That's wrong. And you know it. I am Basque. Basques feel things violently but they say little about it and only to a few.' Whatever Basque credentials he wasn't born with, or which he didn't grow up with, he acquired later.

The view from Ciboure, looking over the bright blue fishing boats bobbing in the harbour towards the historic Maison de l'Infante and the place Louis-XIV in St-Jean-de-Luz, was one that Ravel learned to love in his maturity. There are photographs of him sitting on the sea wall at St-Jean-de-Luz carefully positioned so that the handsome Dutch-style house where he was born, the tallest on the Quai on the other side of the Nivelle, would be in the picture behind him. From Luz, as he called it, he sent his friends picture-postcards of the Church of St John the Baptist, where Louis XIV married the Spanish Infanta in 1660, and he stayed with family friends in a house just opposite the church in rue Gambetta, or just round the corner in rue Tourasse, or on the place Louis-XIV. He enjoyed the spicy food of the region, enthused about its traditional music and dancing, and developed a passion for pelota, the local ball game. Accompanied by his mother, who joined him on many of his trips outside Paris up to 1914, he set out to synthesize the Basque childhood he was deprived of when he was taken to Paris in June 1875.

2

Maurice Ravel at the age
of four

*Those machines fascinated me ... It was their
clicking and roaring, which, with the Spanish
folk songs sung to me at night-time as a*
berceuse *by my mother, formed my first
instruction in music!*

Maurice Ravel

Environment 1875–89

When Maurice Ravel joined the two million or so other inhabitants
of the French capital in 1875 the layout of the central parts of Paris –
after the ruthlessly comprehensive and epoch-making exercise in town-
planning carried out by Baron Haussmann in the 1860s – was much
the same as it is now. The major difference was that two of the most
familiar of present-day Parisian landmarks were still to make their
appearance: on the Left Bank, the Tour Eiffel would be ready only just
in time for the opening of the Exposition Universelle, on the centenary
of the Revolution in 1889; on the Right Bank, at the top of the hill in
Montmartre, building work on the Basilica of the Sacré Coeur,
intended as a symbol of national repentance after the humili-ating end
to the Franco-Prussian War and the horrors of the Commune in 1871,
had just been started but would not be finished until 1910.

Another landmark Montmartre was still to acquire when the Ravels
settled there – a monument almost as famous as the Sacré Coeur but
rather less elevated – was the Moulin Rouge, which opened as a dance
hall on the place Blanche in 1889. In fact, Montmartre in the 1870s
was only just beginning to develop as the centre of entertainment it
was so notoriously to become by the turn of the century. By the time
of the Exposition Universelle most of the celebrated network of
popular dance halls and artistic cabarets was in place, ready to benefit
from the festival atmosphere and the influx of visitors in search of
more or less sophisticated recreation.

When the Moulin Rouge opened for business – on a site previously
occupied not, as legend has it, by an old windmill but by another
dance hall – it was in direct competition with the Elysée Montmartre
and the Boule Noire, both on the boulevard Rochechouart. Near the
top of the hill, known locally as the 'Butte', there was the Moulin de
la Galette, which really had been a flour mill in the distant past but
which, by the time the Ravel family settled in Montmartre, had long
been the popular dance hall so lyrically celebrated by Auguste Renoir
in 1876. There was a thriving café life too. Edouard Manet and like-

minded artistic friends had just deserted the Café Guerbois for the Café de la Nouvelle Athènes, which was not far from similarly busy establishments such as Wepler, Boivin, and Père Lathuile. With the gregarious Marcellin Desboutin prominently installed and ready to engage in conversation, the Nouvelle Athènes would be a congenial meeting place not only for painters but also for writers like Émile Zola and Villiers de l'Isle-Adam and Manet's favourite composer, Emmanuel Chabrier.

Then, in 1881, Rodolphe Salis opened the first of Montmartre's *cabarets artistiques*, Le Chat Noir, at 84 boulevard Rochechouart. It was such a timely inspiration that within three years the original premises, which had been an auxiliary post office, proved to be too cramped and Salis reopened the cabaret in more spacious and more luxurious surroundings in a house recently vacated by the artist Alfred Stevens in rue de Laval. Although the move gave one of his star chansonniers, Aristide Bruant, the chance to open his own cabaret on the spot where the original Chat Noir had been, it also gave Salis the space to operate his famous shadow theatre, which ensured the fascinated attendance of the artistic community as well as more fashionable society. If Bruant's Le Mirliton was to acquire the more exciting reputation – in spite of the discomfort of the place, the

Above, one of several posters designed by Henri de Toulouse-Lautrec for the Montmartre cabaret singer Aristide Bruant. The basic image was conceived by the artist in 1892.
Right, the shadow theatre at Le Chat Noir in 1886, shortly after the move to rue de Laval. The founder of the cabaret, Rodolphe Salis, is delivering a commentary on the play from just below the screen and Emile Zola, Alphonse Daudet and Ferdinand de Lesseps are among the clientèle.

anything but polite welcome extended to its clients, and the street-wise bitterness of the songs – its success, like that of the Moulin Rouge, was due not least to the immensely effective poster designs commissioned from Toulouse-Lautrec. Rodolphe Salis could justly claim that he had 'created Montmartre' but it was Lautrec who, working in his studio there from 1884 until not long before his death in 1901, created its image.

Other, less widespread images by Lautrec, notably his series of studies of women employed in various Parisian brothels, indicate that trade behind the scenes in and around Montmartre extended far beyond the comparatively innocent employment – under the watchful eyes of the censor – of Jane Avril and such evocatively named companions as La Goulue, La Sauterelle and Nini Pattes en l'Air, as dancers on the floor of the Moulin Rouge and the Elysée Montmartre. Even so, Pigalle at that time was far from the cynical centre of the sex industry which it is now. The weekly market of laundry girls from the

A rehearsal at the Moulin Rouge in 1896: as well as the famous dance hall, there was also an outdoor theatre for café-concert and other entertainments in the garden behind the building. The elephant décor was salvaged from the Exposition Universelle.

Latin Quarter selling themselves as artists' models on place Pigalle –
just outside the apartment inhabited by the Ravels between 1886 and
1896 – though an unedifying spectacle, did not amount to wholesale
exploitation. But the nineties were undeniably naughty, the eighties
scarcely less so: the street life observed by Ravel in his teenage years in
Montmartre must inevitably have influenced his perception of women
and must surely have been a factor in forming the contradictory
nature of his own sexuality.

In spite of the changes in the atmosphere and the commerce of the
place in the intervening hundred years or so, the geography of the
streets in the area south of the Butte remains the same. It is not difficult to trace the Ravel family's many house-moves in the ninth
arrondissement, following them from one address to the next on the
lower part of the hill south of the boulevard de Clichy – from rue des
Martyrs to rue de Laval (now Victor-Massé) to rue Pigalle and, after a
singular diversion to the Left Bank, to rue Eugène-Fromentin and rue
de Douai. For the most part substantial examples of the multi-storey
Second-Empire apartment building, the houses are still standing, the
ornate wrought-iron railings of their regularly spaced balconies usually
still in place and the beaux-arts decorative moulding still plainly pro-
filed above the doors and under the windows.

The attraction of this of Montmartre in the late sixties and
seventies was that, after the clearance of the slums and the re-devel-
opment of the area south of the Boulevard de Clichy and the
Boulevard Rochechouart, it was a reasonably cheap, comparatively
quiet, convenient and not unstylish place to live. In 1869, when the
recently married Georges Bizet rented an apartment at 22 rue de
Douai, four doors away from where the Russian poet Ivan Turgenev
was already established with the singer Pauline Viardot, he described
the building in terms which were ironic but not unaffectionate: 'a
façade covered with columns, scrolls, and angels so that it looks like
the work of a delirious mason who has passed through Rome.'
Favoured by writers, musicians, artists and, of course, their models,
this part of Montmartre was certainly bohemian but it was
still respectable.

When the Ravels arrived at 40 rue des Martyrs, halfway down the
street running southwards from Pigalle towards the church of Notre
Dame de Lorette, Bizet had just died, three months after the first

performance of *Carmen*. But Gabriel Fauré, who was to be Maurice Ravel's most distinguished teacher at the Conservatoire, was living just on the other side of the rue de Clichy in rue de Parme. He would soon be moving from there to the Batignolles, which is no more than a few hundred metres away, to share an apartment with fellow composer André Messager in rue Mosnier – a handsome street now called rue de Berne but immortalized under its former name in Manet's painting of 1878.

Emmanuel Chabrier, who was a great friend of Edouard Manet, the subject of two of his portraits and the first owner of one of his greatest paintings, *Un Bar aux Folies Bergère* – and who was to be one of the major influences on Ravel's development as a composer – had moved to rue Mosnier on his marriage in 1873 and was to retain a home in the Montmartre area until his death in 1894. Erik Satie, who was to be another major non-academic influence, was not yet on the scene but would soon be attracted there by the congenial atmosphere of the Chat Noir, conducting Salis's band until he fell out with him, and would be induced to stay in the area by the opportunity to supplement his meagre income as 'second pianist' at the Auberge du Clou. Claude Debussy, who was to be both an inspiration and, at least as far as the press was concerned, a rival to Maurice Ravel, frequented these places too and made a point of befriending Satie, whose eccentric genius he recognized at an early stage, long before he had any kind of reputation as a composer.

So, with an important concert hall, the Salle Pleyel, and the Conservatoire in the same arrondissement (both institutions have moved since then) Ravel grew up in an area and in a community which were not unexciting for a child with musical ambitions. And Maurice Ravel never had any other kind of ambition or, it seems, any other kind of formal education. 'Even as a small child I was sensitive to music – all kinds of music,' he says in a brief but useful autobiographical sketch dictated to his pupil Roland-Manuel in 1928. 'I began to study piano at the age of about six,' he recalls and, though he goes on to detail further stages in his musical education, there is no record here or anywhere else of ordinary schooling. By 1883 secular primary education became compulsory in France for all children over the age of six but not, apparently, for Maurice Ravel. Perhaps his father –

Emmanuel Chabrier

A L'AMI CHABRIER
E. DETAILLE

Emmanuel Chabrier
improvising at the piano as
drawn by Edouard Detaille
in 1873 (and illustrated on
the front cover of the *Revue
Illustrée* on 15 June 1887)

rather than his mother, who was scarcely literate in French – assumed the responsibility for his general education. He also, as Ravel later recalled, took him as a small boy to the factories where he worked: 'Those machines fascinated me ... It was their clicking and roaring, which, with the Spanish folk songs sung to me at night-time as a *berceuse* by my mother, formed my first instruction in music!'

A series of remarkably relaxed family photographs taken in about 1885 (a particularly affectionate one shows Joseph Ravel with his arms round his two sons, the seven-year-old Edouard lolling on his knee and the ten-year-old Maurice with his shoulder-length hair standing leaning against him, his legs elegantly crossed) suggest that this was a close and indulgent family. If this is true and if Maurice really did not attend school, the prominently childish aspect of the adult Maurice Ravel – who so readily identified with children, who loved toys and fairy tales as much as they did, and who never quite matured emotionally – is easier to understand. He was not in the least embarrassed by this side of his personality, incidentally: he would happily demonstrate his mechanical toys to anyone who would take an interest in them. He did all he could, on the other hand, to disguise or compensate for his peculiarly complementary failure to grow up physically: as an adult he was scarcely more than 5 ft 3 ins in height (the famously stunted Toulouse-Lautrec was much the same size) and he was painfully sensitive about such a shortcoming.

Maurice Ravel at the age of six

Both Maurice and Edouard were musically gifted but it was Maurice who was given the professional training, beginning piano lessons with a recognized teacher a few weeks after his seventh birthday. Henry Ghys, composer of a popular *Air Louis XIII* (which featured in Fritz Kreisler's repertoire of encores at one time), noted in his diary for 31 May 1882: 'Today I start a little pupil, Maurice Ravel, who seems intelligent.' It is likely that Maurice had learned something of the rudiments of music somewhat earlier than that, presumably from his father: certainly, as we know from a copy of the *Air Louis XIII* 'transcribed specially for four hands for his little pupil Maurice Ravel by his teacher Henry Ghys, Paris, August 30, 1882' and carefully preserved in Ravel's library at Montfort l'Amaury, Ghys felt he was capable of playing more than the usual beginners' stuff when they were no more than three months into their lessons.

Ravel was never a very diligent piano pupil, even as a student at the Conservatoire, but far from bullying him into practising at this early stage his parents payed him six sous for every half hour he put in – which compares not at all badly with the fifty centimes his teacher received for the same amount of tuition. He apparently needed no such inducement to work when, in 1887, he started studying harmony, counterpoint and composition. His first teacher in these subjects was Charles-René, a pupil and protégé of Léo Delibes and himself expert enough to have twice come second in the Prix de Rome – that much

abused but none the less hotly disputed competition organized by the
the Institut de France. Charles-René believed in getting his students
to work on compositions of their own, as a stimulus to studying the
theory, and in the young Maurice Ravel – who wrote him a sonata
movement and variations on themes by Grieg and Schumann – he
found a willing pupil. Decades later, shortly after the first performance
of *Daphnis et Chloé*, Charles-René recalled those 'really interesting'
early pieces and drew attention to the continuity of Ravel's development since then: 'his conception of music,' he wrote, 'is natural to
him and not, as with so many others, the result of effort.' It is an
interesting comment, bearing in mind that the criticism most com-
monly levelled at Ravel is based on a directly opposite point of view.

Ravel himself considered his composing career to have started at
this point – 'Since I was twelve years old and until now, at the age of
fifty, I have done nothing but compose', he is quoted as saying in an
interview in a Swedish newspaper in 1926. Whether he knew it at that

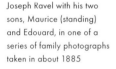

Joseph Ravel with his two
sons, Maurice (standing)
and Edouard, in one of a
series of family photographs
taken in about 1885

time or not, thanks to Charles-René, he had found his vocation. He continued his piano studies, of course, and in 1888 accelerated them by taking on two new courses at the same time. One was with a pupil of Chopin, Émile Descombes, who had the political advantage of a teaching post at the Conservatoire (where Erik Satie had been one of his students); the other, at the Cours Schaller – a specialist establishment for budding virtuosi in rue Geoffroi-Marie, not far from the Conservatoire – was important to him not so much for the instruction he received there as for a formative friendship with one of his fellow pupils.

The Ravel family had moved house twice by now. After 40 rue des Martyrs their next address, from 1880 to 1886, was 29 rue de Laval (now Victor Massé) in the same street as the enlarged and sophisticated version of the Chat Noir cabaret. They then moved to 73 rue Pigalle, not far from place Pigalle, which was so situated in relation to rue Geoffroi-Marie as to make it a convenient place for Ricardo Viñes and his mother to call on the way to or from the Cours Schaller. They probably got to know each other in the first place because Mme Viñes, who had only recently brought her talented son from Spain to Paris to further his musical education, found in Mme Ravel someone she could talk to in Spanish. 'In the evening we went for the first time to the home of the boy with long hair who is called Mauricio, 73 rue Pigalle on the fifth floor,' says the diary of the thirteen-year-old Ricardo Viñes on 23 November 1888. The beginning of a long friendship and professional relationship, this first of many visits to rue Pigalle marked a new stage in Ravel's artistic development.

Though only a few days older than Ravel, Viñes was more advanced as a pianist – he had won a first prize at the Barcelona Conservatoire at an exceptionally early age – and, with his intense intellectual curiosity, knew more of the repertoire. Learning to speak French remarkably quickly, he was to join his friend in an orgy of reading, of books exchanged, books borrowed, books which failed to return. Most of it was by contemporary French writers of the decadent tendency, above all the 'damned poets' as Paul Verlaine identified them in his study of 1884, although they found much to interest them too in Diderot's and Condillac's discussions of art and the process of creation. For Ravel, whose personal style, both in his work and his way of life, was still developing, it was an important experience.

A more immediate cultural experience was the Exposition Universelle of 1889. The exhibition was memorable for the Ravel family in general because of the gold medal awarded to Uncle Edouard, Joseph's artist brother from Geneva, and for Maurice in particular because of the unprecedented variety of folk music that was to be heard there, authentically performed by groups from the various countries represented. Spanish music he knew about but the exotic sounds from China and southeast Asia, particularly the gamelan orchestra which he and Viñes heard in the Javanese Village on the Esplanade des Invalides, were just as fascinating for him as they more famously were for Claude Debussy. He also attended at least one of the two concerts of Russian orchestral music conducted by Rimsky-Korsakov, in the notoriously reverberant acoustic of the Trocadéro, just on the other side of the river from the exhibition site on the Champ de Mars. As Rimsky-Korsakov recorded in his diary, while recalling the impression made on him by the Hungarian and Algerian folk musicians at the exhibition, there was no great demand for Russian music in Paris at this time. For Ravel, on the other hand, these programmes of music by Balakirev, Borodin, Mussorgsky and Rimsky-Korsakov himself were a revelation.

Ravel and Viñes were working hard at the keyboard at this time, since they were both about to compete for entry into the Paris Conservatoire. When he came to play a Chopin concerto in the

Ricardo Viñes (far left) and Maurice Ravel (far right) were to remain good friends for many years. They are photographed here in about 1907 with their 'Apache' associate Abbé Léonce Petit (seated), the pianist Jane Mortier and Robert Mortier.

Conservatoire auditions, however, Ravel was selected for a place only in the preparatory class, whereas Viñes was considered advanced enough to miss out that stage and to go straight on to higher things. Since forty-seven candidates had been competing for nineteen places – all of them free, incidentally – it was a satisfactory result. But only the best was good enough for Ravel and it could be that this decision of the admissions panel caused the first of the many resentments which resulted sixteen years later in his public confrontation with the reactionary forces of the Conservatoire establishment and a considerable upheaval in its administration.

3

A pencil drawing by Jacques
Baugnies of Maurice Ravel
in about 1889 when he
frequented the salon of Mme
René de Saint-Marceaux

*Dandyism is not an immoderate interest in
dressing-up and in material elegance. In the
perfect dandy these things are only a symbol
of the aristocratic superiority of his mind.*

Charles Baudelaire

Conservatoire 1889-99

Ravel worked hard enough in Joseph Anthiôme's preparatory class at
the Conservatoire to catch up with Viñes within two years and to
join him in Charles de Bériot's advanced class in 1891. At the same
time he started attending the harmony course of Charles Pessard
who, though a competent composer and Prix de Rome winner, was
evidently neither as imaginative nor as encouraging as Charles-René
had been. He found his pupil 'very gifted' but also 'somewhat heedless' about his work. In fact, Ravel was so heedless in this subject – or
so lacking in encouragement – that, in spite of his gifts, he failed to
win a prize in three years of harmony examinations and, in accordance
with Conservatoire rules, he was obliged to leave the class.

   He had a better relationship with his piano teacher who – if only
by association with his famous violinist father Charles-Auguste de
Bériot, his mother, the legendary Maria Malibran, and her scarcely less
legendary sister Pauline Viardot – was probably the more interesting
personality. He was certainly the more sympathetic musician and, in
spite of Ravel's tendency not to work hard enough at the piano, Bériot
believed in him: 'You are a criminal,' he told him in 1894, 'you ought
to be the first in the class and you are the last.' It was Viñes who
became the star pupil whereas Ravel, who had no more success in
the piano competitions than he had in the harmony competitions,
was eventually forced out of Bériot's class in July 1895. Choosing not
to exercise his right to attend alternative courses, he left the
Conservatoire for what turned out to be a period of three years of
reflection, of work mainly on his own, and of stimulating friendship
with Viñes.

   The fact is that he had been taking the wrong course. When he
first entered the Conservatoire at the age of fourteen Ravel could
reasonably look forward to growing to at least average height. When
he left the piano class at the age of twenty he knew he would not and,
moreover, that his hands would remain proportionately undersized.
His thumbs, which were uncommonly flexible and almost as long as

his index fingers, were some compensation in this respect but by no means the answer to every technical problem caused by his limited span. It must have been quite clear to him that he would never be able to compete with such brilliantly gifted fellow-pupils as Ricardo Viñes, Alfred Cortot and Marguerite Long – all of whom, incidentally, were later to become distinguished performers of his piano music. We know he didn't give up hope entirely at this stage because, prompted by Viñes perhaps, he took lessons with the Spanish pianist Santiago Riera for as long as two years after leaving the Conservatoire. But the truth was, as Viñes so perceptively pointed out, that 'Ravel didn't love the piano so much as he loved music.'

While he had not increased much in physical stature during his teenage years at the Conservatoire, in intellectual stature he had developed considerably. He might not have had a literary education but he had the enthusiasm of Viñes to stimulate him and the precious example of des Esseintes, the studiously decadent central figure of Joris-Karl Huysmans's novel *A Rebours,* to guide him through a rarefied course in artistic taste. Although he liked nothing else by Huysmans, Ravel confessed in later life that *A Rebours* had 'dazzled my early youth'. It is uncanny how much of his future artistic and personal development is foreshadowed in *A Rebours.* The religiosity of des Esseintes he rejected but his tastes in modern literature – for, among others, Edgar Allan Poe, Charles Baudelaire, Aloysius Bertrand, Paul Verlaine, Stéphane Mallarmé – he wholeheartedly adopted. The last three of those writers were a direct inspiration and all the others influenced him in one way or another. Baudelaire's dictum in *L'Art romantique* that 'inspiration is decidedly the sister of daily work' became one of his own. He had as little faith in the 'fine frenzy' of artistic creation as Edgar Allan Poe, whose *Philosophy of Composition* (in Baudelaire's admirable and widely read translation) impressed him profoundly, even though he rarely aspired to the degree of creative cynicism boasted by that particular text.

In des Esseintes's clockwork fish tangled in artificial weed there is a parallel to the mechanical toys which Ravel so joyfully collected. Just as des Esseintes valued the skilful imitation as highly as the real thing, in the belief that artifice is the distinctive mark of man's genius, so did Ravel, who delighted in the song of the clockwork nightingale on his piano at Le Belvédère. Des Esseintes's Fontenay-aux-Roses was Ravel's

Montfort l'Amaury, his refuge from Paris in the Ile-de-France, where he could create an environment according to his own taste, however eccentric it might seem to outsiders. Unlike des Esseintes, he was not in the least misanthropic, nor misogynist, and he was certainly not malevolent towards children. He was no snob either, although in his student days he did gain a reputation for adopting a superior intellectual attitude: Alfred Cortot remembered him as 'a deliberately sarcastic young man, argumentative and a little distant, who read Mallarmé and associated with Erik Satie.'

He set himself apart from his contemporaries also by extending his natural taste for personal elegance towards the cult of dandyism preached by des Esseintes in *A Rebours*. In his early twenties he was not yet the full-scale exquisite – although he wore his hair moderately long, he sported neither the carefully shaped moustache nor the beard which were soon to be such conspicuous features of his appearance – but he was taking even more care than before with the style and cut of his clothes and the overall harmony of the ensemble. As we know from an elegantly posed full-length portrait of Ravel painted by Léon Tanzi in 1886, he was not indifferent to his image even at the age of eleven. This more recent development was partly a statement of an aesthetic attitude and partly, one suspects, a compensation for his small stature. Certainly, though he would eventually abandon the extravagant extremes, along with the facial hair, he remained an impeccable and style-conscious dresser, the costume always appropriate to the occasion, for the rest of his life.

At the same time there had been rapid developments in Ravel's musical interests, not all of them ideally compatible with the acquisition of a virtuoso piano technique and the learning of respect for the rules of academic harmony and counterpoint. It was perfectly healthy from the keyboard point of view that Ravel and Viñes should exercise themselves for hours on piano duets and piano-duet arrangements of everything they could lay their hands on; and if they were by, say, Mozart, Mendelssohn or Weber – all of whom, but Mozart above all, were to remain among Ravel's favourite composers – no harm would be done to harmonic propriety. But they also had an exotic taste for the Russian 'Mighty Handful' – Rimsky-Korsakov, Balakirev, and Borodin in particular – whose music was as distant from Conservatoire traditions as that of the two French composers they were just beginning to discover, Emmanuel Chabrier and Erik Satie. More dangerous still, as a Viñes diary entry for 15 August 1892 records, they were making their own musical experiments: 'We didn't go out all day but enjoyed ourselves, almost all the time at the piano, trying out new chords and playing over our ideas.'

On that same day, while Edouard – Maurice's technically minded younger brother – went to an exhibition of bicycles on the Champ de Mars, Viñes records, 'we went out on to the balcony and looked at various constellations.' From the balcony on the fifth floor of 73 rue Pigalle, they would have had a good view not only of the stars above but also of place Pigalle below. Even if they were not in a position to see exactly what was going on in the Rat Mort, the nearby restaurant where Toulouse-Lautrec enjoyed sketching the raffish clientele, or in the Nouvelle Athènes, where painters and writers still regularly gathered, their observations of night-life on the streets around them must have been an interesting diversion.

Ravel's experience of cabaret and café life in Montmartre was not long restricted to observing it from the outside, as Dumitriu Kiriac, one of his contemporaries at the Conservatoire, confirmed when he wrote to Ravel in 1925 to remind him of their friendship of three decades earlier: 'I remember the avenue Trudaine, our long nocturnal conversations in the Auberge du Clou and at the Café de Clichy.' In the same letter Kiriac also recalled 'our Saturday meetings at Molard's in Montparnasse.' So, it seems, Ravel made more than occasional contact with that comparatively small but turbulent artistic community centred on the home of William Molard, civil servant by profession and composer by reputation, in the Latin Quarter on the other side of the Seine. Molard and his Norwegian sculptor wife, Ida Ericson, occupied the ground-floor apartment at 6 rue Vercingétorix in the same building where, between 1893 and 1895, Paul Gauguin rented his studio and held his famous Thursday soirées. Whatever Ravel might have learned from Molard's apparently unconventional ideas on music – and according to Florent Schmitt, who was a contemporary of both of them at the Conservatoire, it was more than a little – he could scarcely have failed to find stimulating company in his circle.

Molard being a composer more in theory than in practice, more a talker than a creator – his life's work, inspired by Shakespeare's *Hamlet,* was apparently never put into a performable state – the only

Opposite, Renoir's Le Bal au Moulin de la Galette; right, Frederick Delius, the English composer who befriended Ravel in Paris in the 1890s and whose music had a perceptible influence on Ravel's 1897 Violin Sonata; *far right,* the Norwegian composer Edvard Grieg, who had an important influence on the development of French music round the turn of the century, is pictured with his wife a few years before Ravel met him in Paris.

real composer in the Latin Quarter circle was 'le grand anglais', Frederick Delius, who at this time had an apartment not far away in rue du Couëdic. As is surprisingly but unmistakably clear from Ravel's one-movement Violin Sonata of 1897, Delius made a more than merely passing impression on his younger French colleague. United by a common interest in all things Scandinavian, the Molard circle also extended its hospitality to, among other artists and writers, Edvard Munch and August Strindberg and to the Norwegian composers Edvard Grieg and Christian Sinding whenever they came to Paris. When Grieg visited 6 rue Vercingétorix in 1894, Ravel was invited to meet him and, according to one account, he took the opportunity on that occasion to play one of Grieg's Norwegian Dances: 'No, young man, not like that at all. Much more rhythm.' Grieg is reported as saying, 'It's a folk dance, a peasant dance.' The experience did not diminish Ravel's admiration for Grieg or his susceptibility to his music. When Delius offered the provocative opinion that 'modern French music is quite simply Grieg, plus the third act of *Tristan*,' Ravel agreed with him: 'It's true. We are always unfair to Grieg.'

But Ravel's two greatest composer-heroes, Erik Satie and
Emmanuel Chabrier, were to be found nearer home in Montmartre
and it was there that he got to know both of them personally,
Chabrier scarcely at all but Satie quite well. Satie, who had studied at
the Paris Conservatoire a decade earlier than Ravel and had got
even less out of it – 'he was the laziest student in the Conservatoire,'
according to his piano teacher – was earning a living as 'second
pianist' at the Auberge du Clou, a few yards away from Chabrier's
home in the avenue Trudaine. Ravel's harmony teacher at the
Conservatoire, Charles Pessard, regarded Satie as 'a complete lunatic' –
an opinion which made him all the more interesting to the young
musicians who were aware of him. He was an eccentric, certainly, but
he was no lunatic. A great wit and greater self-publicist, a stylish
entertainer at the piano in cabaret and café-concert, he was also the
composer of four remarkably progressive sets of piano pieces – the
Ogives, the *Sarabandes,* the *Gymnopédies,* and the *Gnossiennes* – which,
though known only to connoisseurs at this time, were a revelation
of music liberated, without recourse to Wagner or any source other
than his own analytical mind, from the limitations imposed by
academic rules. Among the early Satie connoisseurs were Debussy,
Schmitt and Ravel, the last of whom was entertaining his fellow-
students in Pessard's harmony class with the *Gymnopédies* while their
teacher was still insisting that Satie 'has never done anything.'

Through Marcellin Desboutin – who had exhibited his portrait,
Joseph Ravel ingénieur, in 1892 and who was now at work on his *Erik
Satie* – Joseph Ravel introduced his son to Satie in the Café Nouvelle
Athènes some time in the following year. Nothing is recorded of their
conversation but we do know, from a reference to Ravel – 'a kind
of Debussy but more brilliant' – in a letter Satie wrote to his brother
nearly twenty years later, that the younger composer was always conscious of his debt to him: 'Every time he sees me he swears how
much he owes me. That's all right by me.' Satie's benevolence towards
Ravel – it wasn't to last, unfortunately – is reflected in the dedication
of the second of the *Sarabandes* on their publication in 1911, while
Ravel's gratitude to Satie – which did last, in spite of everything – is
reflected in the reciprocal dedication of the last of the *Poèmes de
Stéphane Mallarmé* in 1913.

The Studio of Erik Satie at Montmartre 1890, an oil painting by Santiago Rusiñol. The composer is pictured in the small room he rented 'out of reach of his creditors' on the second floor at 6 rue Cortot.

Emmanuel Chabrier, who cared little more than Satie for the prevailing rules of composition, was an even more seductive influence. He had studied at no conservatoire of any kind and had taken up music as a profession, rather than as an off-duty passion, only after nearly twenty 'wasted years' in the French equivalent of the Home Office. A devastatingly brilliant pianist and as well informed a harmonist as anyone, he was scarcely an amateur but, not having gone through the academic mill, his mind was receptive to new and conventionally unacceptable ideas. If his music is less original than Satie's early piano pieces, in that it was open to influence from everyone from Offenbach to Wagner, it is irresistible for its wit, its poetic sensitivity and, above all, for the exuberance which is such a natural expression of the composer's ebullient Auvergnat personality.

While Ravel and Viñes no doubt enjoyed playing any convenient version of Chabrier's phenomenally popular orchestral rhapsody

España, their favourite piano-duo score was the *Trois Valses romantiques,* an inspired and characteristically reckless work which, as Poulenc once remarked, is 'technically difficult and very exacting in interpretation'. In search of enlightenment before performing that work in a public concert to be given by Bériot pupils, Ravel and Viñes asked Chabrier early in 1893 to hear them play it. They were lucky to be able to make an appointment because, although the Chabrier family home was in Montmartre, he spent most of his time at this period in his life outside Paris at La Membrolle in Touraine. Apart from that he was terminally ill. But they must have known that he would be in Paris for a performance of the *Ode à la Musique* at the Conservatoire in January and, in fact, he was able to meet them a few days later. Viñes was matter-of-fact about the meeting: 'Chabrier pointed out the nuances to us. He stayed for an hour and a half and told us that we played very well, with much taste.' Although Ravel said nothing that anyone remembers about the occasion, his affection for Chabrier is evident in everything he is recorded as saying about him – not least his memory of the performance of *Gwendoline* at the Opéra in December 1893, nine months before his death: 'I saw this poor great man for the last time at a performance of *Gwendoline;* he was already indifferent to everything, even to his own music.'

Ravel's attachment to Chabrier is revealing. It was, it is true, a natural concomitant of his impatience with academic harmony and it coincided too with his developing post-Romantic aesthetic. But alongside the vigour in Chabrier's music, offsetting the pranks and the physical exuberance, there is not only acute poetic observation but also a delicate vein of sentiment. And that 'tenderness', as Chabrier's supporters prefer to put it, is often expressed in harmonies which, though they rarely sound like it, derive largely from Wagner, and from *Tristan und Isolde* in particular. Ravel was not insensitive to this side of Chabrier: he would not otherwise have enjoyed playing the *Trois Valses romantiques* as much as he did and he would not have declared his allegiance to the *Chanson pour Jeanne,* which he singled out in his autobiographical sketch as a formative influence and which is frankly, for all its harmonic and rhythmic interest, sentimental.

Even Viñes, a friend of eight years standing, was surprised by this aspect of Ravel when they went to a concert given by the Lamoureux Orchestra one Sunday afternoon in 1896.

We were listening to the Tristan *Prelude. And what a coincidence! Just when I was saying to myself, terribly moved, that there was nothing in the whole of creation as sublime and as divine as this superb Prelude, at that very moment Ravel touched my hand and said: 'It's always like that, every time I hear it.' And, in fact, Ravel who seemed so cold and cynical, Ravel the eccentric decadent, Ravel was trembling uncontrollably and weeping like a child — but profoundly because, intermittently, he was sobbing too.*

The coincidence that Viñes cannot have been aware of is that at his first *Tristan,* at the Munich Opera twenty-six years earlier, Emmanuel Chabrier was heard sobbing uncontrollably as he waited for the begining of that same Prelude.

Until that *Tristan* experience, Viñes confessed, because Ravel was 'so very secretive about the smallest details of his existence', he didn't really know him.

In spite of the high opinion I had of Maurice Ravel's intellect,
I thought there might be something not quite genuine, something modish,
about his opinions and his tastes in literature. But from this afternoon
I can see that this boy was born with his inclinations, his tastes and his
opinions and that when he expresses them he does it not because he is a
snob and because he wants to follow the fashion but because he really feels
them. And I am taking this opportunity to declare that Ravel is a most
unfortunate and misunderstood person. Everyone thinks he is a failure.
And in fact he is a superior brain and a superior artist, a displaced person
who is really worthy of a marvellous future. He is, moreover, very complic-
ated. There is a mixture of medieval catholicism and satanic impiety in
him but he is guided by a love of art and of beauty and his reactions
are sincere, as he demonstrated today by weeping while listening to the
Tristan *Prelude.*

That display of his feelings — which might well have moved Ravel to redouble his efforts to conceal them in future — was surprising even to his best friend. Just as surprising to us, a hundred years later, is his statement that everyone considered Ravel 'a failure'. But at that time he was regarded as a pianist and was unknown as a composer. As a pianist, by Viñes's virtuoso standards and according to the rules of the Conservatoire, he had failed. It would not be at all surprising if, in these adverse circumstances, he had adopted the dandy aesthetic merely to demonstrate that he was far above it all. But, as Viñes could confirm and as Baudelaire declared, 'Dandyism is not an immoderate interest in dressing-up and in material elegance. In the perfect dandy these things are only a symbol of the aristocratic superiority of his mind.'

Moreover, the marvellous future predicted by Viñes in 1896 was already beginning to take shape. Four years earlier Ravel had attempted his first song, a setting of Verlaine's 'Le Ciel est, pardessus le toit', and had abandoned it after a few pages. In 1893, however, while still in Pessard's harmony class at the Conservatoire, and at about the same time as he met his composer-role models in Montmartre, he completed two works which, though they remained unpublished in his lifetime, he regarded as worthy of acknowledgement in his autobiographical sketch: 'The influence of Emmanuel Chabrier was visible in the *Sérénade grotesque* for piano,' he said, 'that of Satie in the 'Ballade de la Reine morte d'aimer'.'

Valuable and attractive in themselves, these first pieces are particularly interesting as an indication of how early some of the composer's mature characteristics were formed and of how fundamental they were to his creative nature. His career-long tendency to look beyond the standardized major and minor scales for the extra colours obtainable from the older modes of church or folk music, or from artificial scales like the whole-tone scale so favoured by Debussy, is prominently in evidence even at this stage in his development. In the *Sérénade grotesque* he sets out to outdo Chabrier in the dissonance of the harmonies in the outer sections, with whole-tone chords aggressively strummed as though by a whole band of guitars, and to outdo him also in the sentiment of the Andalusian love song in the middle. But there is no precedent in Chabrier for the parody-serenade scenario of the piece which, in both its Spanish idiom and its structure, is a clear anticipation of the *Alborada del gracioso* Ravel was to write more than ten years later. In fact, it is more than an anticipation: it is a first and by no means unsuccessful effort to realize the same concept. The song, *Ballade de la Reine morte d'aimer*, is as remarkable for its Satie-like modal harmonies, which so aptly reflect the ironic and archaic flavour of the text by Roland de Marès, as for the sound of bells in it – the 'great bells of Bohemia and the tiny bells of Thule' tolling 'the supreme hosanna of the Queen who died of love'.

One source of Ravel's lasting fascination with bells must have been those which echo in all their variety in Edgar Allan Poe's famously musical poem *The Bells.* Certainly, Ravel was profoundly impressed by Poe in his student years. Largely because of the passionate advocacy of Baudelaire, who translated much of his work, the American writer had become an intellectual cult in France by this time. He was a source of inspiration not only to Ravel but also, though more for his psychological insights than his aesthetic theories, to Debussy. Poe's claim that he worked on his most successful poem, *The Raven,* calculatedly from the end – 'step by step … with the precision and rigid consequence of a mathematical problem' and without the intervention of 'accident or intuition' – was of particular interest to Ravel. He absorbed that lesson and retained it so firmly that more than half a lifetime later he was able to declare (to an American journalist) that 'my greatest teacher in composition was Edgar Allan Poe.'

Jean-Louis Lefort's portrait of Edgar Allan Poe, the American poet and writer who inspired an intellectual cult in Paris during Ravel's formative years

If Ravel subscribed for a while to Poe's principle that 'melancholy is the most legitimate of all the poetical tones,' he was not long convinced, on the other hand, that 'the death of a beautiful woman is, unquestionably, the most poetical topic in the world.' The Queen who died of love was beautiful, the poet tells us, and one imagines that the dead Infanta, for whom Ravel was to write his famous *Pavane* in 1899, was not ugly. But where he found true melancholy was in the dark despair expressed by Paul Verlaine after he had been sentenced to two years of imprisonment in Brussels for shooting his fellow writer and lover, Arthur Rimbaud, in the arm. In 1892 Ravel had been unable to finish 'Le Ciel est, pardessus le toit' but in 1895 he did complete a setting of 'Un Grand Sommeil noir' ('A Great Black Sleep'), the poem which immediately precedes 'Le Ciel est, pardessus le toit' in Verlaine's *Sagesse* and which was written on the day the poet was tried and found guilty.

In his maturity Ravel declared his early Verlaine settings 'far too juvenile'. He also condemned 'Un Grand Sommeil noir', by implication, in an article he wrote years later on the songs of Gabriel Fauré where he expresses disapproval of the common 'trick' – disdained by Fauré but dear to Massenet among others – of 'suddenly taking off from psalm-like chanting into a flight of lyrical expression'. Fauré's

The poetry of Paul Verlaine
– pictured here in an
engraving published in
Harpers Monthly in 1893 –
was a powerful source of
inspiration for Fauré,
Debussy and, among other
composers, Ravel.

masterful 1894 setting of 'Le Ciel est, pardessus le toit' (*Prison,* Op. 83,
No. 1), which Ravel must have known, is not dissimilar to 'Un Grand
Sommeil noir' but it avoids the extravagant contrast of the Ravel
setting. It could have been that rhetorical gesture, which is actually
alien to the semi-numbed state of Verlaine's poem, that decided Ravel
against publishing the work. Or it could have been what the subject
matter of the song seemed to reveal about him.

The earliest works published in Ravel's lifetime, *Menuet antique*
and *Habanera,* though written in the same year as 'Un Grand
Sommeil noir' are contrastingly full of light and much closer in style
and personality to those of the mature composer. The *Menuet antique*
is the first of his many essays in taking an ancient dance form and
recreating it in his own image. If he failed in this case – making it a
Chabrier minuet as much as a Ravel minuet by piling on the older
composer's harmonies – he was to write other, progressively more
successful minuets in the *Sonatine,* the *Menuet sur le nom de Haydn,*
and *Le Tombeau de Couperin.* The *Habanera* for two pianos is on a
different level. The *Menuet antique* is a brilliant but self-conscious

display of harmonic precociousness. The *Habanera*, headed in the manuscript by a quotation from Baudelaire, *au pays parfumé que le soleil caresse* ('in the perfumed land caressed by the sun'), is pure poetry.

Closely based on Chabrier's piano piece of the same name, the *Habanera* transcends its model not by addition but, in spite of the use of a second piano, by subtraction: the harmonies and textures are refined rather than enriched. Chabrier's *Habanera* is a dance; Ravel's, which uses much the same languorous melodic material in the Andalusian mode, is – to echo Diaghilev's perceptive (though disparaging) comment on *La Valse* – a 'portrait' of a dance. It is, moreover, an impressionist portrait: it is an image of an habanera caught in the clear light of the introduction, floating in on gently nostalgic minor harmonies, its characteristic rhythms rumbling in the bass or ringing in high-pitched echoes, its central and closing cadences suggestive of long-breathed sighs. It is a more economically structured and more sharply defined kind of impressionism than is to be found in *Soirée dans Grenade* in Debussy's *Estampes* of 1905 but the kinship between the two works is quite clear (and, as we shall see, not entirely accidental).

Ravel said that his *Habanera* 'contains the germ of several elements which were to predominate in my later compositions.' He was so happy with it in fact that as long as thirteen years later he orchestrated it and included it, otherwise unchanged, with three newly composed Spanish pieces in his *Rapsodie espagnole*. Other reasons for his youthful authority here, apart from Chabrier's example, are not difficult to find. His Basque background was certainly a factor but, as there is no evidence that he had been anywhere near Spain in the twenty years since the Ravel family settled in Paris in 1875, that was probably less important than his friendship with Viñes and, by extension, his familiarity with the Spanish community in and around Montmartre.

There was also, of course, the influence of his mother – whose knowledge of Spanish so impressed Manuel de Falla and whose memories of a Madrid he had never known so delighted him. Ravel turned to the habanera, Falla said, because that was the

song most in fashion among those his mother heard in gatherings in Madrid in those bygone days. At the same time, Pauline Viardot-Garcia, whose fame brought her into contact with the best musicians in Paris, made them all familiar with it. It is for that reason that the habanera – so surprisingly for Spaniards – continued to live in French music as a characteristic element of our music, while Spain itself had forgotten it half a century earlier.

Circumstances, however unlikely, had conspired to inspire in Ravel his first, though very short, masterpiece.

It is worth recalling at this point that the composer of the fragrant harmonies and evocative two-piano colouring of *Habanera* had been required to leave both the harmony and the piano classes of the Conservatoire only a few weeks before he completed the work. Though this professional setback might well have added another item to a growing store of resentment, it scarcely changed Ravel's way of life, and if it discouraged him at all it was only very temporarily. After all, much the same thing had happened a few years earlier to no less a composer than Claude Debussy, who had gone on not only to win the Prix de Rome but also to write that seminal work, the *Prélude à l'après-midi d'un faune,* which on its first performance in 1894 had been a revelation to him. With the continuing support of his parents, and having been exempted from military service on account of his fragile physique, he was able to carry on much as before. He kept up his friendship with Viñes after the Ravel family's move to the Left Bank (they lived at 15 rue Lagrange, between the Seine and place Maubert, for three years from 1896) and he went on writing music at the same unhurried rate. Actually, in 1896 he composed rather less than he had in the previous year – just two short songs, settings of Mallarmé's 'Sainte' and Marot's 'D'Anne jouant de l'espinette' – but he compensated for that in 1897 by completing not only *Entre Cloches,* to go with *Habanera* in a two-piano suite called *Sites auriculaires,* but also a single-movement Violin Sonata, which is three times as long as anything he had written so far.

Transferring his interest from Verlaine to Mallarmé, the other contemporary poet who found approval with des Esseintes in *A Rebours,* Ravel chose the text which comes just after *L'Après-midi d'un faune* in the Mallarmé collection he was using. Dedicated to St Cecilia and described by the poet as 'a little song-like poem written above all with music in mind', 'Sainte' is Mallarmé's study in the superior sweetness

Opposite, Stéphane Mallarmé, the symbolist poet, as fancifully portrayed in an etching by Paul Gauguin in 1891 with a sinister image of Poe's raven emerging from the shadow behind him

au peintre synthétiste à l'ami Daniel
Paul Gauguin

of unheard music. It was a challenge that Ravel was not yet equipped to meet: his response to the ecclesiastical atmosphere of the poem and the harmonic vacuum described in it – he allies an old church mode with a repeated sequence of bell-like chords derived from Fauré's *Prison* – is highly ingenious; but the conventionally arpeggiated harmonies which arise at the climactic point, where Mallarmé's St Cecilia seems to touch a harp-shaped angel's wing, are more likely to appeal to what Keats in a similar evocation of unheard melody called the 'sensual ear' than to the 'spirit'. Ravel was to return to Mallarmé, much more successfully, nineteen years later.

The colourful setting of 'D'Anne jouant de l'espinette', on the other hand, is appropriate in every way. Defying des Esseintes, whose interest in earlier French poetry was restricted to the 'melancholy ballads' of Villon, he turned to the sixteenth-century poet Clément Marot and found among his epigrams this playfully erotic account of the dark and shapely Anne producing a 'sweet and melodious sound' at her spinet. With its delightfully syncopated melody in quintuple time set against apparently conventional but not always predictably accented broken-chord figuration on the harpsichord (or piano), 'D'Anne jouant de l'espinette' is rhythmically more sophisticated than anything he had written so far. Harmonically too, it is uncommonly resourceful in integrating a modally induced archaic flavour with engaging melodic interest.

Why then, in April 1897, after writing nothing more ambitious than short piano pieces and even shorter songs, Ravel undertook a fifteen-minute Violin Sonata in one movement, no one really knows. He would obviously have felt the need to extend himself sooner or later but in that case he would surely have applied himself to a sonata for solo piano rather than one for an instrument about which he knew comparatively little. Perhaps it was written at the request of George Enescu, the Romanian violinist who was studying in Paris at the time and who is believed to have given the first performance at a Conservatoire concert with fellow-student Ravel at the piano. But as an accomplished composer himself, and not unprolific at this stage, Enescu was not short of material for his recitals. It is more likely that the sonata movement was set as a task in a composition class.

Since Ravel had left the Conservatoire in 1895 there had been significant and, as far as he was concerned, welcome changes.

Théodore Dubois, minor
composer and no friend of
Ravel during his time as
director of the Paris
Conservatoire (1896-1905)

The composer Ambroise Thomas, who had been director since 1871 –
and who was destined never to live down Chabrier's famous division
of music into three types, 'the good, the bad, and that of Ambroise
Thomas' – had died in 1896 and had been succeeded by Théodore
Dubois. The appointment of Dubois, who was a very mediocre
composer, was a good thing not so much in itself as in that it had
provoked the resignation of Massenet who, as a most distinguished
professor of composition, felt that he should have been given the
directorship. And the departure of Massenet left a vacancy which,
contrary to general expectation, was filled not by an in-house candidate but by Gabriel Fauré, who had neither studied at the Conservatoire nor taught there. Ravel's respect for Massenet was limited

but Fauré, whom he surely regarded as the most inspired of the older generation of French composers and who could be trusted to bring fresh air into a notoriously fusty institution, was another matter. Turning down a bizarre offer of a professorship in Tunisia, he made arrangements to return to the Conservatoire, this time as a composition student.

In the meantime, before joining Fauré's composition class at the beginning of 1898, he started taking lessons in counterpoint and orchestration with André Gédalge, a teacher long undervalued in the hierarchy of the Conservatoire (he became a professor only in 1905) but remembered with gratitude by everyone who studied with him, from Enescu to Milhaud and from Ravel to Honegger. 'I am happy to say,' Ravel recorded in his autobiographical sketch, 'that I owe the most precious elements of my craft to André Gédalge. As for Fauré,' he added, 'the encouragement of his artistic advice was no less profit-able for me.' Fauré's classes – at which the master would regularly arrive late, sometimes keeping his pupils waiting for as long as three quarters of an hour while Ravel amused them by playing the latest piano pieces of Erik Satie or Chabrier's *Chanson pour Jeanne* – were civilized discussions or conversations. Gédalge's classes were more like hard work, thorough in the instruction of counterpoint but with artistic effect rather than academic correctness always in mind: 'Do you want a prize in counterpoint,' he would ask his pupils, 'or do you want to learn your trade?' He valued lively rhythms, clarity and logic in construction and, above all, melody: 'Write me eight bars that can be sung without accompaniment' was the supreme challenge he issued to his students.

It could well be that Gédalge set Ravel the task of writing a sonata movement for Enescu, who had been in his class for two years by now and whose violin playing he admired as much as his creative work (Gédalge himself wrote a Violin Sonata for Enescu at about this time). If that is the case, and if he was expecting a conformist student essay, he can only have been surprised by the eleven pages of manu-script Ravel eventually brought him. The sight of the first page alone, where the metre changes nine times in as many bars, must have astonished him – it is unlikely that he had seen anything like it before – and he must have been as impressed by the breadth and spontaneity

John Singer Sargent's portrait (1898) of Gabriel Fauré, one of the greatest of all French composers, composition teacher to Ravel and successor to Dubois as director of the Paris Conservatoire

of the construction as he would have been aware of its untidiness. As for the harmonies, unless Gédalge shared Ravel's interest in both Delius and Chabrier, which is particularly unlikely in the former case, the most extravagant of them must have been a nasty shock to him. The Violin Sonata in A minor came as a surprise also when it was first published, on the centenary of the composer's birth, in 1975: not only was Ravel thought to have written only one work of its kind (the three-movement Violin Sonata in G major first performed in 1927 by George Enescu, by then the leading violinist of his generation), he was also, according to conventional wisdom, considered incapable of expressing himself as passionately as he does in this essentially romantic work. Those who knew and understood him in his student years, like Ricardo Viñes, made no such mistake.

Although Ravel had not definitively abandoned his career as a pianist at this time, he had clearly decided that composing would be his profession from now on. So, having had nothing published or even performed in public as yet, he made moves to correct the situation. The obvious priority was to provide more two-piano music to go with the *Habanera* which, though easily his best work so far, was too short to make a concert item in itself. He intended at first to furnish a suite of three *Sites auriculaires* ('Aural Sites', a paradox worthy of Erik Satie himself) which would add to the Spain he had already evoked in *Habanera* two more scenes, one set in Venice and the other amidst a multitude of bells. Nothing more is known of the Venetian project than its title, *Nuit en gondoles*, but in December 1897 he did complete *Entre Cloches*, which was duly performed, together with *Habanera*, at the 266th concert of the Société Nationale de Musique in the old Salle Pleyel in rue Rochechouart on 5 March 1898.

The first public hearing of music by Maurice Ravel was not a success. Ricardo Viñes, who gave that performance of the two *Sites auriculaires* with Marthe Dron at the other keyboard, confessed that they made a mess of it. He got a crotchet ahead of his partner in *Entre Cloches*, producing what he called an 'indescribable effect'. Pierre Lalo, son of the composer Edouard Lalo and chief music critic of *Le Temps* from 1898 until shortly before his death in 1943, liked neither the title nor the sound of the *Sites auriculaires*. Pierre de Bréville, who was represented as a composer in the same concert, told the readers of the *Mercure de France* that the music was 'revolting'.

It is unlikely that *Entre Cloches* would have found favour even in an ideal performance. Ravel certainly had the inspiration for an extended bell piece in him, as we know from the chiming and tolling allusions in several earlier works, but this was not it. *Entre Cloches* – where the gentle Sunday bells of Debussy's *De Soir* are distorted not quite out of recognition by Ravel's clatteringly dissonant harmonic accretions – was clearly designed to shock. Inspired perhaps by Poe's *The Devil in the Belfry*, it is work of tremendous energy, with a moment of quietly melodic repose in the middle. The composer himself seems to have realized that there must be a more persuasive way of expressing his delight in a counterpoint of all sorts and sizes of bells ringing simultaneously on all sides. Certainly, he kept *Entre Cloches* carefully out of the way after its unhappy first performance and seven years later he, in a sense, replaced it with the masterfully poetic *La Vallée des cloches,* the last movement of his piano suite *Miroirs.*

Not everyone present at the first performance of *Sites auriculaires* was distressed by it. One informed observer was as 'dazzled by the fantasy and originality of these astonishing little pieces' as he was impressed by the Ravel image – 'young and elegant, with large black *favoris* which gave him a romantic sort of appearance.' It seems that Debussy, who almost certainly knew nothing of Ravel's music up to this point, was also impressed, though not so much by the bushy black sideburns or by *Entre Cloches* as by *Habanera.* He was so impressed, in fact, that he borrowed a copy of the latter work and took it home with him. Doubts have been expressed as to the truth of that story and, still more, the embarrassing sequel that he then managed to lose the score and to rediscover it, behind the piano, only

Claude Debussy, whose career was to be more or less congenially interlinked with Ravel's, portrayed by a fellow winner of the Prix de Rome, Marcel Baschet, at the Villa Medici in 1885

when he moved house several years later. But Ravel does seem to have confirmed something of the kind when he claimed that Debussy 'kept it longer than I thought he would. I ought to have to have asked for it back many times.' Anyway, a musician of Debussy's quality would have no need of a score to remind him of the details of a work as clear in texture as *Habanera* and to recall some of them in his own two-piano piece *Lindaraja* in 1901 and, note-for-note in some places, in *La Soirée dans Grenade* in his *Estampes* for piano in 1903.

The other basic qualification Ravel needed in order to confirm his status as a composer was also secured in 1898 when the *Menuet antique* – which was first performed by its dedicatee, Ricardo Viñes in the Salle Érard on 18 April – was issued by Chabrier's old publisher, Enoch.

It was at this time too that Fauré, who knew his way round high society, introduced his pupil into one of the most influential of the artistic salons in Paris. Success at the musical evenings of the formidable Madame de Saint-Marceaux, wife of a fashionable sculptor, was almost as important in establishing a composer's reputation as favourable reviews in the newspapers. The Saint-Marceaux house not far from Fauré's home in the boulevard Malesherbes was open to musical guests after dinner on Wednesdays, when formality was discouraged but any hint of a whisper during the musical performances severely frowned upon. It was here that Ravel first met Colette, future librettist of *L'Enfant et les Sortilèges* and at that time wife of the critic Henri Gauthier-Villars who, under the pseudonyms of Willy and L'Ouvreuse (and not without his wife's participation as a writer), would soon be giving Ravel a hard time in his various columns. Like others who knew him at that time she was particularly struck by the black *favoris* – 'Yes, *favoris*!' she repeated, 'with voluminous hair that exaggerated the contrast between his significantly proportioned head and his tiny body. He liked showy ties and frilly shirts.'

Colette also noted that 'perhaps because he was secretly shy, Ravel adopted a distant manner and spoke with a dry tone … I can recall no particular conversation with him, no demonstration of friendship.' Mme de Saint-Marceaux confirmed Colette's impression: after singing two of Ravel's songs at one of her musical evenings, she asked in her diary, 'Is he pleased to hear his music performed? You cannot tell.

Colette (future librettist of *L'Enfant et les Sortilèges*) in 1897, when she was still married to the music critic Henri Gauthier-Villars and contributing to the columns published under his 'Willy' pseudonym

What a strange man he is. Talented but so sarcastic.' That he was, in fact, pleased to hear his music performed is clear from a stilted and rather pretentious but none the less gracious letter he wrote to her in August 1898 from Granville in Normandy, where he was supplementing his income by playing the piano at the Casino in the holiday season. Assuring her that he was very happy that she deigned to occupy herself a little with his music – she had been the first to perform 'D'Anne jouant de l'espinette' four months earlier – he informed her that he would be taking the liberty of addressing to her his latest composition, which he had written two months earlier and which 'happens to be singable'.

'Chanson du Rouet', which was completed on 2 June 1898, is certainly singable. With its simple folk-like vocal line – appropriately applied to a text taken from Leconte de Lisle's *Chansons écossaises*

('Scottish Songs') – it is salon music of high quality and clearly intended for a singer of no more than average ability. The intrusion of the *Dies irae* melody below the spinning-wheel figuration in the left hand of the piano part, at the sentimental point in the poem where the spinner thinks of making her own winding sheet, is no doubt an example of the 'irony' so acutely observed by Mme de Saint-Marceaux in the Ravel personality. Fauré, who took de Lisle's *Chansons écossaises* rather more seriously, might not have appreciated the irony.

Opposite, Colette's first husband, the critic Henri Gauthier-Villars ('Willy') with canine friend

Though eminently saleable as well as singable, 'Chanson du Rouet' remained unpublished during the composer's lifetime. So did his other song of 1898, 'Si morne' ('So mournful'), a setting of a poem from *Les Débâcles* published by the Belgian symbolist Émile Verhæren ten years earlier. It might not be as attractive a song as 'Chanson du Rouet', in that it reverts to the gloomy manner of 'Un Grand Sommeil noir', but it is of considerably more psychological interest. The choice of text is uncommonly revealing. While it is true that the setting of 'Si morne' has much in common with that of 'Un Grand Sommeil noir', including the anguished climax, Verlaine's poem is an expression of a miserable personal experience whereas Verhæren's is a cry of compassion for an unhealthy state of mind. Rhetorical in expression, replete with whole-tone harmonies and not at all to the taste of Gabriel Fauré, 'Si morne' was surely not intended for Mme de Saint-Marceaux or any other salon performer. It is more likely that it was inspired by the composer's identification of something of his own personality in Verhæren's study of pathological repression. If so, if he recognized in himself a compulsive concealment of 'his evil passions, and his resentments, and his pains, and his errors', 'Si morne' is one of the most intimate confessions he ever made.

Colette's and Mme de Saint-Marceaux's observations of Ravel's demeanour are not inconsistent with the state of mind analysed in Verhæren's poem. On the other hand, while he was not always at ease in their society it was not necessarily because he was 'secretly shy'. He might have seemed ungracious in avoiding being patronized by the portrait painter Jacques-Émile Blanche, who offered to pay him for playing piano duets with him. And he might have been reluctant to accompany Isadora Duncan in her interpretative dancing at the Saint-Marceaux salon. But in his first year as a composition student he had so much more to think about than social niceties. With nothing less ambitious than opera in mind, he turned first to Antoine Galland's translation of *The Thousand and One Nights* and then to E. T. A. Hoffmann's *Der Sandmann* for suitable material.

Only the overture remains of *Shéhérazade* (which is quite separate from the *Shéhérazade* songs with orchestra of 1903) and there is even less of *Olympia*. The projects would still be interesting, however, even if it were only for their subject matter. Ravel's fascination with mechanical objects was such that, in spite of the uncomfortable fact that both Delibes's ballet *Coppélia* and the first episode in Offenbach's *Les Contes d'Hoffmann* are based on the same story, he made a serious start on *Olympia* and, indeed, wrote music good enough to incorporate in the clock-shop introduction of *L'Heure espagnole* several years later. As for *Shéhérazade,* it was probably not inspired in the first place by the Persian stories themselves, much though the composer loved the fairy-tale element in them. As he said in his autobiographical sketch, his work on *Shéhérazade* was 'quite strongly dominated by the influence of Russian music'. It appealed to him above all as a subject that would accommodate his enthusiasm for the exotic language he and Viñes had discovered in the music of Balakirev and Rimsky-Korsakov.

'To Ravel's, with whom I again played Rimsky-Korsakov's *Antar,* arranged for piano duet, superbly oriental music,' Ricardo Viñes recorded in his diary in April 1897; 'at Ravel's we played a duet version of Balakirev's *Tamar,* a beautiful piece,' he wrote eight months later. Ravel knew Rimsky's *Schéhérazade* too, as he demonstrated by making a clear allusion to that score towards the end of his *Shéhérazade* Overture (he was to make a still clearer allusion to a different part of the same score in *Daphnis et Chloé* a dozen years later). It was also through the fairy-tale romances in *The Thousand and One Nights* that Ravel was at last able to release the voluptuous musical instinct stimulated in him by Debussy's *Prélude à l'après-midi d'un faune* – itself a tribute to the liberating influence of Russian exoticism. The *Shéhérazade* Overture luxuriates in sensuous melody of a kind not admitted to Ravel's music before.

When *Shéhérazade, Ouverture de Féerie* ('Fairy-tale Overture') was first performed at the Société Nationale – an opportunity secured against the odds by Fauré, who persuaded fellow committee members to forgive his pupil for the discomfort caused by *Entre Cloches* – the critics did not fail to note the influence both of the Russian school and of Debussy, 'whom one should learn to love but not imitate.' While finding serious faults in the construction, Pierre Lalo in *Le Temps* did at least praise the orchestration for its 'ingenious ideas and its piquant colour effects'. The scoring is, in fact, remarkably accomplished for a composer who had never written for the orchestra before. Ravel agreed that the work has its faults, perfectly clear in construction and thematically well integrated though it actually is, and did not deny the Debussy influence, confessing that the work is 'badly turned out and full of whole-tone scales'. The score was immediately withdrawn and, like that of *Entre Cloches,* remained unpublished until 1975.

Apart from making his début as a conductor to direct the first performance of the *Shéhérazade* Overture on 27 May, Ravel's other major achievements in 1899 were his setting of a second playfully erotic text by Marot, 'D'Anne qui me jecta de la neige' (to make a pair with 'D'Anne jouant de l'espinette' under the joint title *Epigrammes de Clément Marot*) and the composition of one of the most popular of all his works, *Pavane pour une Infante défunte.* Both these pieces are allusions to a fantasy sixteenth century, the song more clearly than the *Pavane* in that, in setting an archaic French text, it employs a similarly archaic musical language. Although Ravel has for the most part abandoned the harpsichord figuration so attractively applied to 'D'Anne jouant de l'espinette', this second Marot setting is a compatible partner to the other at least in the suppleness of its rhythms and its metrical flexibility.

... une Infante défunte – the Infanta Maria Teresa portrayed by Velázquez in about 1653

The *Pavane pour une Infante défunte* – 'Pavane for a Dead Infanta' – is an enigma. Ravel once declared that the title is meaningless and that he made it up simply because he like the sound of it. But then, warning pianists not to attach too much importance to the title and not to dramatize the piece as if it were a funeral lament for a dead Infanta, he went on to say that it is, in fact, 'an evocation of a pavane that a little princess might, in former times, have danced at the Spanish court.' It is not impossible that he had one or more of the familiar Infanta images of Velázquez in mind. Dedicated to the Princesse de Polignac – who, as heiress of the Singer sewing-machine fortune, was even richer than Mme de Saint-Marceaux and still more influential – the *Pavane pour une Infante défunte* must have been performed on several occasions by the composer himself in the Polignac and other salons. Although it was published by Demets in 1900, along with the Marot epigrams, it was not immediately success-ful. The first public performance did not take place until Ricardo Viñes played it in the Salle Pleyel in 1902 and it was only when Ravel arranged the original piano score for orchestra in 1910 that it became, as far as he was concerned, embarrassingly popular.

Reviewing a performance of the *Pavane* by the Lamoureux Orchestra in the *Revue Musicale* in 1912 Ravel confessed that he could 'no longer see its qualities. But – alas! – I can certainly see its faults: the Chabrier influence is flagrant and the form is quite poor.' That is another aspect of the enigma. The *Pavane pour une Infante défunte* surely owes more to Fauré's *Pavane* than to anything by Chabrier, whose *Idylle* has more in common with it for the eye than for the ear; and its rondo structure, though repetitive, is effective above all in that it gives the main theme maximum exposure. Critics who dismiss the work as unworthy of the composer underestimate the quality of that melody which floats above its lute-like accompaniment and its ambiguous harmonies with an enchanting combination of seriousness and serenity.

4

You should remember the name of Maurice Ravel. It is the name of one of the masters of the future.

Jean Marnod, *Mercure de France*

Maurice Ravel, elegantly
costumed in a garden
setting, in about 1898

Controversy 1900–05

Ravel had progressed well in his first two years in Fauré's composition class. A report dated 18 January 1900 refers to his 'very artistic temperament' and his 'notable maturity' and affirms that he is 'less exclusively attracted than before by the pursuit of the excessive'. It seems, however, that in that same month he took part in some kind of academic protest with five other students who, having entered the fugue competition, refused to submit their work for examination. This was not in itself very serious since he had a second chance to achieve the necessary distinction in that most academic of musical forms before the end of the year. But when he submitted his fugue six months later it was rejected as 'impossible' by the director of the Conservatoire, Théodore Dubois. In consequence, as the rules required of any student who failed twice in successive competitions, he was expelled from the composition class. Moreover, on his first entry for the Prix de Rome, he was eliminated at the preliminary stage, his fugue and his choral piece being judged incompetent.

Not surprisingly, bearing in mind that he was by now a published composer with several public performances to his credit, Ravel suspected that there were political motives behind his treatment at the Conservatoire. As early as March 1900, before he had met the worst of his frustrations, he confided to Dumitriu Kiriac that it wasn't really his academic work that was being condemned but, indirectly, his *Shéhérazade* Overture, which Dubois had heard at the Société Nationale the previous May and which he no doubt considered dangerously progressive. When Fauré tried to console his pupil for his disappointments, Ravel's letter to Kiriac goes on, 'Monsieur Dubois told him that he was deceiving himself about my musical nature.'

What is surprising in the circumstances is that, while continuing to attend Fauré's composition classes as an 'auditeur' – as an observer, that is, rather than as an official Conservatoire student – Ravel persisted in his laborious efforts to win the Prix de Rome. He would have known that, as an indication of a young composer's potential, the prize meant not very much. Of the modern French composers he admired or for whom he had at least a little respect at the time – Fauré, Saint-Saëns, Chabrier, Massenet, Debussy, Dukas, Koechlin, Satie – not all of them had entered for it and only two of them had won it. In fact, since 1803, when the Prix de Rome was first made available (to unmarried French nationals under the age of thirty), it had been awarded to no more than five composers of real distinction: Berlioz, Gounod, Bizet, Massenet and Debussy.

Obviously, the Prix de Rome brought its benefits, not least the opportunity to spend two years at work at the Villa Medici in Rome. And there was the money of course. The prospect of a regular income, modest in scale but guaranteed for four years and renewable in certain circumstances for three more, must have been a powerful attraction to a young composer with no means of support outside his immediate family and the pupils he took on at twenty francs an hour. So he no doubt felt that being confined to the Palais de Compiègne and being constantly invigilated, for a week at the preliminary stage and for a whole month at the second stage, was worth it. Photographs taken at Compiègne in May or June 1901 show the five unsmiling finalists

The five candidates for the Prix de Rome 1901 watched over by two uniformed invigilators on the steps of the Palais de Compiègne: from right to left, Maurice Ravel, Albert Bertelin, André Caplet (first prize-winner), Aymé Kunc and Gabriel

artistically arrayed on the steps of the palace with their two uniformed minders – Ravel aloof from the others, cigarette in hand and, in one case, displaying the striped socks and white shoes he had chosen to match his white boater.

In 1901 Ravel got safely through the preliminary stage and submitted a cantata, *Myrrha,* which won the consistent support of Massenet in the prolonged judgement of the final round. Massenet was outvoted, however, by those jurors (some of them non-musicians) who preferred settings of the same text by André Caplet and Gabriel Dupont. After much discussion as to whether a first prize should be awarded at all, Caplet was given the 1st Grand Prix, Dupont the upper 2nd Grand Prix and Ravel the lower 2nd Grand Prix. Although Ravel allowed himself to express some surprise at Caplet's success, he did concede that his colleague's orchestration was 'remarkable' whereas his own, because he hadn't left himself time to do it justice, was 'botched'. So he tried again and, in successive years, yet again, reaching the final stage on both occasions but without securing any kind of prize for either of his (thoroughly unremarkable) cantatas, *Alcyone* in 1902 and *Alyssa* in 1903. Wisely, in 1904 he refrained from competing but then in 1905 – his last chance, since he was now in his thirtieth year – he submitted himself to the process all over again. The result was embarrassing, though not so much for Ravel as for the jury which stopped him at the preliminary stage and for the Conservatoire and the Institut de France.

If Ravel had won the Prix de Rome in 1901 it is difficult to imagine what professional benefit two years at the Villa Medici would have been to him – let alone the following year which (according to the conditions laid down) was to be spent in either Germany or Austria. No young composer was ever better placed than Maurice Ravel in Paris in the twenty years round the turn of the century.

In 1900, for example, Ravel had been invited to Debussy's home in rue Cardinet to hear him play excerpts from his major work in progress, his opera *Pelléas et Mélisande,* and he remained on visiting terms with Debussy for two or three years at least. Delius, who knew them both, was overstating the case when he declared that 'without Debussy, Ravel would not exist' but there can be no doubt at all that in these years round the turn of the century – when he wrote the String Quartet, the *Nocturnes* for orchestra, and *Pelléas et Mélisande* –

Jules Massenet (1842–1912), leading French opera composer of his day

Opposite, Claude Debussy photographed by Pierre Louÿs (in the writer's home in Paris) round about the time he completed the *Prélude à l'après-midi d'un faune* in 1894

Debussy was the most exciting phenomenon in French music since
Berlioz. If Debussy had not existed, Ravel would have grown out of
his allegiance to Chabrier and Satie sooner or later but, having
emerged from the same background himself, Debussy set an
irresistible example. Unfortunately for the more jealous of the older
composer's supporters, Ravel was 'even cleverer' than Debussy, as
Delius acknowledged and as Satie agreed, and was soon able to catch
up with him in technique and even, though he would never have
anything like the breadth of Debussy's creative vision, anticipate some
of his ideas.

It was also at the beginning of the new century that Ravel joined a
group of friends who met regularly on Saturdays at the home of Paul
Sordes, a painter and excellent pianist who (like William Molard,
Delius's friend across the river in rue Vercingétorix) spent more time
enjoying art and talking about it than actually creating it. His studio
facing Montmartre from the fourth floor of 39 rue Dulong was a more
fertile and more natural place for the exchange of ideas than the Villa
Medici could have been. There was a preponderance of visual artists
here too but there were writers who came to read their latest work
and musicians who played their latest compositions or their latest discoveries on the fringes of the repertoire. One of the most influential
members of the group was Léon Leclère, professionally known by
his Wagnerian pseudonym of Tristan Klingsor, who dabbled in music
and painting but who is best known as a writer, above all for the
Shéhérazade poems which Ravel set to music in 1903. The most
charismatic was the journalist and poet Léon-Paul Fargue, who was
admired everywhere for his brilliant conversation and for his extra-
ordinarily handsome appearance. Said at this time to resemble Arthur
Rimbaud at his best, he must have been particularly interesting to
a composer drawn, as Ravel was, to the Verlaine of 'Le Ciel est,
pardessus le toit' and 'Un Grand Sommeil noir'. Certainly, he retained
a lifelong affection for Fargue, whose *Rêves* he set to music a quarter
of a century later. Some of the musicians in the circle – Ricardo Viñes,
Lucien Garban, Marcel Chadeigne – he had known before, but the
friendships he formed or confirmed at about this time with critics
M. D. Calvocoressi and Emile Vuillermoz and the conductor D. -E.
Inghelbrecht were, in spite of a period of coolness in the last case, to
be of lasting value.

One of Ravel's closest
friends, Léon-Paul Fargue,
past his youthful best here
as far as his looks are
concerned but in his
prime as poet, journalist
and conversationalist

In the course of time the group took on some of the aspects, not all of them attractive, of a secret society. They gleefully welcomed the unflattering label stuck on them by a newspaper seller who, when they bumped into him on the rue de Rome one day, responded by shouting at them, 'Attention les Apaches!' ('Look out, hooligans!'). They had their individual nicknames, too, and Ravel, who was known as 'Rara', invented the imaginary character 'Gomez de Riquet' as someone they urgently had to meet whenever they wanted to get away from boring company. It was no doubt Ravel also who chose the opening theme of Borodin's Second Symphony as the Apache signature tune, which members would whistle to identify themselves to the others. When their gatherings – from which women were rigorously excluded – became too noisy for the neighbours in rue Dulong they took place mainly in the studio of Maurice Delage, one of Ravel's few pupils, who rented a kind of summer house at the bottom of a garden in rue de Civry in Auteil.

Ravel did frequent other artistic circles at the time, including that of the *Revue blanche* to which Fauré introduced him and where he found congenial company on the liberal side of the long-running and bitterly contested Dreyfus affair. At the *Revue blanche* in rue Laffitte he met its co-founder Thadée Natanson and, among its contributors, he got to know the poet Henri de Régnier, who was a source of inspiration to him on more than one occasion, Jules Renard, author of the *Histoires naturelles* that Ravel was to set to music in 1906, and Franc-Nohain, whose one-act comedy *L'Heure espagnole* was to become the libretto of his first opera. When the *Revue blanche* closed down in 1903 Ravel could still look forward to the Tuesday receptions of the *Mercure de France,* where he found less congenial political company perhaps but also a good friend and valuable ally in its music critic, Jean Marnold. Even so, until they were dispersed by World War I, it was from the Apaches that Ravel drew most encouragement and artistic stimulation.

In their turn the Apaches were privileged to witness at close quarters the extraordinary developments in Ravel's music in the early years of his maturity. When he first played *Jeux d'eau* to them, presumably towards the end of 1901 (it was completed on 11 November), it was, Léon-Paul Fargue declared, 'a revelation'. If they had heard anything at all like it before it would have been in Liszt's *Les Jeux*

Henri de Régnier, poet and long-term friend of Ravel whose *Jeux d'eau* might well have been inspired by Régnier's poem 'Fête d'eau'

Pierre Bonnard's design
(1894) for a poster for the
Revue blanche

d'eau à la Villa d'Este, where a similar technique of arpeggios at the top of the piano keyboard is used to simulate the sound and the movement of the play of water in a fountain. But, whereas Liszt's piece, for all its impressionistic introduction, is an effusion of religious symbolism, Ravel's is a celebration of physical sensation, as the composer affirmed by heading the published score with the evocative line *Dieu fluvial riant de l'eau qui le chatouille* ('river god laughing at the water that tickles him') from Régnier's 'Fête d'eau'. Ravel actually asked the poet to inscribe that line in his own hand on the manuscript of *Jeux d'eau,* which suggests that he might have seen 'Fête d'eau' before it was published in Régnier's collection of poems inspired by

Versailles, *La Cité des eaux*, in 1902. If so, the poem could be more
intimately connected with the music than as just a convenient source
for an appropriate superscription. Inspired by the Bassin de Latone,
the one fountain in working order at Versailles at that time, Régnier's
'Fête d'eau' might in its turn have been the original inspiration of *Jeux
d'eau*, with which it has both descriptive and structural features
in common.

It surely took more than a hint from Liszt to stimulate this sudden
and unprecedented surge in Ravel's imagination. The watery experience in *Jeux d'eau* is certainly more realistic than in *Les Jeux d'eau à la
Villa d'Este*. Ravel's arpeggios rise and, unlike Liszt's divine aspirations,
naturalistically fall. There are bubbles of whole-tones and sprays of
tiny droplets in chromatic scales. Finely calculated dissonances splash
in the bright light of the piano's top register or, at the centre of the
piece, hover on a glittering tremolando before a dramatic glissando
plunges to the very bottom of the keyboard. Variations in the light
and the wind are reflected in changing harmonies and subtle rhythmic
distortions. In a cadenza towards the end conflicting currents struggle
to the surface in a clash of two opposing harmonies. The one melodic,
rather than colouristic, theme is presented in the pentatonic mode (on
the black keys only), as though Ravel wanted to emphasize the pagan
aspect of his inspiration and to distinguish it from Liszt's specifically
Christian sentiment.

Jeux d'eau was a revelation to Ravel's friends because, as Fargue
recalled, they were at that time 'soaked body and soul in the impressionism of Debussy' and this impressionism was quite different.
Ravel's was more precisely drawn and, as he himself pointed out, it
was cast in a classical form. He too believed he had discovered something new: '*Jeux d'eau* is,' he said, 'the origin of all the pianistic
innovations people have claimed to find in my work.' Although it has
more than a little in common with the piano music Debussy had
written up to that time, this is more a matter of modality, in the use
of pentatonic melody and of the whole-tone scale (which, incidentally,
Ravel claimed to have abandoned after the *Shéhérazade* Overture),
than in the piano writing. Debussy, who had demonstrated little
enthusiasm for watery scenes in his piano music before 1901 –
although there is a picturesque fountain in his Baudelaire song 'Le Jet
d'eau' of 1889 – seemed to acknowledge Ravel's inspiration in this

The first page of the autograph of Ravel's *Jeux d'eau* with the superscription in the hand of the poet Henri de Régnier

area in his *Jardins sous la pluie* (the third of the *Estampes* of 1903) which plainly echoes the dramatic plunge from the top to the bottom of the keyboard in the middle of *Jeux d'eau*.

What passed between the two composers by way of Viñes, who was in regular contact with both of them at this time, perhaps not even he could have said. Certainly, such exchanges between contemporaries are not uncommon in the history of music and usually they take place with little or no acrimony on either side – which, unfortunately, was not to be the case as far as Debussy and Ravel were concerned. For the present, however, they were on good terms. Ravel demonstrated his respect for the older composer by sharing in the task of making a two-piano arrangement of what he described as the 'admirable' *Nocturnes* for orchestra. 'Having revealed some skill in this kind of work,' Ravel told Florent Schmitt in April 1901, 'it has fallen to me to transcribe unaided the third of them, *Sirènes,* which is perhaps the most perfectly beautiful and certainly the trickiest, all the more so because it hasn't been performed yet.' Then, on 30 April 1902, just a few days after Viñes introduced Ravel's *Jeux d'eau* and *Pavane pour une Infante défunte* to the audience of the Société Nationale in the Salle Pleyel, there was the first night of Debussy's epoch-making *Pelléas et Mélisande* at the Opéra-Comique. Ravel and some of his Apache friends were there and they religiously attended every one of the following twenty-nine performances of the opera, always ready to defend Debussy's poetic but controversial score from its many reactionary enemies and detractors while, in private, amusing themselves by parodying the mannerisms of Maeterlinck's text.

It was on the crest of this wave of enthusiasm for Debussy that Ravel started work on his String Quartet in F, completing the first two movements before the end of the year. Although there were other reasons for choosing this particular form – the *Allegro moderato* was originally intended as Ravel's contribution to a composite quartet written in tribute to Fauré by four of his pupils – the inspiration behind it was clearly Debussy's Quartet in G minor. Ravel's alignment with Debussy here did not escape the attention of Théodore Dubois, who not only declared the *Allegro moderato,* the first movement of what has since become one of the most popular of all string quartets, unworthy of a Conservatoire prize but also saw to it that Ravel would no longer attend classes at that august institution, even as an 'auditeur'. Annoyed perhaps but creatively undeterred, Ravel went on to complete the work, much the longest he had written so far, within four months. In dedicating it to 'my dear master Gabriel Fauré' he was drawing attention not so much to the paternity of the score as to his continuing gratitude to his old teacher after his dismissal from the Conservatoire. Whereas Fauré was unhappy about the last of the four movements of the work, Debussy is said to have advised him, 'in the name of the gods of music, and in my name too, do not change anything in your quartet.'

One of the clearest indications of Ravel's debt to Debussy in the String Quartet in F is, paradoxically, the phantom presence of César Franck, a composer with whom Ravel had little in common but whose influence is perceptible here in some colouristic and melodic details and, above all, in the conscientiously 'cyclic' construction. Inspired directly by Franck's String Quartet in D major, Debussy's in G minor follows its model in its use of a theme which not only recurs, on a cyclic basis, from movement to movement but which also lends itself to melodic and rhythmic transformation to supply much of the rest of the material of the work. And so, in its turn, does Ravel's Quartet in F. Each of the three composers has his own approach to the cyclic procedure but the line of descent between the three works – written at ten year intervals, incidentally – is quite clear.

Where Debussy departs from Franck, and where Ravel departs with him, is in the freshness of the modal melody and the colouring. With some help from Grieg, whose String Quartet in G minor is never very far from his own, and with seductive echoes from a variety of exotic sources, Debussy created a new sound. Ravel drew on that sound extensively, adding much from his own fertile imagination for instrumental sonority and a little also from the voluptuous textures of Borodin's Quartet in D major. But even where he is most successful – as in the brilliant scoring for plucked strings and the ingenious thematic transformations in the *Assez vif* scherzo – Debussy has been there before him. Ravel's melodic line had never been as supple and as expressive as in the first movement of the Quartet in F but it needed Debussy's example to achieve its new freedom.

Surprisingly, while he is generous enough in his autobiographical sketch to acknowledge the influence of Debussy on his next major work, the *Shéhérazade* song cycle, and although he is frank enough to admit to some doubt about the construction of the String Quartet, Ravel makes no mention of Debussy in relation to this particular score. But when it was first performed, by the Quatuor Heyman at a concert of the Société Nationale in the Schola Cantorum on 5 March 1904, the critics certainly did. 'In its harmonies … its sonority and form … in all the sensations which it evokes,' wrote Pierre Lalo in *Le Temps,* 'it offers an incredible similarity to the music of Monsieur Debussy.' 'Its new and delicious harmony evokes that of Claude Debussy,' said Jean Marnold in the *Mercure de France.* Marnold did, on the other hand, have the perception to recognize the developing personality of the composer and, firmly declaring his allegiance, he

Opposite, the Scottish soprano Mary Garden as Mélisande, the role she created in Debussy's *Pelleas et Mélisande* at the Opéra-Comique in 1902. Ravel attended every one of the first thirty performances of the opera.

MARY GARDEN (Melisande)

added, 'You should remember the name of Maurice Ravel. It is the name of one of the masters of the future.'

This public taking of sides after the first performance of the String Quartet in 1904 – the defenders of Debussy led by Lalo, the supporters of Ravel led by Marnold – marked the beginning of the deterioration of the relationship between two composers who, if left to themselves, would surely have remained on speaking terms at the very least. Indeed, with characteristic candour, Ravel was always willing to express his admiration for Debussy. Not long before the end of his life, listening to a broadcast performance of the *Prélude à l'après-midi d'un faune,* Ravel confessed to a close friend, his eyes filling with tears, that it was not until he heard that work that he understood 'what music was all about'. Because he had been so much under the spell of Chabrier and so fascinated by Satie, it took some time for him to submit to the Debussy influence. When he did, in the String Quartet and the *Shéhérazade* song cycle in 1903, it not only reawakened his sensual instinct. It also encouraged him – after a brief and unwise diversion of his time in setting Paul Gravollet's uninspiring little poem 'Manteau de Fleurs' – to risk working on a larger scale again.

Tristan Klingsor's recently published verse collection, *Shéhérazade,* might have been designed specifically to appeal to Maurice Ravel at this time. Named after the Rimsky-Korsakov symphonic suite which Ravel admired so much, it offered in its hundred oriental fantasies ample opportunity for him to satisfy the longing for exotic gratification left unfulfilled when he abandoned the *Shéhérazade* opera project five years earlier. He was attracted too by the form of the poems, their unrhymed but rhythmical free verse, which, as Klingsor said and as Ravel could only have agreed, 'seems particularly suitable for music.' According to Klingsor, what setting a poem to music meant to Ravel was 'transforming it into an expressive recitative, intensifying the inflexions of the words into song, heightening all the possibilities of the words without subordinating them to the music,' and he recalled how the composer got him to read the poems aloud so as to be sure that he had not misunderstood his intentions.

It is generally assumed that Ravel was referring to this approach to word-setting – which has more than a little in common with that of Debussy in *Pelléas et Mélisande* – when he confessed to the 'at least

Tristan Klingsor (Léon Leclère), poet, painter and composer who wrote the *Shéhérazade* poems Ravel set to music in 1903

spiritual influence of Debussy' on the *Shéhérazade* songs. But Ravel's vocal line here is actually closer to song than Debussy's and, besides, this is a technical matter rather than a spiritual one. The more likely meaning, though clearly not in so many words, is that he had created something nearer to the spirit of the suggestive haze of Debussy's kind of impressionism than he had ever done before and would ever do again. In fact, Ravel was so deeply immersed in Debussy's music at this time that *Shéhérazade* not only betrays echoes of his *Nocturnes* and his *Chansons de Bilitis* but also foresees a little of the seascape imagery Debussy was sketching at much the same time in the early stages of his work on *La Mer.*

The fact that Ravel chose the same title for his new song cycle as he had already used for his *Schéhérazade* Overture suggests that he intended to consign the earlier piece to permanent oblivion. He had not completely forgotten it, however, as is indicated by the similarly allusive quality of the oboe solos at the beginning of the two works, and he had not forgotten Rimsky-Korsakov either. But this is by far the more accomplished score. Where Klingsor's verse lapses into banality, as it does in several lines in 'Asie' – 'I would like to see fine silk turbans on black faces with bright teeth' and 'I would like to see velvet clothes and coats with long fringes' – Ravel is reduced to well-meaning generalizations. At his best, on the other hand, where he evokes the 'bewitching rhythm of the sea' in 'Asie' for example, the poet inspires correspondingly evocative music.

Not the least interesting aspect of the *Shéhérazade* cycle is the question why, out of the hundred Klingsor poems he had to choose from, Ravel selected 'L'Indifférent'. The appeal of 'Asie', the first song in the set as published, would have been its far-and-wide invocation of an abundance of oriental images. 'La Flûte enchantée', where the sound of the flute is felt as a lover's kiss, is a fascinating metaphor of music as an erotic experience and it inspired a song of correspondingly melodious sensuality. The primary attraction of 'L'Indifférent', on the other hand, is neither oriental nor musical: it is the sexual ambiguity of the young stranger whose 'eyes are as soft as a girl's' and whose 'hips sway a little with his languid and feminine gait'. Though notoriously unwilling to reveal anything of himself in such intimate matters, Ravel – who cannot have been unaware of Klingsor's homosexual orientation – obviously found 'L'Indifférent' irresistible. 'I sincerely hope you'll have it sung by a girl,' said the conductor Camille Chevillard on seeing Ravel's setting and noting perhaps the languid gait of the muted strings, the voluptuous longing in the vocal line and the way the composer identifies himself with it in the melodic allusions to the String Quartet. Ravel left few clues to the nature of his sexuality but 'L'Indifférent' is one of the more significant.

The first performance of *Shéhérazade* was, as Chevillard sincerely hoped, given by a woman, Jane Hatto of the Paris Opéra, with Alfred Cortot conducting the orchestra of the Société Nationale in the Nouveau Théâtre on 17 May 1904. The three songs are all dedicated to women – 'Asie' to Jane Hatto, 'La Flûte enchantée' to Mme de Saint-Marceaux, 'L'Indifférent' to Emma Bardac (Fauré's former mistress and Debussy's future second wife) – and they have nearly always been sung by women ever since, though not necessarily in the published order: Ravel himself apparently preferred to present 'L'Indifférent' as the centrepiece, preceded by 'La Flûte enchantée' and followed by 'Asie'. It was in that order that *Shéhérazade* was first performed and gratifyingly well received. Even as committed a Debussyist as Louis Laloy, while noting what Debussy and Ravel had in common, insisted in the *Revue Musicale* that the comparison should not be taken too far and that no one should dismiss as an imitator a composer with this 'finesse' and 'exquisite lightness of touch'.

When Ravel made the decision to compete for the Prix de Rome in 1905 his intention was to win the First Prize. His entry was not, as has sometimes been suggested, a political move calculated to provoke his early elimination and the consequent embarrassment of the reactionary forces of the Conservatoire and the Institut de France – although, if it had been, they could scarcely have played into his hands more effectively. A more likely calculation would have been that if he won the First Prize he would enhance Fauré's reputation as a teacher and, with Théodore Dubois about to retire, help secure his succession to the directorship of the Conservatoire. Besides, he still needed the money. He was making some kind of income from teaching, accompanying cabaret singers and perhaps even ghosting popular songs (he is said to have written Raoul Marchetti's highly successful 'Fascination' at about this time) but only at the expense of the resources he would rather have been spending on serious composition.

This was his last chance to win the Prix de Rome and, in a statistical sense at least, his best: the previous winner, Raymond Pech, having chosen to get married rather than live in celibacy at the Villa Medici, there were two First Prizes to be won this time. Moreover, as the composer of the by now quite popular *Pavane pour une Infante défunte,* of *Jeux d'eau,* the String Quartet and *Shéhérazade,* and as 'one of the masters of the future', he was surely worthy of a modest state pension.

Why, on the other hand, he ended his Fugue in C in the preliminary test with an unacceptable discord, and why he so clearly broke the rules of four-part writing in his choral piece *L'Aurore,* it is difficult to say. Perhaps he had calculated that, since he was scarcely likely to fail at this stage, he could afford to take a risk and issue a little academic provocation. Certainly, he provoked one of the jurors to declare that 'Monsieur Ravel might well consider us old-fashioned but he is not going to take us for imbeciles.' When they declared him unfit to proceed to the competition proper they no doubt felt fully justified in doing so. But it was an unwise move and, as the newspapers were not slow to point out when the *affaire Ravel* erupted, an inconsistent judgement: since Ravel had been awarded a second prize in 1901 and had duly passed the preliminary tests in 1902 and 1903, how could he have become so incompetent in 1905? And there was more to it than that. Journalists not known to be supporters of Ravel, like Pierre Lalo in *Le Temps,* joined with his friends, like Jean Marnold in the *Mercure Musical,* in condemning one particular member of the jury. Of the three teachers of composition at the Conservatoire, Charles Lenepveu was the only one who was a member of the Institut de France and therefore the only one entitled to sit on the jury of the Prix de Rome. In 1905 Lenepveu entered eight students for the competition. While all Fauré's and Widor's students – including two second prize winners in previous years, Maurice Ravel and Hélène Fleury – were eliminated at the preliminary stage, all six of the places in the second stage were allocated to Lenepveu students and so, in consequence, were the two first prizes available this year and the two second prizes.

The injustice was so obvious that the scandal assumed political proportions. At an early stage in the controversy Romain Rolland –

A 1902 caricature by 'Aroun Al Rascid' of Charles Lenepveu, professor at the Conservatoire and member of the jury of the Prix de Rome in 1905 when, scandalously, all six finalists were selected from his composition class and Ravel was excluded

already an authority on music though not yet the heavyweight novelist
and Nobel Prize-winning thinker he was to become – wrote to the
Director of the Académie des Beaux Arts:

> *I am not a friend of Ravel. I cannot even say that his subtle and*
> *refined art has any appeal for me personally. But justice requires me to*
> *say that Ravel is not only a promising student; he is one of the most*
> *prominent of the young masters of French music, which does not have*
> *many of them … I admire the composers who have dared to judge him.*
> *Who will judge them in their turn?*

The answer to that very pertinent question is that the Government
Minister responsible saw to it that on the departure of Théodore
Dubois his place as Director of the Conservatoire was taken not by
his heir apparent, Charles Lenepveu, who had done all he could to
secure the succession, but by Ravel's teacher Gabriel Fauré.

5

Chloe garlanding Daphnis,
a lithograph illustration
by Pierre Bonnard for a
French edition of Longus's
Daphnis and Chloe (1902)

*We went down to the factories as night was
falling. I don't know how to describe the
impression made by these castles of smelting,
these incandescent cathedrals, this marvellous
symphony of conveyor belts, whistles, and
massive hammer blows that envelop you.*

Maurice Ravel,
on a cruise in the Rhineland

Celebrity 1905-7

The period between Ravel's final disqualification from competition for the Prix de Rome and the outbreak of World War I were the most fruitful nine or ten years of his adult life. The death of his father in 1908 was a severe blow and, although it did reduce his energy for work for several months, it did not have the traumatic effect that the loss of his mother was to have nine years later. Always a meticulous craftsman, always a composer whose best ideas were more likely to be stimulated by prolonged confrontation with a technical or stylistic challenge than by sudden inspiration, he was never prolific. In spite of his comparatively slow productivity, however, and in spite of breaks necessitated by the death of his father in 1908 and by overwork in 1912, it was during this time that he wrote not only two of his longest scores – the opera *L'Heure espagnole* and the ballet *Daphnis et Chloé* – but also the most important of his piano works, the most challenging of his songs and some of the most popular of his chamber and orchestral pieces.

He was particularly encouraged at this time by the fact that, far from being left in financial hardship by his failure to win the Prix de Rome, he was now a celebrity prized by the most ambitious of music publishers, Auguste and Jacques Durand, who were enlightened enough to secure sooner or later the allegiance of most of the leading French composers of the day – Saint-Saëns, Fauré, Debussy, D'Indy, Dukas, Schmitt and Roussel prominent among them. The first Ravel work they added to their catalogue was the *Sonatine*, which they published in 1905, and soon after that, in return for the right of first refusal on anything he was to write in future, they offered to pay the composer a retainer of 12,000 francs a year – the same as they were paying Debussy. With characteristic integrity, and so as not to feel pressurized into sacrificing quality for quantity, Ravel preferred to accept only half that amount.

The contract with Durand did not make him rich but it did mean that he could afford to cultivate his dandyism more authentically and more convincingly than he had done before. A fellow student had noted, somewhat maliciously, that the stylish frock coat Ravel wore at the Conservatoire was actually too long and made him look even smaller than he was. But no one, surely, could describe him as anything but impeccably presented by now. A photograph of Ravel and Viñes taken in 1905 – the former standing with the inevitable cigarette in his hand, the latter modestly sitting on a chair arm so as to conceal the discrepancy in height between the two of them – shows both men smartly dressed in three-piece suits but with Ravel, in his ultra-fashionable, ultra-high stiff collar and elaborate tie with a jewelled stud in it, much the more extravagantly turned out. Even the pianist's luxuriant moustache is outdone by the composer's newly grown beard – a feature which was to remain famously with him for five years or more.

It cannot be said, on the other hand, that Ravel was altogether happy about his family's recent house-moves. For reasons of economy and because of the location of Joseph Ravel's motor manufacturing business, they had by now had to leave Montmartre for less attractive

Ricardo Viñes and Maurice
Ravel in about 1905

areas of the capital. For Edouard, who was involved in the same business as his father, the moves were probably not inconvenient. For
Maurice, whose interest in heavy industry did not extend to living in
the midst of it, they were most unwelcome. He went along with them
partly because of the financial advantage of staying with his parents
but mainly because of his reluctance to separate himself from the
emotional security represented by his family in general and the 'dear
silent presence' of his mother in particular. In 1901 the Ravels had
moved to 19 boulevard Péreire, in an unfashionable part of the
seventeenth arrondissement, where, 'lulled by the warbling of
locomotives' on the railway line outside, Ravel could only resort to
irony in describing the atmosphere as 'charming'. Four years later they
moved again, beyond the city boundary this time, to rue Chevallier
(now rue Rouquier) in the industrial suburb of Levallois-Perret:
according to Maurice Delage who visited him there, it was 'populated
by sheet-metal workshops rolling their theatrical thunder and shaken
by deafening waggons passing by in the din of steam hammers and
sirens of the least poetic kind.'

The consolation was that in the meantime they had rediscovered
the Basque country. Their first documented return visit to St-Jean-de-
Luz was in 1902 – when, perhaps out of admiration for the 'grand
anglais' as well as for the fee he offered, Ravel undertook the holiday
task of reducing Delius's one-act opera *Margot la Rouge* to vocal score.
But it seems likely from a letter he wrote in 1901 to Jane Courteault, a
family friend in St-Jean-de-Luz, that he had returned to his birthplace
on at least one earlier occasion. Anyway, however little he might have
seen of St-Jean-de-Luz and Ciboure before, it was from this time that
the Basque country assumed an ever growing importance in the life of
the composer. It was not only a place of recreation, where he could
take long walks and go sea-bathing or boating, and of comparative
quiet, where he could work without too much distraction; it became a
spiritual home for him, a country which he could think of as his own
inhabited by a people with whom he could identify, a refuge to which
he could resort when the stresses of professional and metropolitan life
became too much for him.

There were refuges for Ravel in Paris too, not least among the
mutually supportive brotherhood of Apaches. One of the warmest of
all his long-term relationships outside his own household was with the

Polish Godebski family – Xavier Cyprien Godebski, familiarly known as Cipa, who was forty when Ravel first met him in 1904, his attractive blonde wife Ida, who was eight years younger, and their two children, Mimie and Jean, for whom he wrote *Ma Mère l'Oye* in 1910. Though not rich, Cipa was a great friend to the arts: he had been particularly supportive of Toulouse-Lautrec, who had painted his portrait, and he owned canvases by Vuillard, Bonnard and Roussel among others.

Invitations to the Godebskis's Sunday evenings at home were highly prized by the artistic community, musicians included. A painting executed by Georges d'Espagnat in about 1910, *Réunion de musiciens chez Monsieur Godebski*, shows the heavily bearded Cipa and his son Jean in the foreground, the composers Florent Schmitt, Déodat de Séverac and Albert Roussel standing with the critic M. D. Calvocoressi to the left, while Ricardo Viñes plays the piano at the centre of the picture and Maurice Ravel leans in characteristically solitary elegance on the piano lid at the far right. 'I think my parents were Ravel's adopted family,' wrote Mimie in 1938, recalling that 'when they moved to rue d'Athènes he rented a room in a very modest

Georges d'Espagnat's painting *Réunion de musiciens chez Monsieur Godebski*

hotel opposite their apartment where he stayed whenever he came to Paris from Montfort l'Amaury.'

The Godebski influence was extended into the higher circles of society by way of Cipa's half sister, Misia. A famous beauty who was admired by Mallarmé, painted by Bonnard and Renoir and featured by Toulouse-Lautrec as a skater on a celebrated poster for the *Revue blanche* in 1895, she was married in turn to Thadée Natanson, co-founder of the *Revue blanche*, Alfred Edwards, editor of *Le Matin*, and

Misia Natanson (née Godebska) featured as a skater in Toulouse-Lautrec's poster for *La Revue blanche* (1896)

Henri Matisse painted his *Luxe, calme et volupté* in 1904, not long before Ravel, in an apparently similar frame of mind, wrote his *Introduction and Allegro*.

the Spanish painter José Maria Sert. At this time she was in her Edwards period and it was at least partly because of Godebski pressure that *Le Matin*, which was not noted for its arts coverage, took an exhaustive interest in the scandal of Ravel and the Prix de Rome, interviewing the composer and several other principal protagonists in the affair. And it was probably because of the Edwards's gratitude to Ravel for providing such valuable front-page material that they invited him to accompany them on a yachting cruise which would take him, together with the artists Pierre Bonnard and Pierre Laprade, to Belgium, Holland and Germany and away from the controversy for nearly the whole of June and July.

Before he could board the Edwards's yacht, however, Ravel had his first major commission to fulfil. It had come from Albert Blondel, director of the instrument manufacturer Erard, who was eager to promote his company's double-action pedal harp in competition with Pleyel's chromatic harp, for which Debussy had recently written his *Danse sacrée et danse profane*. The result of the eight days and three sleepless nights Ravel devoted to the task was the *Introduction and Allegro* for harp, flute, clarinet and string quartet. A work of apparently effortless spontaneity, it is all *luxe, calme et volupté* – a

musical equivalent of the Matisse painting which bears that line from
Baudelaire as its title and which was executed at almost exactly the
same time. Critics who disapprove of the *Pavane pour une Infante
défunte* tend to disapprove also of the septet, as though here too the
qualities that make the piece so popular should count against it.
It is true that the *Introduction and Allegro* is shamelessly melodious,
seductive in harmony and alluringly coloured. But, shaped as a concerto movement with a slow introduction and a harp cadenza near the
end, it does not lack the classical virtues of a perfectly proportioned
and thoroughly integrated construction. It was also most effectively
written for its immediate purpose. Though Ravel can scarcely take the
credit for rendering the chromatic harp redundant, he did demonstrate what poetry the pedal harp is capable of and how well it blends
with woodwind and strings. In terms of sound, Debussy's chastely
scored dances for the chromatic harp – which, significantly, are
nowadays played on the pedal harp – could not compete.

One other thing Ravel had to do before joining the Edwards and
their other guests on board the luxury yacht *Aimée* was to pay a
visit to his outfitters and get himself appropriately costumed for the
voyage. This last-minute activity caused him not only to miss the
boat but also, in his excitement with what a friend described as an
'unforgettable' yachting cap, to leave the manuscript of the
Introduction and Allegro on the shop counter. *Aimée* he caught up with
by road in a lock at Soissons; the manuscript was taken good care of
by the chemisier who, fortunately, was a music lover and knew what
a precious document it was.

Once he was safely on board and embarked on what he called 'this
fairy-tale' cruise, Ravel was 'perfectly happy'. He had little in common
with Alfred Edwards, a notorious vulgarian and a prominent leader
of illiberal opinion in the Dreyfus affair, but the very much more
sympathetic Ida and Cipa Godebski were on board too. As for
Bonnard and Laprade, though he makes no mention of them in the
cards and letters he posted en route, their presence seems to have
sharpened his observation of the passing landscape. It was perhaps as
a counterpoint to their painterly perceptions that he somewhat self-
consciously insisted on drawing attention to the industrial scenery.
What an artist might have seen as a conventionally picturesque scene
of a lake surrounded by windmills – 'whichever way you look nothing

but turning sails' – Ravel saw as 'a mechanical landscape' where
'you end up feeling you are a machine yourself.' Just outside Liège he
interrupted a letter to rush onto the deck for a better view of
'a peculiar and magnificent factory'. At Arhaus he took ecstatic
pleasure in

*a gigantic foundry where 24,000 workers labour night and day … a
prodigious spectacle. We went down to the factories as night was falling.
I don't know how to describe the impression made by these castles of
smelting, these incandescent cathedrals, this marvellous symphony of
conveyor belts, whistles, and massive hammer blows that envelop you.
Everywhere a sky glowing dark red. Then a storm broke. We went back
horribly soaked and in different moods. Ida was terrified and wanted
to cry. So did I, but with joy. How musical all that is! I certainly intend
to make use of it.*

The direct result of that and similar experiences, beginning with
'the clicking and roaring' of the machines in Joseph Ravel's workshop, should have been in an opera based on *Die versunkene Glocke*
('The Sunken Bell') by the German playwright Gerhardt Hauptmann.
Ravel discovered the play – in a French translation, *La Cloche
engloutie*, by Ferdinand Hérold – on a bookstall by the Seine in 1905
and was attracted immediately by the mixture of supernatural with
everyday life in this 'fable-drama'. According to Hérold, who col-
laborated with Ravel on creating the libretto, the scenes which take
place in the workshop of its central figure, a bell-founder, 'would have
been of singular power. Ravel did not have a little craftsman's studio in
mind; he was thinking rather of a vast factory, equipped like the most
grandiose of those we see today, and he would have used innumerable
sounds of hammers, saws, files, sirens …' Unfortunately, although two
of the five acts were substantially sketched by 1909 when a contract
was signed by Ravel, Hérold, Hauptmann and the publisher Durand,
progress on the work was slow and was abandoned entirely when
Germany declared war on France in 1914. Some of Ravel's music for
La Cloche engloutie was used in *L'Enfant et les Sortilèges* in 1925 but
most of it was eventually discarded.

The priority in 1905 was not the opera project, which was to
make a major claim on the composer's attention in 1906, but the

completion of two piano works, the *Sonatine* and *Miroirs*, which – because of the distractions of the Prix de Rome affair, the yachting cruise, a more modest boating holiday with Maurice and Nelly Delage at Mary-sur-Marne and a trip to Brittany in August – he had had to put on one side for a while.

Actually, he was able to complete the *Sonatine*, which he had begun in 1903 and which must have been well advanced by now, in the few days he spent in Paris before leaving for Brittany. If, as the next piano work after *Jeux d'eau*, the *Sonatine* seems an anomalous act of self-denial, the facts are otherwise. It is true that in *Jeux d'eau* Ravel had joyously discovered a new kind of impressionism. It is also true that the first movement of the *Sonatine* was written as a kind of neo-classical exercise, in response to a competition sponsored by a short-lived Anglo-French periodical called *The Weekly Review*. But it is not true that the *Sonatine* and *Jeux d'eau* are essentially and irreconcilably different. *Jeux d'eau*, for all its poetry and its picturesque imagery, is basically a sonata-form construction. Conversely, for all the classical allusions of the *Sonatine*, the lyrical main theme of the opening 'Modéré' movement is carried on the current of something not unlike the running-water arpeggio figuration of parts of *Jeux d'eau*.

The 'Mouvement de Menuet', the second movement of the *Sonatine*, is not cold pastiche but another stage in Ravel's compulsion to recreate the minuet in his own image. For all its charm, it is another example of the ghost of Chabrier getting in the way, though far less intrusively here than ten years earlier in the *Menuet antique* of 1895. What is anomalous, stylistically, is the 'Animé' finale, which is more closely related to the 'Toccata' finale of Debussy's *Pour le piano* of 1901 than anything Ravel himself had written up to that point; structurally, in its ingenious integration of the main theme of the first movement with its own impulsive momentum, it is perfectly in place.

In *Miroirs*, on the other hand, in *Noctuelles* and *Une Barque sur l'océan* at least, there is a direct and progressive development of the impressionist technique of *Jeux d'eau*. The activity of lepidoptera rather than the splashing of water is the subject of *Noctuelles* ('Night Moths'): 'The moths which take clumsy flight from barn to barn to tie themselves to other beams,' runs a line from Léon-Paul Fargue, the Apache poet to whom the piece is dedicated. The rhythms and harmonies are correspondingly even less predictable than those of

Jeux d'eau – so much so that a comparatively static passage of gently tolling bells is introduced in the middle to stabilize the construction – but the fluttering keyboard figuration of the outer sections is clearly related to that of the earlier work.

Paradoxically, the earliest of the five pieces, *Oiseaux tristes* ('Sad Birds'), was written in quite a different spirit. Ravel was working on it in 1904 when Viñes told him that Debussy was thinking about writing music which was so free in form that it would seem improvised or torn straight out of a sketch book. Ravel welcomed the idea: 'I would really like to do something to free myself from *Jeux d'eau*,' he is quoted as saying. Based on the song of a blackbird noted down on a walk in the woods at Fontainebleau and evoking, in the composer's own words, 'birds lost in the torpor of a very dark forest at the hottest time of summer', *Oiseaux tristes* does indeed seem so spontaneous that it might have been improvised. According to Ravel, it is the 'most typical' piece in the set, which, if he meant musically typical, is very difficult to understand. He had written nothing at all like it before and – although the structure of *Oiseaux tristes* is simply the reverse of that of *Noctuelles* – he was to write nothing very like it later. What he might have meant to say, in his characteristically reticent way, is that the sound of the blackbird sadly repeating its two-note motif against dark and alien harmonies reflects something of his own loneliness. Its nearest relation, *Le Gibet* in *Gaspard de la nuit*, is even more desolate.

The next *Miroir* piece in order of composition after *Oiseaux tristes* was *Une Barque sur l'océan* ('A Boat on the Ocean'), which most successfully develops the scope of *Jeux d'eau* to a full-scale seascape. Written in March 1905, at the same time as Debussy was working on *La Mer* and several weeks before the yachting cruise, it calls to mind perhaps the little blue fishing boats in the harbour at St-Jean-de-Luz. At first it seems that the boat is rocking gently at its moorings: the opening theme is repeated over and over again, at the same pitch and against much the same gently rippling arpeggios, before getting into deeper harmonic water. Winds, signalled by double-trilled crescendos high in the right hand, carry it into swirling squalls. An apparent restoration of tranquillity proves to be illusory. It is only in the last bars that the theme returns to the security of the harmonies in which it set out.

If *Alborada del gracioso* ('The Fool's Aubade') seems out of place in *Miroirs*, brilliant piano music though it is, the reason could be that it is the only one of the five scenes with a human presence. It might also have something to do with the fact that it derives from a concept Ravel had explored more than ten years earlier in his *Sérénade grotesque*, which is also vigorous Spanish dance music articulated in guitar-like figuration and offset by expressive if caricatured vocal melody. It is presented very much more effectively here, of course, with a stylish seguidilla framing a vividly characterized middle section where the gracioso (the pathetic jester of classical Spanish comedy) sings his lugubrious serenade. The Spanish serenade concept achieved its ultimate realization in Ravel's masterful orchestration of the *Alborada* thirteen years later.

La Vallée des cloches ('The Valley of the Bells') is also a return to an earlier concept, this one having been first tried out in 1897 in *Entre Cloches*, the highly clangorous partner of *Habanera* in *Sites auriculaires*. Though based on the same idea of a counterpoint of bells ringing with the same salient intervals and similarly insistent repeated notes, *La Vallée des cloches* is a very much more poetic and persuasive composition. The sonorously harmonized middle section enshrines one of the most beautiful and most sustained melodies to be found anywhere in Ravel's music.

'My *Miroirs*,' said Ravel, 'marked such a considerable change in my harmonic development that it disconcerted those musicians who were most familiar with my style up to that point.' In fact, not even the Apaches, including the specially favoured five of them associated with *Miroirs* as dedicatees, understood them immediately. *Oiseaux tristes* was particularly problematical: Ricardo Viñes, dedicatee of that piece, confessed that he was the only one who actually liked it. As for the general public, when Viñes gave the first performance of *Miroirs* at a Société Nationale concert in the Salle Erard on 6 January 1906, although they encored *Alborada del gracioso*, according to one witness they hissed other parts of the work. While some critics, like Marnold and Calvocoressi (dedicatee of the *Alborada*), greeted *Miroirs* with enthusiasm, Pierre Lalo praised it faintly and accused the composer in an oblique sort of way of exploiting Debussy's keyboard innovations: 'After Chopin, after Schumann, after Liszt, Monsieur Debussy has created a new way of writing for the piano ... You scarcely hear anything these days without the arabesques, passage work and arpeggios invented by Monsieur Debussy.'

Annoyed by the implications of what he was saying, Ravel wrote to Lalo, politely but firmly and quite properly insisting on the priority of his *Jeux d'eau*. That work was published, he said, 'at the beginning of 1902, when all there was of Debussy was the three pieces *Pour le piano* – a work which, I don't have to tell you, I admire passionately but which, from a *purely pianistic* point of view, has nothing new in it.' If it was indiscreet of Ravel to say what he did, it was highly mischievous of Lalo to publish what was actually a personal letter in *Le Temps* two years later. The relationship between the two composers, already severely strained by Ravel's taking sides with Debussy's first wife when he left her for Emma Bardac, could not then survive such a setback.

Claude Debussy and his second wife Emma Bardac: Ravel's support for Debussy's first wife was the final cause of the rift between the two composers.

It was unfortunate that *Miroirs* was presented in Paris before the slightly earlier and much less challenging *Sonatine* which would surely have predisposed the audience in Ravel's favour. Sensitive though he was to adverse criticism, however, Ravel was never put off his work by anything but ill health or the most devastating of personal tragedies. Just before he wrote to Lalo he told Jean Marnold that he was thinking about writing 'a grand waltz, a sort of homage to the memory of the great Strauss, not Richard, the other, Johann. You know how much I love those wonderful rhythms.' In fact, *La Valse* would not be written until fourteen years later. But he had his Hauptmann opera, *La Cloche engloutie*, to occupy him and more new works to introduce.

On 24 March he and the soprano Jane Bathori gave the first performance of 'Noël des Jouets' ('The Toys' Christmas'), for which, presumably during the previous December, he had written both the music and the words. It is not great or even good verse but it is revealing. There is no human or divine presence in this nursery-crib Nativity, only toy animals and Christmas-tree angels, a doll Virgin, a Child of coloured sugar and, lurking in the woods, a sinister dog. It is a scene perfectly suited to the bright enamelled surfaces, the jewelled detail, and the mechanical rhythms so characteristic of his music. A charming song, which anticipates *Ma Mère l'Oye* in places, Ravel liked it so much that he immediately made an arrangement for voice and orchestra. As though to compensate for that little self-indulgence, he turned in April to a contrastingly bleak poem by Henri de Régnier,

The soprano Jane Bathori, who appeared in many concerts with Ravel and gave first performances of several of his songs, was also an excellent pianist and frequently accompanied herself at the piano.

his winter townscape 'Les Grands Vents venus d'outre-mer' ('The Great Winds Coming from Overseas'), and during the next few months wrote a song which, though appropriately sombre, does not escape the rhetorical trap he had already fallen into in 'Un Grand Sommeil noir' and 'Si morne'.

The most successful and most substantial of the works completed in 1906 were two very different sets of songs. The earliest of the *Cinq mélodies populaires grecques* ('Five Greek Folksongs') were written in 1904 at the urgent request of Pierre Aubry who needed to illustrate a lecture he was giving on Greek folksong. Their mutual friend, M. D. Calvocoressi, who was of Greek descent, found five choice examples and Ravel supplied piano accompaniments for them in a mere thirty-six hours. Calvocoressi, who was most impressed by this 'extraordinary feat', then produced three more Greek folksongs and commissioned Ravel to arrange these as well. The new collection, selected from eight arrangements in all, was first performed (probably in Greek) by Marguerite Barbaïan and published as *Cinq mélodies populaires grecques* in Calvocoressi's French translations in 1906. Surprisingly, considering how brief the songs and how minimal the accompani-ment – with the entertaining exception of the bagpipe-style ritornello in 'Qual galant m'est comparable?' – Ravel immediately set to work on orchestrating them. Less surprisingly, he lost interest after 'Chanson de la mariée' and 'Tout gai!' and the orchestration remained incomplete until 1935 when Ravel's last pupil, Manuel Rosenthal, undertook the task.

Charming though they are, the *Cinq mélodies populaires grecques* entered the repertoire almost unnoticed. The *Histoires naturelles*, on the other hand, caused a scandal almost equal in proportion to that of the 'affaire Ravel' in 1905. The composer did not expect the first performance of *Histoires naturelles* to take place entirely without opposition: it was to be given at a concert presented by the Société Nationale, which was becoming more and more reactionary as it fell more and more under the control of Vincent D'Indy and like-minded representatives of his Schola Cantorum. A devotee of everything Ravel preferred to avoid in his music – Beethoven, Franck, Wagner, a Christian aesthetic – D'Indy could surely be relied upon to disapprove of a work as radically opposed to his high-minded principles as *Histoires naturelles*. So on the day of the concert, in the hope of winning the public support of the author of his songs, Ravel called on the irascible and aptly named Jules Renard to invite him to the Salle Erard in the evening. Unfortunately, Renard, who had only reluctantly given his permission for the setting a few weeks earlier, pleaded an indisposition and sent his wife and daughter in his place. Ravel, whom he described as 'dark, rich and elegant', had not impressed him. If he had known that Ravel was not rich but, because of his dandified appearance, only looked it, and if he had been aware that he shared some of his socialist principles, he might have been more sympathetic. As it was, he grumpily asked Ravel what a composer could add to the *Histoires naturelles* and was not convinced by Ravel's answer that it was his intention not to add but to interpret, 'to say with music what you say with words.'

Jules Renard, author of
the *Histoires naturelles*,
caricatured by Sem in 1903

Ravel was probably attracted to the *Histoires naturelles* in the first place by the high quality of the artists – Toulouse-Lautrec in 1899, Bonnard in 1904 – who had illustrated the earliest editions. On reading Renard's text, which consists of dozens of short characterizations of the birds and animals of the farm and the surrounding countryside, he must have been delighted to find a kindred spirit: Renard's unsentimental and often ironic attitude to his subjects offsets but does not conceal his affection for them. While not forgetting Chabrier's delightful farmyard songs, *Les Cigales* least of all, Ravel decided not to emulate them in imposing even the most subtle

La Pintade

One of Toulouse-Lautrec's lithograph illustrations for the 1889 edition of Renard's *Histoires naturelles*

of melodic and metrical patterns on the words. On the contrary, it was his intention to shape the vocal line entirely according to the natural inflections and rhythms of Renard's calculatedly prosaic language. And since he was setting prose rather than verse, he determined to ignore the mute 'e' which is counted as a syllable in conventional French musical prosody but which remains silent in everyday speech.

This last technical detail, which in academic opinion reduced the songs to café-concert or music-hall status, was a disproportionately significant factor in stimulating the outraged reaction to the *Histoires naturelles* on their first performance on 12 January 1907. Bathori and Ravel encored the last song in the set, 'La Pintade', but this was more an act of defiance than anything else. It was quite clear from the booing, whistling and derisory laughter directed at the singer and the composer-pianist from an early stage in the performance that the songs had not given the audience the gratification it expected. Worse still, the unique qualities they offered in their place had not been appreciated. Word-setting so sensitive and so natural that those who knew the composer could recognize his ironic tone of voice was no compensation for the absence of old-fashioned vocal melody.

The major musical interest in *Histoires naturelles* is in the extravagantly witty, brilliantly colourful and discreetly affectionate piano part. In 'Le Paon', strutting about in his best clothes as though it were his wedding day and waiting in vain for his bride, the peacock is accompanied in his progress by the stately dotted rhythms of the Baroque French overture; his 'diabolical cry' of 'Léon! Léon!' is heralded by a crescendo of discords and his ceremonial display of his tail feathers signalled by a dramatic glissando in both hands. Perhaps the most inspired setting from the colouristic point of view is 'Le Grillon', where Renard associates the cricket's chirping with some domestic activity, like winding his tiny watch or turning a key in a delicate lock, and where between disconcerting silences Ravel reflects its metallic sound in glittering high-pitched dissonances. In 'Le Cygne', chasing reflections of clouds in the water, the swan floats on ripples of Debussy-like impressionism until its poetic pretensions are drily dismissed at the end. 'Le Martin-pêcheur', where a kingfisher robs an angler of his breath by perching on his fishing rod, is a precarious study in suppressed motion and scarcely whispered commentary. 'La Pintade' is just the opposite: the self-consciously ugly and aggressive guinea-fowl attacks the chickens and the turkey-hen in a vigorous Spanish dance rhythm and utters her piercing cry in a volley of repeated notes.

Echoing something of Mussorgsky's *Nursery* songs in their naturalistic word setting and vivaciously detailed piano part, while anticipating something of Janácek's *Cunning Little Vixen* in its anthropomorphic imagery, the *Histoires naturelles* seem to us now an entirely appropriate development in their time. But for many of Ravel's contemporaries they were not just unacceptably progressive: they were positively offensive. Pierre Lalo made the inevitable deprecatory comparison with the café concert while a Schola Cantorum critic went so far as to declare war on such 'musical decomposition'. Debussy, who clearly missed the point of the impressionist parody in 'Le Cygne', admitted to finding some 'very attractive music' in that particular song but took his friend Louis Laloy to task for finding genuine comedy in these 'conjuring tricks'. Even Fauré, who had always been able to support his former pupil up to now, was alienated:

'I like him very much but I wish he wouldn't set such things to music.'
Ravel – whose side was taken in this new controversy by Jean-Aubry,
Calvocoressi and Marnold as well as Laloy – was quite unrepentant of
course. Indeed, as he said later, his experience with Renard's *Histoires
naturelles* prepared him for his operatic setting of the scarcely less
prosaic text of Franc-Nohain's *L'Heure espagnole*.

What caused Ravel to interrupt work on *La Cloche engloutie* for a
less ambitious opera project was the seriously declining health of his
father. Joseph Ravel had suffered a slight stroke in the summer of 1906
and, while still preoccupied by *La Cloche engloutie*, Maurice had taken
him to recuperate in Hermance near Lake Geneva. Unfortunately,
although the holiday in Switzerland restored his spirits somewhat,
Joseph's health continued to deteriorate to the extent that by June of
the following year he could scarcely walk. By now, as the central figure
of two very public scandals within two years, Maurice Ravel was a
celebrity and, although his genius was recognized by only a minority
in the musical world, that group was growing. But for Joseph Ravel
success in the concert hall meant nothing like as much as success in

Joseph Ravel at Hermance
on Lake Geneva in August
1906 with his sister Louise
Perrin, his son Maurice
and his niece Hélène Perrin

the opera house. It was to please the old man while there was still time that the composer turned his attention to *L'Heure espagnole*, a one-act comedy which should not take too long to set and would surely be easier to get performed than the five-act opera *La Cloche engloutie* was intended to be.

Before he could apply himself to *L'Heure espagnole* he had a song or, more accurately, a vocal study to write. *Vocalise-Étude en forme de habanera* was commissioned for a collection of wordless songs intended to familiarize singing students with the problems of modern vocal writing. Better known as *Pièce en forme de habanera* in a variety of instrumental arrangements (none of them by Ravel himself), it amounts to little more than a decorative reworking of the early *Habanera* for two pianos and is of correspondingly little significance in the composer's development. It was, on the other hand, a useful preparation for *L'Heure espagnole* where one of the characters is much given to vocalizing in the Spanish idiom and not least in habanera rhythms. The other song Ravel completed in 1907, a setting of Verlaine's tipsy little rococo parody, 'Sur l'herbe' in *Fêtes galantes*, was also relevant to his work on his *comédie musicale*. There is nothing Spanish about 'Sur l'herbe' but it does have other characteristics in common with the *L'Heure espagnole*: in its naturalistic observation of the inflections of spoken dialogue, its provocative flirting with dance rhythms, and its ironic characterization the song is closer to the opera than the stylistic division between Verlaine's delicately witty poem and Franc-Nohain's robust comedy might suggest.

Ravel could have seen *L'Heure espagnole* during its long run at the Odéon in 1904 but it seems from something he wrote later that he first came across it in book form rather than on the stage. Explaining that he had 'long thought of composing music that would be funny,' he said that 'in reading *L'Heure espagnole* by Franc-Nohain, I realized that this comic fantasy would be suitable for my purpose.' He went on to describe 'a heap of things' that attracted him in the text: 'the mixture of everyday conversation and deliberately ridiculous lyricism; the atmosphere of unusual and amusing sounds surrounding the characters in the clock shop; finally, the opportunity to make good use of the picturesque rhythms of Spanish music.' For a composer brought up, as he once said, 'on the clicking and roaring of my father's machines' and 'the Spanish folk songs sung to me by my mother',

Franc-Nohain, dramatist and author of the comedy which furnished the text for Ravel's first stage work, *L'Heure espagnole*

L'heure Espagnole

L'Heure espagnole, le brillant petit acte de M. Franc Nohain, pour lequel M. Maurice Ravel écrivit une partition du plus curieux intérêt, peut se prévaloir justement d'une interprétation hors de pair. En effet, Mlle Vix, étrange et troublant Zuloaga, a apporté dans la composition du rôle de Conception l'originalité précieuse qui la classe parmi les meilleures comédiennes lyriques de notre époque. M. Jean Périer, dont le talent multiple se plaît dans la variété, est toujours l'admirable chanteur et l'admirable acteur que chacun sait. MM. Delvoye, Coulomb et Cazeneuve contribuèrent certes pour beaucoup à la réussite de cet ouvrage très applaudi. Au milieu de la page : M. PÉRIER ; à gauche en haut : M. PÉRIER ; en bas : Mme VIX ; à droite en haut : M. COULOMB ; en bas : M. DELVOYE.

L'Heure espagnole, set in a clockmaker's shop in Spain, was ideal material. All he had to do to fabricate a libretto from it was change a few words and make a few cuts. Franc-Nohain's comically clumsy rhymes he was happy to retain.

The plot of *L'Heure espagnole* revolves round Concepcion, wife of the sexually inadequate clockmaker, Torquemada, who lives above the shop in Toledo. At home during the rest of the week, every Thursday Torquemada goes out to regulate the municipal clocks, leaving Concepcion a precious hour in which to entertain her lovers. This Thursday she is put out by the presence in the shop of Ramiro, the postal muleteer, who has come to have his watch repaired and has to wait for Torquemada's return. The only way she can discreetly get her lovers to her bedroom – first the student Gonzalve and then the corpulent old banker Don Inigo Gomez – is to conceal them in clocks in the shop and get the unsuspecting Ramiro, who would much rather move furniture than make polite conversation, to carry them up and down for her. To her frustration Gonzalve proves to be more poetic than potent and Don Inigo too fat to extricate himself from his clock. So, with both clocks and their contents returned to the shop, she invites Ramiro upstairs again, but this time 'without a clock'.

Costume designs for Franc-
Nohain's one-act comedy,
L'Heure espagnole

Torquemada returns, finds the severely embarrassed Gonzalve and
Don Inigo apparently taking a deep interest in the two long-case
clocks, and triumphantly makes a sale to both of them. The moral
of the story, we are told on the return of Ramiro and Concepcion, is
that 'every muleteer has his day.'

If Ravel identified with any one of these characters, it was not
Torquemada, whose status as a cuckold is signalled even by his own
cuckoo clocks, or the more rounded figure of Don Inigo Gomez, who
struts about to much the same vainglorious rhythms as the peacock
in the *Histoires naturelles*, or even the poetic Gonzalve, whose
impromptu vocalizations are patently absurd. As for Concepcion and
Ramiro, the sturdy rhythms repeatedly associated with the muleteer
are certainly more engaging than the exasperated vocal line of the
clockmaker's wife. But there is more of Ravel in Gonzalve than in
Ramiro. Except in one or two clearly heartfelt episodes, where he is
enchanted by the magic of the clock shop and endearingly confused
by the coincidence of the mechanical and the erotic, Ramiro is just
another counter in an elaborate board game.

Ravel is interested not so much in people here as in their language,
the natural inflections of which determine the rhythm and melodic
shape of the vocal line, just as in the *Histoires naturelles* and 'Sur
l'herbe'. The composer's instructions in the score are explicit in this
respect: 'Except in the final quintet and, for the most part, in the
affectedly lyrical role of Gonzalve, *speak* rather than *sing*.' The sole
precedent, Ravel wrote in an open letter published in *Le Figaro* just
before the first performance in May 1911, was Mussorgsky's unfinished
opera *The Wedding*. In fact, that work could have had no influence on
L'Heure espagnole since Ravel had only just got to know it through
the writer Robert d'Harcourt, who had asked him to orchestrate it
(a task he would gladly have carried out if he had been offered an
adequate fee). Besides, as he said in the letter to *Le Figaro*, his first
intention was to 'regenerate Italian *opera buffa*' – which has sung
recitative where the French *opéra comique* has spoken dialogue.
L'Heure espagnole is 'a *musical* comedy', Ravel emphasized, 'in
which the laughs are not in the comically arbitrary accentuation of
words, as in operetta, but in unusual effects in harmony, rhythm,
melody and orchestration.'

The score of *L'Heure espagnole* is abundant in such effects, many
of the wittiest of them having to do with the lower instruments of the
orchestra – portentous bassoons, derisory trombones, a lugubrious
tuba. The most sustained example of the composer's extraordinary ear
for instrumental colour, and the most important, since it sets the
clockwork scene and recurs from time to time to confirm it, is the
orchestral introduction. Over an eerie background of slowly shifting
shadows on wind and strings in parallel motion, three metronomes
tick at different speeds, bells ring out of time, a mechanical trumpeter
sounds a fanfare, puppets dance to a musical-box celesta, an imitation
cock crows on the detached mouthpiece of a sarrusophone, a metallic
bird utters a shrill call on the piccolo. It is the mechanical equivalent
of the luxuriant nature imagery in the daybreak episode in *Daphnis
et Chloé.*

If this introductory material was originally conceived for
Coppelius's workshop in Ravel's unfinished opera, *Olympia* – and it
is generally believed that it was – it is scarcely less apposite here in
Torquemada's clockwork emporium. It does mean, on the other hand,
that there is no specifically Spanish allusion until the entry of Ramiro
in the first scene, where his account of how his watch saved the life
of his toreador uncle at a bullfight in Barcelona inspires a surprisingly
vigorous jota. The main source of Spanish dance rhythms is not the
heavy-treading muleteer, however, but Gonzalve, who makes his first
appearance on a prolonged flamenco vocalization and whose feeble
poetic improvisations are based either on the habanera or, in a last
inappropriate gesture, the malagueña. Concepcion very briefly joins
him at one point in an habanera, though more in anger than sym-
pathy, and expresses the extreme of her frustration in an aggressively
percussive and highly coloured seguidilla with an ironically pathetic
bassoon obbligato. Torquemada is clearly not interested in dancing
and Don Inigo, when his baroque pompousness so disarmingly melts
into romantic sentiment, prefers the waltz to anything Spanish. At
the end, when the story is over and its moral is to be drawn, all five
singers join in an extravagantly overloaded habanera, the one and only
ensemble in fifty-five Spanish minutes.

Driven by the failing health of his father, Ravel all but completed
L'Heure espagnole in less than three months in the summer of 1907.
On 16 August he wrote to Jane Courteault from Morgat in Brittany,

where he had gone to recover from what he described as this 'insane amount of work', to tell her that the opera 'will probably be presented at the Opéra-Comique this winter, the director having declared that we won't have to wait very long.' In fact, he was in for a disappointment and had to wait for as long as four years for his *L'Heure espagnole* to be performed. His father, who at least had the satisfaction of seeing the vocal score of his son's first opera published by Durand, died on 13 October 1908.

6

Mikhail Fokin from a drawing
by V. Serov

*Things are even more complicated because
Fokin doesn't know a word of French and all
I know of Russian is how to swear in it ... You
can imagine the atmosphere of these meetings.*

Maurice Ravel on *Daphnis et Chloé*

Maturity 1907-12

Ravel's holiday in Brittany in July and August 1907 was so effective
in restoring his creative energy after the intense effort he had put
into *L'Heure espagnole* that by September he was already at work on
another major score. Reluctant, evidently, to spend longer than
necessary in the heavy-industrial surroundings of the family home
at Levallois-Perret, he installed himself for a second time on the
Edwards's yacht, which was now moored alongside the Godebskis's
country home, La Grangette, at Valvins near Fontainebleau. With
Misia's grand piano on board and with only swimming, boating and
a sudden craze for diabolo to distract him from work, he was in
the ideal situation to apply himself to a new project. The vocal
score of the opera was not quite finished and he would be working
on that until October. But at the same time, his interest in the
Spanish idiom stimulated rather than stifled by his work on
L'Heure espagnole, he made a start on the three pieces which together
with *Habanera*, the astonishing two-piano masterpiece of 1895,
would become the *Rapsodie espagnole*. Although the new movements
were written first in two-piano form, it was always intended that
the rhapsody would ultimately be scored for orchestra – in
preparation, perhaps, for the scoring of *L'Heure espagnole* which he
would complete when there seemed to be a firm prospect of a
performance.

It was in the midst of this activity that, towards the end of 1907,
Ravel was introduced to his only British pupil. In search of what he
called 'a little French polish', Ralph Vaughan Williams had turned first
to Delius and finding little encouragement there, apparently, was put
in touch with Ravel by their mutual friend M. D. Calvocoressi. It was
agreed that Vaughan Williams would come to Paris for a course
of four or five lessons a week over a period of three months. After an
initial misunderstanding – the English composer had to make it clear
that he had not come to Paris to write anything as elementary as a
'petit menuet dans le style de Mozart' – they became great friends. 'I

learned much from Ravel,' he declared: 'for example, that the heavy
contrapuntal Teutonic manner was not necessary. "Complexe mais pas
compliqué" was his motto. He showed me how to orchestrate in
points of colour rather than in lines … I practised chiefly
orchestration with him. I used to score some of his own pianoforte
music and bits of Rimsky and Borodin to which he introduced me for
the first time.'

It is interesting that they concentrated on orchestration in these
lessons. Although Vaughan Williams had written little orchestral
music at that time, Ravel, who was three years younger, had written
even less: excluding Prix de Rome pieces, the only orchestral works he

Ravel's only British pupil,
Ralph Vaughan Williams in
about 1910

had completed were the *Shéhérazade* Overture, the *Shéhérazade* songs and a version of *Une Barque sur l'océan* which had proved such a miscalculation on its performance a few months earlier that he had immediately withdrew it. In studying *Antar* and other favourite Russian scores with Vaughan Williams, consciously or not Ravel was also giving himself an advanced course in orchestration. While the pupil was being taught a basic impressionist technique the teacher was developing a different orchestral sound. Concerned more with primary colours than suggestive shading, more with firmly defined outlines than vaguely poetic shapes, it had less in common with impressionism than with the Fauvist vision recently realised on canvas by Henri Matisse, André Derain and, among others, Henri-Charles Manguin. Ravel, who admired Manguin enough to have sat for a portrait for him in 1903, cannot have been unaware of this latest development in French painting. Indeed, he had observed it for himself at the Salon d'Automne, if not in 1905 – when the colour-intoxicated Matisse and his similarly uninhibited colleagues were first described by a journalist as *fauves* or 'wild beasts' – then certainly

Maurice Ravel as portrayed in 1903 by Henri-Charles Manguin a painter who would be associated with Matisse, Derain and the Fauves a couple of years later

in 1906, when the Gauguin retrospective in the same building also
made an impression on him.

Creating an equivalent Fauve effect in music was a considerable
technical problem, in spite of the discoveries he was still making in the
scores of his favourite Russian composers. Although the three new
movements of the *Rapsodie espagnole* were written in the two-piano
version within a few weeks, the preparation of the orchestral score
took much longer and was completed only in March 1908, after
Vaughan Williams's return to London. Ravel had by no means
rejected impressionism: *Prélude à la nuit* ('Prelude at Night') – its
exotically shaped four-note motif passing stealthily through the
shadows, its distant hints of a languorously syncopated dance rhythm
developing into a fragmentary serenade – is highly atmospheric and,
except in the brightly illuminated cadenzas on clarinets and bassoons,
it is by suggestion rather than by definition. Much the same applies to
the third movement, the *Habanera* of 1895, which is presented here
virtually unchanged, its impressionist poetry and its peculiar static
quality both reflected in the pointillistic orchestral colouring of 1908.

The pieces which frame *Habanera*, on the other hand, *Malagueña*
and *Feria*, are remarkable for their vivid and rhythmically mobile
splashes of primary colour. Presumably in order to reserve the most
sensational effect for the end of the work, *Malagueña* is cut off at its
climax by the intervention of a soulful cor anglais projecting its *cante
flamenco* into the gathering shadows amid renewed repetitions of the
nocturnal four-note motif from the first movement. *Feria*, a vigorous
and comparatively extended jota, is interrupted by a similar night-
time episode: the cor anglais solo is this time accompanied by
seductively feline voices on a double bass with two cellos and
gradually merges into a more comprehensive memory of the *Prélude à
la nuit*. Unlike *Malagueña*, however, and in spite of the continuing
presence of the four-note motif, *Feria* is resumed in its full daylight
brilliance and finally transcends the previous climax in a burst of
colour so intense in its whole-tone dissonance that it anticipates the
violent, expressionist gestures at the end of *La Valse* and *Boléro*.

In its day, before Diaghilev had formed the Ballets Russes and
before the first of Stravinsky's ballets had been written, the liberation
of primitive rhythmic instincts offered by the *Rapsodie espagnole* was a
rare phenomenon. So it is surprising that after its performance in the

Théâtre du Châtelet on 15 March 1908 Pierre Lalo could describe the work in *Le Temps* as 'a parsimonious *España*'. *Rapsodie espagnole* obviously does have elements in common with Chabrier's *España*, not least the malagueña and jota rhythms, but while it is less jovial in character it is certainly no less abundant in energy. In the *Mercure musical*, on the other side of the critical divide, Jean Marnold was perceptive enough to recognize the revolutionary aspect of the instrumental colouring, the like of which he had never heard before. Writing (as Willy) in his column in *Comoedia*, Henri Gauthier-Villars compared Ravel's skill in orchestration to that of Richard Strauss – a comparison which Ravel, who admired Strauss's orchestral technique above that of any other living composer, would not have found at all unflattering.

Favourable publicity of this kind and the private encouragement given him by the Spanish composer, Manuel de Falla, who was impressed by the authentically Spanish qualities of *Rapsodie espagnole* as well as the 'unsurpassed ingeniousness and virtuosity' of the orchestration, would have been particularly welcome to Ravel at this time. In his campaign to get *L'Heure espagnole* performed he needed all the support he could find. Two months earlier he and Jane Bathori had played and sung through the score for Albert Carré, director of the Opéra-Comique, who aroused the composer's indignation by declaring the subject too provocative for the innocent ears of his subscribers. To a young man brought up in view of place Pigalle such prudishness was incomprehensible. 'This nun's mentality is very surprising in Carré. Isn't he still very young to be thinking of becoming a hermit?' wrote Ravel to one woman friend while turning to another, whose husband had recently been appointed a Government Minister, to intercede for him.

Albert Carré, director of
the Opéra-Comique from
1898 to 1913

While negotiations went on with Carré at the Opéra-Comique, Ravel was not sure what work he should be getting on with. '*Cloche engloutie*, trio, symphony, St Francis of Assisi? Don't know yet,' he wrote to Cipa Godebski shortly after the first performance of *Rapsodie espagnole*. In fact, his next major undertaking was not the Hauptmann opera project he would never finish, not the Piano Trio he would complete in 1914, not the symphony he had been working on intermittently for years and would eventually discard, and not the setting from *The Little Flowers of St Francis of Assisi* which he would probably not even sketch. The direction in which he actually chose to move, returning to the piano for the first time since *Miroirs*, proved in some ways to be a reversal of the radical departure he had made in the meantime in *Histoires naturelles* and *L'Heure espagnole*.

Aloysius Bertrand's collection of spooky prose poems *Gaspard de la nuit* was an enthusiasm of Ravel's student days. First published in 1842, a year after the poet's early death, the book had become a collector's piece until the *Mercure de France* issued a new edition in 1895 and Ravel was able to borrow a copy from Viñes. It was presumably the 1908 reprint of the *Mercure de France* edition that now revived the composer's interest. The hallucinatory intensity of Bertrand's vision overwhelmed him now just as it had in his impressionable youth. 'Perhaps I got carried away,' said Ravel to Vlado Perlemuter, confessing that in the first place he had actually intended 'to make a caricature of romanticism'. To another young musician taking a course of instruction on the interpretation of his piano music, he offered the advice that – although Bertrand's 'Ondine', 'Le Gibet' and 'Scarbo' are printed in the published score, next to the pieces they inspired – she should read the whole *Gaspard de la nuit* collection: 'It's marvellous, all the romanticism of the nineteenth century is contained in that little book.' 'Ah!' exclaimed the seventeen-year-old Henriette Faure, delighted to have discovered a crack in the armour, 'So you are sometimes a romantic after all?'

The composer's reply to the question is not recorded but the implied answer is clearly confirmed in at least *Ondine* and *Scarbo*, the first and last of what Ravel, echoing Liszt, described as his 'three poems of transcendental virtuosity'. If his pupil had compared *Ondine* with Ravel's earliest study in the sound of running water, *Jeux d'eau*, and then with Liszt's *Les Jeux d'eau à la Villa d'Este* and *Au Bord d'une source*, she would have found that it is actually closer to Liszt in poetic spirit than it is to *Jeux d'eau*. The tender melody which runs throughout *Ondine*, below or above or intermingling with the continuously rippling water figuration, betrays not a trace of irony. Representing no doubt the seductive voice of the water sprite heard in the rain falling on the window panes, the melody finally disappears in a flurry of splashing tears and laughing arpeggios, her volatile spirit clearly not too depressed by the brief but firmly uttered recitative which had rejected her advances.

The more malevolent laughter in *Scarbo* represents only one aspect of the many-sided and mercurial dwarf apparition which haunts the poet's sleepless nights. 'I wanted to write something more difficult than *Islamey*,' said Ravel, referring to Balakirev's notoriously demanding oriental fantasy – and, incidentally, revealing one of the sources of his solution to the problems of reproducing Fauve colouring in terms of the piano. He might also have mentioned Chabrier's *Bourrée fantasque*, which is a similarly challenging demonstration of the percussive energy contained in rapid repeated-note figurations like those which buzz, creak, rattle and rumble through *Scarbo*. Melodically, *Scarbo* is identified by a frantic kind of waltz tune beginning with a rising three-note motif associated in Ravel's mind with the words 'Quelle horreur!' ('What a fright!'). Rhythmically, he is unpredictable, drumming his feet to patterns of repeated notes, darting backwards and forwards in a variably vigorous skipping motif, pausing in motionless silence, dancing in defiance of the beat and, towards the end, expanding his thematic images into grand romantic gestures. Finally, like *Ondine*, *Scarbo* quietly evaporates.

Technically, *Le Gibet* ('The Gibbet'), the second of the three *Gaspard* pieces, is quite different in that it requires something other than Lisztian 'transcendental virtuosity' in its execution. In fact, whereas *Ondine* and *Scarbo* are dedicated to pianists, *Le Gibet* is dedicated to the critic Jean Marnold – 'not because you deserve the noose,' the composer reassured him, 'but because it is the least difficult of the three.' Poetically, it has no antecedent in Liszt or Balakirev or anything but Ravel's own most personal music. Its nearest relation is *Oiseaux tristes*, the lonely second movement of *Miroirs*. Whereas the earlier piece expresses nothing more alarming than a claustrophobic kind of melancholy, however, the later one is deliberately macabre. The salient feature, a motif of two or more repeated notes obsessively reiterated, is much the same in the two pieces, but in *Le Gibet* it is heard without interruption in every bar from the first to the last. 'What is it I hear?' asks the poet. 'Could it be the north wind howling in the night, or the hanging man sighing on the gibbet? ... It is a bell ringing on the walls of a town below the horizon and the hanging carcass turned red by the sun.' Whatever the changes in harmony in the slow-moving sarabande-like material in the outer sections and the sighing melody in the middle, and however disturbing the resulting dissonances, the bell continues to ring inexorably at the same pitch.

In the piano-roll recording of *Le Gibet* allegedly made by Ravel in 1922 (though actually made by Robert Casadesus under his supervision) the composer's expressive intentions are made painfully explicit by the persistently high profile of the bell notes in the otherwise subdued textures and by the sharply exaggerated crescendos. The transition from Fauvism to Expressionism seems so clear that it is tempting to speculate whether Ravel was directly influenced here by the distressing experience of watching his father gradually fade away in the family home at Levallois-Perret. But then, between the completion of *Gaspard de la nuit* in September 1908 and the death of Joseph Ravel only a month later, he retreated once more to the riverside delights of La Grangette and took refuge in the fairy-tale world of the *Pavane de la Belle au bois dormant* ('Sleeping Beauty's Pavane') – which, ostensibly at least, was written as a piano duet to amuse the two Godebski children while their parents were away in Spain. Far from indulging in bizarre fantasies about his father's imminent death, he was preserving himself from anticipating its effect until it actually hit him.

It was surely in a state of shock that Ravel, a non-believer according to everyone who knew him, was persuaded to send for the cleric among the Apaches, Abbé Léonce Petit, to administer the last rights to his dying father. Joseph Ravel had had little more to do with the Church than his son had; Manuel de Falla, on the other hand, who happened to be with the Ravels at this time, was a devout Catholic and, unwilling as ever to accept his friend's agnosticism, it was he who undertook to go and find the priest. The effects of the bereavement were prolonged. It would be eighteen months before Ravel's next major work, *Ma Mère l'Oye* ('Mother Goose') would be ready. Although such fallow seasons were to become more common as he grew older, it was a long time at this otherwise fruitful period in his life. Besides, the children's piano duet pieces of *Ma Mère l'Oye*, which consisted of the *Pavane de la Belle au bois dormant* and four new fairy-tale inspirations written in April 1910, did not amount to the hardest work he had ever undertaken.

At the same time, it is true, he had various domestic and political distractions to cope with. Within a month of Joseph Ravel's death,

The Spanish composer Manuel de Falla got to know Ravel and his music during the seven years he spent in Paris before World War I and they remained on the best of terms – in spite of Ravel's agnosticism and Falla's fervent Catholicism.

The composer at the piano in the Ravel family's 'charming' apartment at the top of the avenue Carnot, near the Arc de Triomphe, in about 1912

Roland-Manuel, a composition pupil who became one of Ravel's closest friends and his first biographer

his widow and two sons had left Levallois-Perret and had taken up residence at 4 avenue Carnot, just off the place de l'Etoile, in the much more fashionable seventeenth arrondissement. Maurice Ravel was delighted, not least with the view of the Arc de Triomphe from the drawing-room window, as he said when he reported this 'lucky find' to the Godebskis: 'a magnificent view, a delicious apartment, everything ready, even the electricity.' He saw to it that it was also furnished to his taste, the Desboutin portrait of his father occupying pride of place on the watered-silk wallcovering together with a gouache by his Apache friend Paul Sordes, two Japanese prints and, as he insisted wherever he lived, no sign at all that it was the workplace of a busy composer. Now at last he was able to invite friends and colleagues to his home: Edgard Varèse called on him shortly after he moved in; it was at 4 avenue Carnot that Roland-Manuel, his future pupil and biographer, was introduced to him by their mutual friend

Erik Satie; and the English novelist Arnold Bennett, who had first met Ravel through the Godebskis in 1908, dined there in 1911.

Professionally too, he was contemplating a move. Although he had little trouble in getting his own work into the programmes of the Société Nationale de Musique, he was becoming increasingly unhappy about the reactionary way in which it was being run by the increasingly influential Vincent D'Indy from his power-base at the Schola Cantorum. On 16 January 1909 Ricardo Viñes gave the successful first performance of *Gaspard de la nuit* at a concert presented by the Société Nationale in the Salle Érard. Only a week later Ravel resigned from the committee in protest at the exclusion of works submitted by three of his pupils, including one (Maurice Delage's *Conté par la mer*) which he considered 'particularly interesting'. As he explained with full-scale irony to his colleague Charles Koechlin, Delage's score 'didn't offer those solid qualities of incoherence and boredom which the Schola Cantorum has baptized as construction and profundity.'

Within months Ravel, Koechlin and several other former pupils of Gabriel Fauré were to form the Société Musicale Indépendante and to persuade Fauré himself to become its president while, somehow, he retained the equivalent position with the Société Nationale and, moreover, remained on friendly terms with D'Indy. In the meantime, in April 1909, Ravel gave his first concert abroad, performing the *Sonatine* and (with Emile Engel and Jane Bathori) the *Cinq Mélodies populaires grecques* and the *Histoires naturelles* for the Société des Concerts Français in London. Well received by the British public, he was also well entertained by Ralph and Adeline Vaughan Williams in Cheyne Walk where, he gratefully told them on his return to Paris, he had felt quite at home and 'almost a Londoner'.

The one piece Ravel managed to start and finish during the first seven months after the death of his father was an arrangement of another Greek folksong, *Tripatos*, for the soprano, Marguerite Barbaïan, who had given the first performance of his *Cinq Mélodies populaires grecques* three or four years earlier. Various hopeful signals from the Opéra-Comique got him working on the orchestration of *L'Heure espagnole* and, though they proved to be false alarms, he persevered with what was surely not an uncongenial task and had the full score ready in time for its publication by Durand early in 1911. But what he really needed, to set the adrenalin flowing again, was a

major challenge – which, in the form of a most timely commission
from Serge Diaghilev, he duly received. 'I have to tell you that I've just
had a mad week,' he wrote to Mme de Saint-Marceaux in June 1909:
'preparation of the libretto for a ballet to be performed by the
Russians next season, work every night until three in the morning.
Things are even more complicated because Fokin doesn't know a word
of French and all I know of Russian is how to swear in it … You can
imagine the atmosphere of these meetings.'

Difficult thought the situation clearly was, it must have been exciting too. Ravel had known about Diaghilev since 1906, when he organized an exhibition of 'Two Centuries of Russian Art' at the Salon
d'Automne (alongside the Gauguin retrospective and Matisse and the
Fauves). He first met him in 1907 when, having engaged Calvocoressi
as one of his advisers, the impresario returned to Paris to present a
season of five concerts of Russian music at the Opéra. Although the
public and the press did not much appreciate what Diaghilev had to
offer that year, they were generally overwhelmed by the production
of *Boris Godunov* which he presented at the Opéra in 1908. Most
of the major French composers, predictably excluding Saint-Saëns
but including both Debussy and Ravel, were no less profoundly
impressed. 'We did something tonight,' said Chaliapin to Diaghilev
after his sensational first night in Paris as Boris. 'I don't know what,
but we did something.'

Then, in 1909, Diaghilev mounted his first ballet season which,
though based on a largely undistinguished miscellany of music, was
another Parisian sensation, above all for the stage designers Alexandre
Benois and Léon Bakst and the dancers Anna Pavlova, Tamara
Karsavina, Ida Rubinstein and Vaslav Nijinsky. Financially, the season
at the Théâtre du Châtelet was a disaster but that did not deter
Diaghilev from planning another at the Opéra for the following year
and, in an effort to improve the quality of the music in the repertoire,
seeking to commission new scores from French composers. Encouraged no doubt by Misia Edwards, a major Diaghilev patron in Paris,
Ravel was one of those who accepted. In agreeing to compose a ballet
on the story of Daphnis and Chloe – based on the second-century
Greek pastoral romance by Longus – he had put himself in an awkward artistic situation, however. This was the first time he had under-

Serge Diaghilev who, as founder and director of the Ballets Russes had a profound influence on the development not only of ballet but also of music and visual arts in the first quarter of the twentieth century. His relationship with Ravel was not a uniformly happy one.

taken to work on a subject he had not himself chosen and, as he observed during his discussions with Diaghilev's choreographer Mikhail Fokin, he did not like it. He was not ready for the project and the project was not ready for him.

According to Fokin's *Memoirs of a Ballet Master*, the scenario of *Daphnis et Chloé* as we know it from Ravel's one-act ballet is much the same as it was when the choreographer first presented it to the composer (and not very different either, he claims, from the multi-act libretto he had offered to the Imperial Theatre in St Petersburg in 1904). This is a questionable statement. Having chosen a text celebrated for its eroticism – and intending, moreover, to base his choreography on the pagan scenes depicted on ancient Greek vases and friezes – would Fokin then have proceeded to render it as chaste as any fairy tale? It was surely Ravel who could not face the frank sexuality of Daphnis and Chloe and Ravel who – 'in many night-time hours writing the libretto' – reduced them to something not far short of the conventional rococo shepherd and shepherdess.

The likelihood is that the scenario described in Fokin's memoirs represents not the original concept, as it was before the composer was consulted, but the extent to which he was finally prepared to go along with Ravel in his emasculation of the story. 'I planned to make an elaborate dramatic sequence out of the attack of the pirates,' says Fokin. 'Ravel, however, wanted to produce a lightning attack. I yielded … I later came to reproach myself for not having insisted on this point.' So he left the full-scale attack in his account of the scenario, together with one or two details he was reluctant to part

Vaslav Nijinsky as the Faune, the role he created to his own choreograohy in the Ballets Russes production of *L'Après-midi d'un faune* in 1912

with but which were actually changed in the ballet. He goes on to say that 'with the exception of the scene just mentioned, which was even shorter than I expected, I loved the score from the first time I heard it.' But then he adds, 'I must admit that in some places I somehow felt a lack of virility which, in my opinion, was necessary for a projection of the world of antiquity.' This is surely getting nearer to the truth of the situation. Fokin obviously did not intend to make his choreography as explicit as Nijinsky's in the scandalous interpretation of Debussy's *Prélude à l'après-midi d'un faune* which was introduced into the repertoire of the Ballets Russes in the same Paris season as *Daphnis et Chloé*: he disapproved of it, though more for the Faune's notorious auto-erotic gesture at the end than anything else. But, in basing his choreography on the same sort of erotic imagery in ancient Greek art as that which inspired Nijinsky's, very different in style though they were, the two ballets would surely have had more in common than, after Ravel's intervention, they actually did.

The erotic was a sensation which Ravel had touched on only briefly in his music and, as in the *Shéhérazade* songs, discreetly rather than overtly even then. Overt sexual passion – which is obviously not the same thing as the clockwork manoeuvres of *L'Heure espagnole* – was basically alien to his art. Faced with a concept which did not suit him, he had had to persist with adapting Fokin's archaeological image of second-century Lesbos until it became compatible, as he said, with 'the Greece of my dreams, which is not unlike that imagined and depicted by French artists at the end of the eighteenth century.' Even if Bakst would not adapt his authentic-Greek vision for the sets and costumes – and, in fact, he did not – Ravel needed to be able to imagine a setting he could identify with. More important, by taking Daphnis and Chloe out of their authentic background and displacing them into a neo-classical landscape by some such artist as Jacques-Louis David, he was separating Longus's goatherd and shepherdess from their pagan sexuality.

Ravel was still not ready to embrace them even so. People, men and women as distinct from the caricature figures of *L'Heure espagnole* or the supernatural visitants of *Gaspard de la nuit*, had featured little in his music, love scenes between them not at all. Just as in preparation for his first opera he had developed certain aspects of his word-setting technique, in preparation for his first ballet he needed to extend his

Set design by Léon Bakst for
the Ballets Russes
production of *Daphnis et
Chloé* in 1912

expressive range. He also needed time to recover his creative energy –
which is why, instead of applying himself immediately to the most
important commission he had ever received, he devoted himself to
a variety of undemanding projects on a considerably smaller scale.

In September 1909, three months after his discussions with Fokin,
he 'tailored', as he dismissively put it, a minuet for a special edition
of the *Revue musicale* to be published as a centenary tribute to Joseph
Haydn – 'tailored' because, in company with other leading French
composers, he had been invited to construct the piece on a five-note
theme derived (by a common form of musical cryptography) from the
five letters of Haydn's name. It is a small but nonetheless remarkable
token of Ravel's genius that his *Menuet sur le nom de Haydn*, though
stitched together by a network of scholastic devices, is melodically
charming, harmonically fascinating and especially witty in that its
most prominent motif is not the cryptic one but a cheerful little tune
reflecting the rhythm and natural pitch inflections of the four syllables
of 'Joseph Haydn'. Any composer who appreciated Haydn's music

as much as Ravel did would have found time for a short tribute, however busy he was. It is difficult, on the other hand, to understand why if he was not procrastinating he undertook to arrange music by Rimsky-Korsakov for Chékry-Ganem's five-act play *Antar* which (with Mata Hari starring in a dancing role) was to be performed in Monte Carlo in January 1910 and at the Odéon in Paris a month later.

It was also at the beginning of 1910 that Ravel delivered his piano-duet arrangement of Debussy's *Prélude à l'après-midi d'un faune* to Fromont, the publisher who had issued his two-piano arrangement of the same composer's *Nocturnes* a year earlier. If it is true that he had to do no more than revise an earlier arrangement of the *Prélude* – a friend recalled playing a Ravel keyboard version of the piece with Debussy himself in 1898 – it cannot have taken him very long. By bringing him into intimate contact with this most vivid reaction to pagan sensuality, it might even have helped to equip him for *Daphnis et Chloé*. But for a composer with his reputation and his commitments to enter the 1910 folksong-setting competition of the Maison du Lied in Moscow can only have been more prevarication. He was good at harmonizing folk tunes, as he had demonstrated in his Greek songs, and his competition entries were duly adjudged the best in four of the seven national categories. The winning numbers now published as *Chants populaires* – the stylish 'Chanson espagnole' with its guitar-like accompaniment, the charmingly pastoral 'Chanson française', the ironically tragic 'Chanson italienne' with its discreet hint of Puccini at the end, the eloquently idiomatic 'Chanson hébraïque' – are among the most attractive of Ravel's works for voice and piano. But, with the possible exception of the story of the playful shepherd and shepherdess from Limousin, they were scarcely relevant to *Daphnis et Chloé*.

The truth must be that both Ravel and Diaghilev knew at an early stage, though without saying anything to each other, that *Daphnis et Chloé* would not be ready in time for the 1910 season. Certainly, by November 1909 Diaghilev had asked Igor Stravinsky to provide the score for the ballet which was to replace it in the Russian repertoire at the Paris Opéra seven months later. Inspired move though that turned out to be when *The Firebird* was first performed, at the time it was commissioned, when the young Russian composer had done no more for Diaghilev than orchestrate a total of three short pieces by Grieg and Chopin, it can only have been an emergency measure.

So, although he did get to work, intermittently, on *Daphnis et Chloé* in the winter months, Ravel allowed himself to be tempted into yet another distraction when he installed himself at La Grangette in the spring of 1910. This time the diversion was both more fruitful in itself and more to the point as far as *Daphnis et Chloé* was concerned. It was at La Grangette, shortly before the death of his father in 1908, that he had written the *Pavane de la Belle au bois dormant* for the Godebski children. Finding himself in the same situation, except that he now had his widowed mother with him, and perhaps experiencing similarly mixed emotions about the loss of his own childhood and his delight in that of Mimie and Jean Godebski, he again took refuge in fairy tale and the domesticity of the piano duet. Jacques Durand, who had heard Mimie and Jean play the *Pavane de la Belle au bois dormant* at La Grangette, had encouraged the composer to write more such pieces but even he must have been surprised by the depth of expression Ravel was able to secure by such simple means in *Ma Mère l'Oye*. There is at least as much adult nostalgia as childish joy in these five pieces and far more Ravel than Perrault or the other tellers of the tales featured therein.

The loneliness of *Pavane de la Belle au bois dormant* ('Sleeping Beauty's Pavane') derives largely from the simplicity of the texture which exposes its wistful melody to the small consolation of the modal harmonies that go with it. There is not much comfort either in the wandering chromatic lines and uncertain metre of *Petit Poucet* ('Tom Thumb') where, after a brief allusion to the calls of the cuckoos and the high-pitched flourishes of the songbirds attracted by Tom's trail of crumbs, the gently reassuring main theme is resumed only to lose its way at the end. *Laideronnette, Impératrice des Pagodes* ('Little Ugly, Empress of the Pagodas') is contrastingly brilliant in colour, cheerfully extrovert in character and not a little parodistic of *Pagodes* in Debussy's *Estampes*: while the Empress takes her bath, the tiny inhabitants of the island entertain her with exotic tunes on walnut-shell theorbos and almond-shell viols; but even here, at the heart of the gamelan ceremonial in the middle of the piece, a private thought disquietingly arises. Though Ravel was generous enough to acknowledge Satie as the 'grand-papa' of *Les Entretiens de la Belle*

et de la Bête ('Conversations of Beauty and the Beast'), and though
it does begin as if in imitation of that composer's *Gymnopédies*, its
development is dramatic: Beauty's slow-waltz poise, unsettled by the
gruff pleas of the Beast rising in passion from the bass of the piano, is
restored in a harmoniously amorous duet and finally transcended with
the transformation of the Beast in the closing bars. As for *Le Jardin
féerique* ('The Fairy Garden'), Manuel de Falla found it so 'splendidly
religious in character' that, in another effort to make Ravel a Catholic,
he declared it to be based on material from the once-planned setting
of *The Little Flowers of St Francis of Assisi*.

If there is any religious feeling in *Le Jardin féerique* – in what could
be described as a hymn-like beginning and, amid pealing bells and
joyful glissandos and triumphant fanfares, an assertion of faith at the
end – it is in the worship of nature rather than of God. That is one
reason why *Ma Mère l'Oye* was so important a stage on the way to
Daphnis et Chloé, where the unity of man and nature is an essential
element. Materially, apart from their shared allusions to birdsong
and a relationship of a sort between the middle section of *Le Jardin
féerique* and the music associated in the ballet with Pan and the
Nymphs, the two works have little in common. Emotionally, however,
in the liberation of inhibitions in *Les Entretiens de la Belle et la Bête*,
which was Ravel's first ever love scene, and in the rejection of irony in
Le Jardin féerique, these children's piano-duets were a breakthrough.

Within days of its completion, *Ma Mère l'Oye* was introduced
to the public at the opening concert of the recently formed Société
Musicale Indépendante in the Salle Gaveau on 20 April 1910 – not
by its Godebski dedicatees, who were not up to it unfortunately, but
by two other young pianists, Jeanne Leleu and Geneviève Durony.
The composer, who performed Debussy's *D'un cahier d'esquisses* in the
same concert, was so pleased with the playing of the eleven-year-old
Mlle Leleu (who was to win the Prix de Rome thirteen years later)
that he wrote to thank her for her 'understanding in interpreting a
rather special work with exactly the right sentiment'.

It is difficult to believe that in the midst of this activity Ravel was
able to complete a version of *Daphnis et Chloé*, however imperfect,
by the beginning of May. In fact, there is a manuscript of an early
piano version signed and dated 1 May 1910; but there is also a letter
addressed to the Godebskis on 10 May with the contradictory indi-

cation that '*Daphnis* is not progressing very quickly.' Assuming that
1 May was the deadline agreed with Diaghilev – and it was about this
time that he received a deputation from the Ballets Russes at La
Grangette – the use of that date on the manuscript has probably more
to do with contractual formality than concern for chronological accur-
acy. Durand must have been similarly motivated when he rushed that
first version into print without actually publishing it. Arnold Bennett
heard Ravel play extracts from this proof, incidentally, but not until
1911, when he recorded in his journal that he was 'much pleased' by
the new score. The composer himself was happy enough with the first
two scenes, a sizeable fragment of which (*Nocturne, Interlude* and
Danse guerrière) he now offered as a concert suite to Gabriel Pierné,
conductor of the Orchestre Colonne. He was not at all happy, on the
other hand, with the end of the last scene, which he had written in a
hurry presumably towards the end of May, and he must have been
even less happy with it when he heard Stravinsky's *Firebird* so successfully performed by the Russians at the end of June. It was going to
cost him immense trouble to put it right and, even when he knew
that Diaghilev was determined to present Stravinsky's *Petrushka* the
following season and that *Daphnis et Chloé* would not be needed until
1912, it remained a constant source of anxiety.

For the present the pressure was off and Ravel was able to turn his
mind to other problems, like getting *L'Heure espagnole* staged at the
Opéra-Comique at last. A major item in the strategy was a private
performance organized by the musicianly wife of an important
Government Minister, Mme Jean Cruppi, who had taken up Ravel's
cause at the Opéra-Comique as soon as Albert Carré had turned it
down. Details of the private performance are confused – there might
even have been more than one – but it seems that it took place at
Mme Cruppi's home in the summer of 1910, that she herself sang the
role of Concepcion, that Ravel and Philippe Jarnach accompanied at
the piano, and that Carré was present. The director of the Opéra-
Comique stubbornly declared even then that he would put it on only
if he was ordered to – which moved the Minister's wife to make the
exquisitely diplomatic reply that 'You will produce *L'Heure espagnole*
and, I hope, you will do it for music and not for the Republic!' From
then on Carré became rather more positive about the work and,

Maurice Ravel in a
portrait etching by Achille
Ouvré (1909)

although there were further delays, the opening of *L'Heure espagnole*
was eventually scheduled for May 1911.

In the meantime, after undertaking another concert tour in Britain,
this one extending to Newcastle and Edinburgh as well as London,
and organizing and performing in an unprecedented all-Satie concert
at the Société Musicale Indépendante, he had two other first performances to attend to. At the Châtelet on 2 April 1911 Gabriel Pierné
conducted what is now known as the First Suite from *Daphnis et
Chloé* – which severely irritated Serge Diaghilev; in the Salle Gaveau
on 9 May Louis Aubert introduced the *Valses nobles et sentimentales* –
which severely distressed Maurice Ravel. Diaghilev's irritation, on
learning that the audience at the Concerts Colonne had got to hear a
substantial excerpt from a score he had commissioned, was only to be
expected. Ravel's distress at a performance of one of his own piano
works at, so to speak, his own concert society, the Société Musicale
Indépendante, came as a nasty shock.

Being a progressive organization, the SMI was interested in trying out new ways of presenting its programmes, one of which, as
adopted on this occasion, was to identify the items by their titles only

and to ask the audience to name the composers at the end. Ravel was probably not too worried that the *Valses nobles et sentimentales* were attributed to Satie, Kodály and even (someone was joking, surely) the dreaded Théodore Dubois. What distressed him was the howls of protest and derision which accompanied Louis Aubert's performance of the work, some of them coming from people who were supposed to know and like his music, including Cipa Godebski, who was sitting next to him and asking what idiot could have written such a piece.

Godebski (who was quickly forgiven) should have known better, but there were mitigating circumstances for all concerned. Few people at that time would have associated Ravel with the waltz. If anyone had noticed that the waltz was replacing the minuet as Ravel's favourite dance form – there are more or less clear waltz-time allusions in *L'Heure espagnole, Gaspard de la nuit* and *Ma Mère L'Oye* – there was still the question why he applied himself at this time to what he was to describe as a 'sequence of waltzes in the manner of Schubert'. The question remains unanswered: perhaps it was inspired by the discovery or rediscovery of Liszt's 'valses-caprices after Schubert', the *Soirées de Vienne*; or perhaps it was no more than an indulgence in 'the delightful and always novel pleasure of a useless occupation', as Régnier puts it in a phrase quoted at the head of the score.

Another problem for the first audience of the *Valses nobles et sentimentales* was the steely brilliance of the harmonies. Comparing this work with the virtuoso pieces of *Gaspard de la nuit*, Ravel referred to 'a style that is simpler and clearer, in which the harmony is harder.' Obviously, he had underestimated the effect those actually quite logical but apparently aggressive harmonies would have, particularly in a work explicitly inviting comparison with the Schubert *Valses nobles* and *Valses sentimentales*. Ears suffering from the shock of the percussively articulated dissonances of the opening number were evidently deaf to such reassurance as the hints of the modality of the *Belle au bois dormant* in the next waltz and of *Laideronnette* in the one after that. The composer himself believed the seventh and last waltz to be the most characteristic – which it is but, in its stylistic alignment to Johann Strauss rather than to Schubert and its anticipations of *La Valse*, only in hindsight. The least predictable section of all, the *Epilogue*, is the most inspired: recalling all except the fifth of the preceding waltzes in a poetic succession of fleeting dream-like images, it is the supreme example of the impressionist recapitulation.

The long-awaited first performance of *L'Heure espagnole*, in a double bill with Massenet's *Thérèse* at the Opéra-Comique on 19 May, was much more encouraging. There seemed to be some support for Carré's original attitude to the work when Gaston Carraud in *La Liberté* called it a 'pornographic vaudeville' but that lasted only as long as it took Franc-Nohain to protest and Carraud to issue a public apology. The other critics were less hysterical and, though mixed in their opinions, generally in favour, Gabriel Fauré in *Le Figaro* more than most. The production ran for only seven or eight performances but the box-office receipts from the second night onwards were enough to impress even Albert Carré.

So, in spite of the moral setback caused by the all-too innocent reactions of his friends and colleagues to the *Valses nobles et senti-mentales* at the SMI, Ravel ought to have been able to look forward to the summer and his customary holiday in the Basque country in a reasonably happy frame of mind. In fact, he was still worried about the finale of *Daphnis et Chloé*, although he was not quite as desperate by now as he had been a few weeks earlier. According to Louis Aubert, who was in the midst of preparing for the first performance of the *Valses nobles et sentimentales* at the time, Ravel told him that he had had enough of *Daphnis et Chloé* and asked him, in all seriousness, if he would rewrite the finale for him. Aubert, although he too had studied composition with Fauré at the Conservatoire, very wisely declined the offer: Aubert's own music is all but forgotten whereas the finale of *Daphnis et Chloé*, as definitively completed on 5 April 1912, is one of the most frequently performed items in the concert-hall repertoire.

Ravel solved the problem not by a stroke of inspiration but by his usual process of attrition, remorselessly working at it over and over again for as long as it took to get it right. Fortunately for his health, the weather in the Basque country, where he arrived with his mother and brother Edouard in the middle of July, was particularly good that summer. They were staying not in St-Jean-de-Luz this time but on the other side of the river in Ciboure, just a few yards away from where he was born in rue du Quai, and the beauty of the countryside, the walking and the sea-bathing proved so distracting that, as he said, he 'didn't do masses of work.' He even found time to go to Spain and, perhaps for the first time, for more than a day-trip across the border at San Sebastián. That he was also working on *Daphnis et Chloé* we know from a memory of this summer recorded by his friend, critic and fellow-composer, Gustave Samazeuilh, who had a house on the hill at Bordegain overlooking Ciboure. He was used to hearing Ravel working at the piano as he called on him on the way down to St-Jean-de-Luz but he was surprised on one occasion to hear from the staircase 'a theme which was alike as a twin brother, in its melodic line and its harmony, to one of those in a piano piece of mine, *Naïades au soir* ("Evening Naiads"), which Alfred Cortot had played at the Société Nationale … It had become the theme of the nymphs in *Daphnis*.'

Following a sensible suggestion from Durand, Ravel had also been working, probably since March or April, on an orchestral version of *Ma Mère l'Oye*. The scoring must have been well advanced towards the end of the year because it was only then that Jacques Rouché, the newly appointed director of the Théâtre des Arts in Paris, asked Ravel for a ballet which was to be based on the music of *Ma Mère l'Oye* and to be performed at the end of January 1912. In not much more than a month Ravel not only devised a scenario which would incorporate the five movements of the suite, though in a different order and with slightly different story-lines, but also wrote an atmospheric new *Prélude*, a new first episode, *Danse du rouet* ('Spinning-wheel Dance'), and new material to link the various scenes. Even allowing for the probability that the orchestration of the original suite was complete by then and the possibility that the *Danse du rouet* derives from the abandoned sketches for *La Cloche engloutie*, it was a remarkable achievement. It was also a masterful achievement, as far as the magical orchestration is concerned, and an ingenious one from the dramatic point of view: after pricking her finger in the *Danse du rouet* at the beginning, Princess Florine falls asleep in *Pavane de la Belle au bois dormant* and, thanks to the providence of the Good Fairy, is entertained in her dreams by the stories of the *Entretiens de la Belle et de la Bête*, *Petit Poucet* and *Laideronnette*, before she is lovingly awakened by Prince Charming in *Le Jardin féerique* at the end.

The success of *Ma Mère l'Oye* at the Théâtre des Arts brought another urgent request for ballet music. The commission came this time from the dancer and choreographer Natacha Trohanova, who needed a fourth work to complete a programme including Vincent

Ravel and Nijinsky – in what the composer mischievously described as 'a most surprising posture' – at the piano in the Ravels's avenue Carnot apartment

D'Indy's *Istar*, Florent Schmitt's *La Tragédie de Salomé* and Paul Dukas's *La Péri*, each score to be conducted by its composer, at the Châtelet towards the end of April. Since *Daphnis et Chloé* was to be performed by the Ballets Russes at the same theatre only a few weeks later, and since Trohanova was the mistress of Dukas, whose *La Péri* – in which she was to have danced the starring role – had been accepted and then dropped by Diaghilev in 1911, Ravel could scarcely have failed to be aware that he was being drawn into an awkward political situation. Even so, in little more than two weeks in March 1912 he orchestrated his *Valses nobles et sentimentales* and drew up a scenario under the title *Adélaïde ou le langage des fleurs* ('Adélaïde or the Language of Flowers') to go with it.

Of the two, the orchestration is more successful than the scenario. The story, set in the salon of the courtesan Adélaïde in Paris in about 1820 and told through symbolic exchanges of flowers, is a pale echo of the first act of *La traviata* – although its initial inspiration, as a succession of waltzes allied to a flower theme, might well have been *Le Spectre de la Rose* in which Nijinsky had enjoyed such a great success in the Ballets Russes season in 1911. The orchestration, on the other hand, is a brilliant reflection of the original piano version, the initial truculence of which provokes liberal use of percussion while its seductive qualities are intensified above all by sensuous violin sounds and its poetry is heightened by the delicately pointillistic scoring for strings and wind in the *Epilogue*. Debussy, in a rare demonstration of generosity towards his colleague, described it as 'a product of the most refined ear there has ever been.'

If he could have seen it objectively, the success of *Adélaïde* might have been an encouragement to Diaghilev as his company got involved in preparations for staging *Daphnis et Chloé*. In fact, worried that the latter score was more symphonic than choreographic, suitable more for the concert hall than for dance, he announced to Durand that he was thinking of cancelling the whole project. According to the publisher's memoirs, it was only his diplomacy that persuaded the impresario to go through with it – although the fear of losing the support of Misia Edwards was probably more to the point. So, in spite of assurances that Ravel's orchestration and his atmospheric use of wordless chorus would make all the difference, Diaghilev still had less than complete faith in the score, which is no doubt one reason why the rehearsal period proved to be such an unhappy one. Fokin was convinced, not without reason, that Diaghilev was much more interested in Nijinsky and his work on *L'après-midi d'un faune* and that he was devoting a disproportionate amount of time and attention to that far less ambitious project. Less reasonably perhaps, he suspected that while Diaghilev was encouraging Nijinsky's work he was actually attempting to 'wreck' his own. Since Nijinsky was also rehearsing the part of Daphnis, it was a dangerous situation – which resulted, in fact, in Fokin's early departure from the company and Nijinsky's appointment as choreographer for *The Rite of Spring* a year later.

Daphnis et Chloé opened at the Théâtre du Châtelet on 8 June 1912 with choreography by Fokin, sets and costumes by Bakst, Nijinky and Karsavina in the title roles and Pierre Monteux conducting. Those members of the audience who were familiar with Longus's pastoral romance must have been amazed by what they saw – not so much by the drastic abbreviation of the story, which was inevitable in a one-act ballet, as by the transformation of the whole ethos behind it. The goatherd and shepherdess who, according to Longus, spend long hours locked in naked frustration in the pastures of Lesbos, attempting to consummate their love for each other but without knowing how, are seen in the ballet to meet in no more than three chaste embraces. Daphnis's erotic adventure with the farmer's wife who takes it upon herself to teach him the technical details – most successfully, according to Longus – is reduced in the ballet to the short episode in

After Nijinsky's departure
from the Ballets Russes, Fokin
was persuaded to return to
the company. In 1914 he
danced the part of Daphnis in
Daphnis et Chloé, sometimes
with Karsavina and sometimes
(as seen here) with his wife
Vera Fokina. *Below*, costume
designs by Léon Bakst for the
Ballets Russes production of
Daphnis et Chloé in 1912

which Lyceion attempts to seduce him and, failing to make her veil-dropping intentions understood, leaves him to his own devices. Most extraordinary of all, Daphnis and Chloe are denied the amorous pas de deux which any choreographer and any other composer would have considered basic to the whole enterprise. On the one occasion they do get to dance more than briefly together it is not as themselves but as Pan and Syrinx in a re-enactment of their unhappy story – which ends not in consummation, of course, but in the nymph's escape from the god's unwelcome attentions by taking refuge in a reed-bed. According to his libretto, Fokin would have had Daphnis and Chloe dance together throughout this episode; Ravel separates them at an early stage by having Daphnis rather than one of his companions mime Pan's forlorn reed-pipe improvisation. Chloe is left to dance alone.

It is significant that none of the most amorous moments in the ballet is more than a few bars long. Ravel's economy is such, moreover, that the same theme is used on each occasion. On the other hand, though basically only two short phrases, that theme is so voluptuously shaped that its symbolic significance is unmistakable: in its tender curve downwards and its yearning upward intervals it is one of Ravel's greatest melodic inspirations. It is first heard on a solo horn just after the curtain rises and, always passionate but more or less agitated depending on the dramatic circumstances, it reappears in an infinite variety of transformations. Its most ingenious variant is the flute melody which, rather surprisingly, accompanies Lyceion's unsuccessful effort to seduce Daphnis. Its most romantic manifestations are reserved for the three embraces: in the first scene, after gracefully outdancing his clumsy rival Dorcon, Daphnis is rewarded with a kiss from Chloe as the love theme is slowly and very quietly drawn by strings in luminous octaves over a gentle harp glissando; in the third scene, where Daphnis welcomes Chloe after she has been delivered by Pan from the hands of the pirates, it is presented in stronger colours on the same string instruments again in octaves; the emotional climax of the ballet occurs between the Pan-and-Syrinx episode and the closing bacchanal, at the point where Daphnis and Chloe are formally united and the love theme is taken up once again by the strings but now with more expressive harmonies and at a meltingly supple tempo.

Another problem Ravel had to solve in *Daphnis et Chloé*, the articulation of religious sentiment – which was even more alien to him and his music than erotic passion – gave him less trouble. Christianity inspired him not in the least. Nature worship was another matter, as he had demonstrated in *Le Jardin féerique* at the end of *Ma Mère l'Oye*, and it was probably not too difficult for him to extend that kind of feeling towards the pastoral deities who preside over the idyllic setting of *Daphnis et Chloé* and play a major role in the story. As the curtain rises on the stone images of three nymphs and the god Pan in the opening scene, three horns very quietly intone a simple but curiously eerie echoing motif while a solo flute improvises a reed-pipe melody high above them. Separately or together, the first of them echoing mainly in the chorus, these two ideas have as prominent a part in the score as the love theme which is introduced immediately after them.

By the standards of, say, Stravinsky's *Petrushka*, the sensation of the previous season at the Châtelet, Ravel's *Daphnis et Chloé* was not a great success for the Ballets Russes. Diaghilev himself was partly to blame: as Fokin resentfully declared, and as Ravel can only have agreed, *Daphnis et Chloé* was always 'a stepchild of the company', scarcely given a chance to prosper. In his eagerness to capitalize on the scandal associated with Nijinsky's *Prélude à l'après-midi d'un faune*, Diaghilev confined *Daphnis et Chloé* to two performances at the very end of the season. Some of Bakst's costumes were not ready even then and his sets, brilliant though they were in their own right, were inspired by a more realistic vision of Greece than the French neo-classical Greece which Ravel had in mind. The score was not without its problems either. It offered less opportunity than *Petrushka* for set-piece choreography, as Diaghilev was well aware, and yet it was not the 'choreographic symphony' the composer claimed it to be. True, it is to a large extent unified by the pervasive presence of two or three main themes but there are several picturesque episodes which, thematically or structurally, are not integrated with the rest. Moreover, in expanding the scope of his music to meet Fokin's requirements, Ravel all too obviously helped himself out by drawing on the experience of other composers – Debussy, Borodin and, most prominent of all, Rimsky-Korsakov. As usual, when he was aware that he had modelled his work on that of another composer, he was perfectly frank in acknowledging it. Asked how he was eventually able to complete the troublesome finale of the ballet, he replied, 'It's quite simple: I put Rimsky-Korsakov's *Scheherazade* on the piano and copied it.'

Where Ravel succeeded above all was in creating what he described as 'a vast musical fresco', the like of which he had never achieved before and would not attempt to achieve again. In the third and last scene, which is frequently performed in the concert hall as the Second Suite, he excelled himself. The dawn beginning – the dew running off the rocks in rippling arpeggios on flutes and clarinets, the sun rising melodiously on lower strings and wind, dawn-chorus birdsong on flutes and violins, shepherds playing their pipes in the distance – is magically atmospheric. At the same time, as the sun-rise melody is gradually transformed into the love theme to assume its authentic shape just at the moment Chloe is restored to Daphnis, it is both structurally functional and dramatically effective. The Pan and Syrinx episode, where an elaborately eloquent flute plays the part of the frustrated god's panpipe soliloquy, is an ideally proportioned interlude before the bacchanal. This last episode – which is twice as long as in the 1910 version and immeasurably more dangerous in its use of a pagan five-in-a bar metre rather than a civilized three-in-a-bar – remains one of the most exciting passages in the choral and orchestral repertoire.

Recalling his 'whirlpool' choreography for the bacchanal with particular pride, Fokin declared the ballet 'a tremendous success'. Even so, the bitterness left over from the rehearsal period was still too strong for those who had created the work to enjoy its first perform-ance. Ravel – who had arrived marginally but deliberately late and had made a little ceremony of giving a present to Misia Edwards just as the curtain was rising – refused to appear on stage at the end. Fokin did take a curtain call, alongside Nijinsky and Karsavina, but immediately afterwards he quietly left the company.

7

Stéphane Mallarmé's
'hermetic sonnets' (as Ravel
described them) were the
ultimate challenge to song
composers of the day

*With me composition bears all the symptoms of
a serious illness: fever, insomnia, loss of appetite.
After three days of that there emerged a song to
words by Mallarmé.*

Maurice Ravel

Adversity 1912–17

Severely stressed by the problems associated with completing and
staging *Daphnis et Chloé*, Ravel once again escaped to La Grangette at
Valvins – this time on doctor's orders. As in his previous crisis, after
the death of his father in 1908, it took him seven months to recover
enough energy to start creative work again. Much of the intervening
time, from early August to mid October at the earliest, was spent in
the Basque country with his mother: 'The various works I had put on
last season, *Daphnis et Chloé* above all,' he wrote to Vaughan Williams
from St-Jean-de-Luz in August 1912, 'left me in a pitiable state. I had
to be sent to the country to take care of an incipient neurasthenia. I
am now completing my recovery in my native country.' Although he
toyed with the idea of writing another ballet for Jacques Rouché, he
seems to have done no work of any kind until, at the beginning of
1913, he took the opportunity to write the occasional column of music
criticism and to score a few points off his old enemies in the pages
of *Comoedia illustré* and *Les Cahiers d'aujourd'hui*.

The return to actual composition was, as before, a gradual process,
beginning with an offer so attractive that he could scarcely turn it
down. Stravinsky had recently been commissioned by Diaghilev to
make a new performing version of *Khovanshchina*, the opera which
Mussorgsky had left incomplete and largely unorchestrated on his
death in 1881 and which was known to the public only in the well-
meaning but much-cut edition published by Rimsky-Korsakov in
1883. Having first met Ravel in 1910, when he came to Paris for *The
Firebird*, Stravinsky knew his French colleague very well by now and
was as conscious of his skill in orchestration as he was aware of his
love for Russian music in general and that of Mussorgsky in particular.
It was Stravinsky who suggested to Diaghilev that Ravel should
collaborate with him on the task and it was Diaghilev who paid for
Ravel (and his mother) to spend a couple of months in the spring of
1913 at the Hôtel des Crêtes – just across the road from where

Igor Stravinsky in about
1916 from a portrait by
Jacques-Émile Blanche

Stravinsky was staying at the Hôtel du Mont Blanc – in Clarens on
Lake Geneva.

A happy collaboration, it was important more for what the two
composers learned from each other than for the future of Mussorgsky's
opera. At Clarens Ravel first saw the epoch-making score which was
to be so spectacularly introduced to the world by the Ballets Russes at
the newly opened Théâtre des Champs-Elysées in May: 'You must
hear Stravinsky's *Rite of Spring*,' he wrote to Lucien Garban from the
Hôtel des Crêtes at the end of March: 'I really believe that the first

night will be as important as that of *Pelléas et Mélisande*.' He also got
to know Stravinsky's *Three Japanese Lyrics* and was so impressed by
them, particularly in the version with a mixed instrumental accompaniment (two each of flutes and clarinets with piano and string
quartet) that he was inspired to write something similar. It was a large
and painful step from orchestrating music by Mussorgksy to creating
music of his own again but, as he wrote from Clarens to Mme Kahn-
Casella – wife of the Italian composer Alfredo Casella and assistant
to him in his capacity as Secretary General of the Société Musicale
Indépendante – he achieved it: 'With me composition bears all the
symptoms of a serious illness: fever, insomnia, loss of appetite. After
three days of that there emerged a song to words by Mallarmé.' That

Arnold Schoenberg's music
was admired by Ravel for its
'very interesting discoveries'
– which influenced his
own music and which he
defended from chauvinistic
attack during World War I.

was 'Soupir', the first of the *Poèmes de Stéphane Mallarmé*. He was so
confident by now of his returning powers that in the same letter he
proposed that the SMI should present a 'scandal concert' including
Schoenberg's *Pierrot Lunaire*, Stravinsky's *Japanese Lyrics* and two of
his own Mallarmé songs. His ironic sense of humour was also fully
restored: *Pierrot Lunaire* and the *Japanese Lyrics*, he said, would
'make the audience howl' while his Mallarmé songs would 'calm
them down and have them going home humming the tunes'.

There are no hummable tunes in the *Poèmes de Stéphane Mallarmé*.
There is melody – the first of the songs, 'Soupir', contains one of the
most shapely and most sustained of all Ravel's melodic lines – but,
as in *Histoires naturelles*, it observes no regular pattern and it is determined entirely by the natural rhythms and pitch inflections of the
text. Indeed, anyone moved to howl by *Pierrot Lunaire* and the
Japanese Lyrics would be unlikely to find consolation in a score which
has so much in common with both of them. While the three works
are quite distinct in character, the line of descent from *Pierrot Lunaire*
by way of the *Japanese Lyrics* (the last of which is dedicated to Ravel)
to the Mallarmé songs (the first of which is dedicated to Stravinsky)
is quite clear. Ravel did not know *Pierrot Lunaire* at this time but
Stravinsky did. He had been present at the first performance in
Vienna in 1912 and had been particularly impressed by Schoenberg's
instrumentation. It was only after he had heard it that he settled on
the definitive instrumental ensemble for his *Japanese Lyrics*, which
is much the same as that of *Pierrot Lunaire*. Ravel's instrumental
ensemble is the same as Stravinsky's and, while the three works have

little in common as far as word-setting is concerned, Schoenberg's radical harmonies encouraged both Stravinsky and Ravel to proceed in the same direction.

Ravel was quite frank about it. 'You should never be afraid of imitating,' he said years later. 'I joined the Schoenberg school to write my *Poèmes de Mallarmé* ... If it didn't become quite Schoenberg it is because, in music, I am not so wary of charm, which is something he avoids to the point of asceticism, martyrdom even.' The public was duly charmed when – with the *Three Japanese Lyrics* but without *Pierrot Lunaire*, which was replaced by Maurice Delage's *Quatre Poèmes hindous* – the *Poèmes de Mallarmé* were first performed and well received at an SMI concert on 14 January 1914. However obscure Mallarmé's texts might be, Ravel's settings, inspired by an intense lyricism and illuminated by an exquisitely calculated vocal and instrumental sound, proved irresistible to the ear.

The luminous colouring of the arpeggio harmonics reflecting the poet's 'white fountain sighing towards the Azure' in the first half of the autumnally lingering 'Soupir' ('Sigh') is only the first example of Ravel's magical scoring in this work. Stravinsky was so charmed by the opening bars of 'Placet futile' ('Futile Petition') that he recalled them at the beginning of the *Pastorale* section of his *Soldier's Tale* in 1918. Itself an evocation of a pastoral scene, 'Placet futile' echoes in Ravel's setting with tantalizing half-reminders of *Daphnis et Chloé*. Ravel confessed that it was a 'great audacity to have attempted to set this sonnet'. He had to match not only the preciosity and elegance of the text, he said, but also 'the profound, adorable tenderness which suffuses it'. This he certainly succeeded in doing in music which at one point, where the recurring instrumental melody and the vocal line coincide, touches on pure romantic sentiment.

It is clear from Ravel's letter from the Hôtel des Crêtes to Mme Kahn-Casella that it was his original intention to write only two Mallarmé songs. According to the manuscript scores, 'Soupir' was completed at Clarens on 2 April 1913 and 'Placet futile' in Paris in May. The first anyone heard of 'Surgi de la croupe et du bond' was in the following August, when Ravel wrote from St-Jean-de-Luz to Roland-Manuel to inform him that he had just finished another Mallarmé setting and, most intriguingly, to announce that 'a Debussy Ravel contest' was about to take place. By an extraordinary

coincidence, Ravel and Debussy had been working on the same
Mallarmé texts at exactly the same time. It is not so surprising that
they both turned to Mallarmé in the early months of 1913: an important complete edition of Mallarmé's poetry had just been published
by the *Nouvelle Revue française* and both composers had no doubt
acquired a copy. It is very strange, on the other hand, that out of the
dozens of poems at their disposal they both chose 'Soupir' and 'Placet
futile'. Debussy claimed that it was 'a phenomenon of auto-suggestion
worthy of interest to the Academy of Medicine'. Ravel got to know
about it only when Durand, publisher of both composers, wrote him
a desperate letter asking him to interecede with Mallarmé's son-in-law
and literary executor, Dr Edmond Bonniot, who, having authorized
Ravel's settings of 'Soupir' and 'Placet futile', quite rightly felt unable
to do the same for Debussy's.

Ravel, who was a patient of Dr Bonniot, a country-villa neighbour
of the Godebskis at Valvins, did intervene and did secure the necessary
authorization for Debussy. What is not certain is whether it was
before or after he found that Debussy had set a third Mallarmé poem,
'Eventail', that Ravel decided that he would add 'Surgi de la croupe et
du bond' ('Rising from the rump and the bound') to the other two.
'The strangest if not the most hermetic of the sonnets', according
to Ravel himself, 'Surgi de la croupe et du bond' has few obvious
attractions for a composer and it is difficult to understand why he
chose to set this most obscure of Mallarmé's poems unless it was in a
spirit of competition or, at least, in an effort to demonstrate that he
was clever enough to cope with it. The tenuous hold on meaning in
the text is reflected by a similarly tenuous hold on tonality in the
music. The conclusion is achieved not by a harmonically definitive
cadence but by the ingenious device of having the voice agree to adopt
the winding melody of the instrumental accompaniment and, finally,
to echo the repeated notes which have been the one stable element
in the flux. '"Surgi de la croupe" is an incredible thing,' Maurice
Delage reported to Stravinsky after the first performance, 'beyond
any music that he has composed.'

'Surgi de la croupe et du bond' represents in fact the limit to which
Ravel would go with the modernists of the day. Firmly in support of
progress on the famously riotous first night of *The Rite of Spring* –
'Genius! Genius!' he called from his seat in the Théâtre des Champs-

Elysées; 'Dirty Jew! Dirty Jew!' retaliated his neighbour – he stayed
with the avant garde only as long as he was under Stravinsky's
influence, which would survive Ravel's prolonged periods of isolation
in the Basque country up to the outbreak of World War I in the
summer of 1914 but not the war itself.

The Basque summer of 1913 was a particularly happy one. 'What
bathing we are having!' he wrote to the Godebskis from St-Jean-de-
Luz at the end of July, 'The weather is hot and it rains only at night.'
A few days later he wrote a generous letter to Jeanne Leleu, the young
pianist who had taken part in the first performance of *Ma Mère
l'Oye* in 1910 and who had now won the sight-reading competition for
piano students at the Conservatoire. As a member of the jury on
that occasion and as the composer of the test piece – the tiny *Prélude*
for piano, where the technical problems are not so much imposed on
its sentimental slow-waltz charm as an integral part of it – Ravel had
been so 'sincerely touched' by her playing that, he told her, he was
going to dedicate the work to her on its publication. It was at St-Jean-
de-Luz that he wrote 'Surgi de la croupe et du bond' but at the same
time his surroundings were drawing him in quite a different creative
direction. As he wrote to Stravinsky at the end of August: 'I have just
finished the third Mallarmé poem. I am now going to revise the
second and then I shall immediately get to work on *Zazpiac bat*.' If
Stravinsky was sceptical about the wisdom of his modernist colleague
writing a Basque rhapsody called, in Basque, 'The Seven are One' – in
reference to the unity of the four Spanish and three French Basque
provinces – he was not entirely wrong. Ravel had actually been
thinking about writing such a work for piano and orchestra since, one
day in what might have been 1911, he had climbed to the top of
Mount Aya and 'tired but awed' had seen three of the Basque
provinces at his feet. 'That gave me the idea,' he is quoted as saying to
Elisabeth Anchochury, in whose house in Ciboure the Ravels were
lodging in 1911, 'of writing a piece which I shall call *Zazpiac bat*!' In
fact, although Ricardo Viñes and Alfred Cortot were both looking
forward to having the work dedicated to them, it was never finished.

Zazpiac bat was abandoned not because of any loss in affection
for the Basque country but, on the contrary, out of respect for the
folk tunes he had assembled as thematic material for the work. 'One
shouldn't treat folk tunes in that way,' he explained later: 'they do not

lend themselves to development.' It took him some time to realize that, however. For perhaps as long as fourteen months from August 1913 he continued at least to think about the rhapsody and he did make some progress. During this period he was as Basque as he ever would be – to the extent that in, in February 1914, he exchanged Paris at the height of the musical season for St-Jean-de-Luz in mid-winter, which is not the most favourable time to be there.

The English novelist Arnold Bennett, who lived in Paris for ten years from 1902, met Ravel through the Godebskis and took a keen interest in his music.

The last months of 1913 were spent in Paris except that in the middle of December he was in England again. He was there primarily to give a recital of his own music at the London Music Club but he also took the opportunity to visit Arnold Bennett and his French wife in their new home at Thorpe-le-Soken in Essex and to go antique shopping with them in Ipswich. The day before he left, Alfredo Casella gave the first performance of two little piano pieces under the joint title of *À la manière de …* at the SMI. Ravel probably thought little of these miniatures 'in the manner of' Borodin and Chabrier and was no doubt happy to entrust them to Casella who, as a specialist in pastiche himself, had encouraged him to write them. The Borodin piece, a waltz which has something in common with the Intermezzo in Borodin's own *Petite Suite* for piano but which displays more key-board elegance than the Russian composer could ever have achieved, is not a particularly good characterization. The other piece, an ingeniously conceived evocation of what Chabrier might have done if he had been persuaded to sit down and improvise on a favourite melody (*Faites-lui mes aveux*) from Gounod's *Faust*, is outstandingly good value: a wonderfully witty and touchingly affectionate inspiration, it says more about Chabrier than any amount of harmonic or stylistic analysis.

Back in Paris for the New Year and the preparations for the first performance of the *Trois Poèmes de Stéphane Mallarmé* at the SMI, Ravel also took the opportunity to do a little more music criticism for *Comoedia illustré*. He did not shrink from scolding his enemies again, praising his friends and treating *Parsifal* at the Opéra with a mixture of respect and journalistic irreverence: Wagner's music he considered 'magical', the opera as a whole 'less entertaining than *La Vie Parisienne*' but 'not as boring as the *Missa Solemnis* even so'.

Before the end of the first week in February he had installed himself in St-Jean-de-Luz. He set to work first on orchestrating

Schumann and Chopin piano pieces for Nijinsky who, after his
marriage to Romola de Pulszky and his consequent break with
Diaghilev, had formed his own ballet company in London and
needed new scores for *Carnaval* and *Les Sylphides*. But his major
preoccupation throughout the winter and summer would be a Trio
for violin, cello and piano. He had been contemplating a piano trio
ever since 1908, although at that time it was just one of several
projects, like the *Cloche engloutie* opera, the symphony and the
setting of *The Little Flowers of St Francis*, which were never finished
or never even started. Why, when *Zazpiac bat* still excited him, he
chose to devote himself to the Trio it is impossible to imagine –
unless, that is, he had previously committed himself to writing such
a work and was now under pressure to complete it. The more he saw
of his Basque surroundings the more enthusiastic he was about
Zazpiac bat – 'I have just come in from the countryside,' he wrote to
a friend on a sunny spring day in St-Jean-de Luz, 'My country really
is one of the most beautiful of all ... Throughout my walk I was
thinking of nothing but *Zazpiac bat*' – but he was working on both
Zazpiac bat and the Trio by now and would continue to do so for
several months.

There is no record of the Trio having been formally commissioned
but if friends and fellow-composers as distinguished as, say, Alfredo
Casella and George Enescu had asked him to write something of the
kind for them to perform at the SMI he would surely not have
refused. It is significant perhaps that the first report of actual progress
on the Trio was made in a letter to Mme Kahn-Casella in terms which
suggested that she already knew about the work: 'I am working on the
trio in spite of the cold, the tempest, the storms, the rain and the hail,'
he wrote on 21 March 1914. It is surely also significant that the pianist
in the eventual first performance of the Trio, in Paris on 28 January
1915, was Alfredo Casella. The violinist should have been George
Enescu who, although he had left France for Romania on the
outbreak of war and would not be returning until May, has actually
been credited by some authorities with the distinction of having taken
part on that occasion. It does seem moreover that Ravel had Enescu in
mind: the resemblance between the first movement of the Trio and
the Violin Sonata he had written for Enescu in 1897 is striking and the
dedication of the new work to André Gédalge, the Conservatoire

teacher to whom they both owed so much, is as interesting in this
context as it is touching.

Before the first performance of the Trio could take place, however,
there was much creative agony and even more emotional stress to go
through. At first there was no great urgency. He told Ida Godebska on
25 March that he had 'finished the first bit' of the Trio and then
departed on a complicated itinerary to give concerts in Lyon and
Geneva. He even found time to make voice-and-piano arrangements
of two Jewish songs for Alvina Alvi – a soprano in the St Petersburg
Opera and, no doubt, an admirer of the *Chanson hébraïque* in the
Chants populaires of 1910 – and to join her in their first performance at
the SMI in Paris in June. It is unlikely that work on the *Deux Mélodies
hébraïques* ('Two Hebrew Songs') detained him very long. As in his
earlier settings of traditional melodies, he does nothing to deflect the
vocal line from its natural development: the cantorial elaboration on
the Aramaic text of *Kaddisch* is accompanied by a rhythmically neutral
succession of sustained chords which, though they accumulate in
harmonic intensity, are based on the same note throughout; the comic
element in the setting of the Yiddish folk-song 'L'Enigme éternel'
('The Eternal Enigma') derives from repetitive primitive harmonies
and an obstinate rhythmic ostinato.

In Paris in June Ravel also took the opportunity to go and see
Stravinsky's new opera *Le Rossignol* and, in a both perceptive and
pugnacious article in *Comoedia illustré*, to defend the work from the
critics who had attacked it. Unfortunately neither this display of sol-
idarity with his Russian colleague nor his praise of the production by
the Ballets Russes – he drew particular attention to the conducting of
Pierre Monteux and the designs of Alexandre Benois – seems to have
endeared him to Diaghilev. Within days of the appearance of that
article he was writing in *Comoedia* again, this time in the form of
a letter to the editor, in protest at Diaghilev's decision to perform
Daphnis et Chloé in the Ballets Russes season at the Drury Lane
Theatre in London in what he described as a 'makeshift arrangement'
without chorus. He had the letter translated in order to have it
published also in *The Times*, the *Morning Post*, the *Daily Mail* and
the *Daily Telegraph*. Diaghilev replied that he considered the chorus
'not only useless but actually harmful' – which, of course, impressed
Ravel not in the least.

Before the end of June he was back in St-Jean-de-Luz. The Trio which he had started in March in rain and hail he was now working on again in a temperature, he claimed, of 35 degrees. Still in a Basque frame of mind in spite of 'the heat and the fleas of my country' he was thinking about *Zazpiac bat* as well. The official opening of the bathing beach on 1 July brought some relief from the heat and the presence of Alexandre Benois, who was holidaying with his family at St-Jean-de-Luz and no doubt rejoicing in the success of his sets and costumes for *Le Rossignol*, brought congenial company. Just over two weeks later – after several more days of swimming and sunbathing, to judge by the number of Benois sketches of Ravel on the beach – the composer was writing guiltily to Mme Kahn-Casella to confess that 'the Trio has made no progress for three weeks, and it disgusts me.' But, he immediately reassured her, 'I realized today that it isn't so distasteful after all … and the carburettor is repaired.' In spite of his problems with the Trio – and he was never without problems of this kind – Ravel was happier in July 1914 than he would ever be again.

The outbreak of war with Germany and Austria at the beginning of August came as a profound shock to Ravel. He cannot have failed to anticipate it – the obviously precarious political situation would have been a frequent subject of conversation and newspaper reports even in St-Jean-de-Luz – but he must have been at least as surprised as everyone else by the speed at which, after the assassination of the Archduke Franz Ferdinand at Sarajevo on 28 June, the crisis developed. On 3 August, two days after the church bells had rung throughout France to signal the mobilization of the nation's forces, he wrote to Cipa Godebski to express the anguish aroused in him by 'that tocsin, those weeping women, above all the horrible enthusiasm of the young men, and all my friends who have had to join up and my not knowing what is happening to them.'

More painful still was the moral dilemma in which he now found himself. On the one hand, he was so obsessed by 'this nightmare … the horror of this fighting which never stops for a second' that he felt he would go mad thinking about it without being able to take part in it. On the other hand, the idea of leaving his 'poor old mother' seemed to him 'frightful and cruel' and he was afraid it might even kill her. When his brother Edouard decided to enlist the situation was

Just four weeks before the
outbreak of World War I:
a photograph taken by
Alexandre Benois on the
beach at St-Jean-de-Luz on
2 July 1914 shows Maurice
Ravel in bathing costume, his
mother on what was to be
her last visit to the Basque
country, Mme Benois and her
son Nicholas Benois.

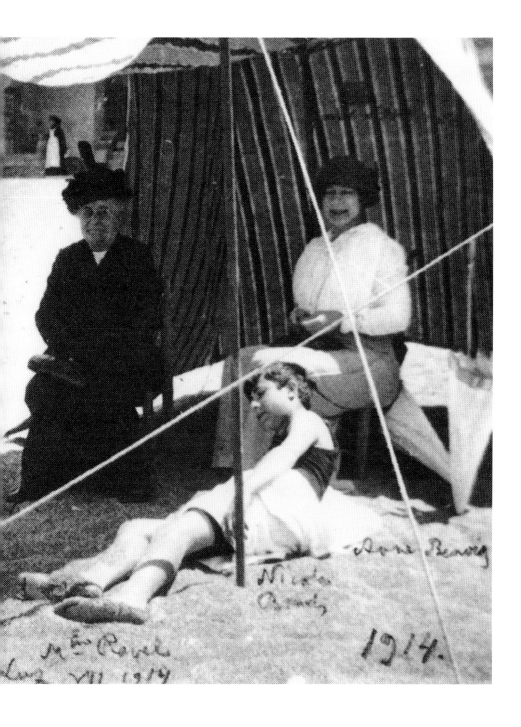

even worse. 'She is a poor old woman with neither religion nor high principles to sustain her,' he wrote again to Cipa.

Her one ideal has always been the love of her husband and her children and she wouldn't be in the least ashamed of holding on to what is left of them. She's a sort of monster, isn't she? If only there were more monsters like her! And you know how much I love this one! I don't know how she would bear it if I told her what I am hiding from her, that Edouard has enlisted as a driver; but I know, I am sure what will happen when she finds out that we are both leaving her. It won't be hunger she dies of.

In fact, within a week of the beginning of the war and in spite of the fact that he had long since been declared unfit for military service, he had already decided – without saying anything to his mother – to attempt to enlist. None of the arguments his friends put forward could make him change his mind: 'I know I am working for the nation in writing music … but that's no consolation,' he said to Roland-Manuel; 'France doesn't need me to save her … but that's just rationalization,' he said to Maurice Delage. 'Everyone has his faults and mine is to act only with a clear conscience.' It wasn't so easy, however. The authorities at the nearest recruiting centre in Bayonne rejected him because he was two kilograms underweight – which, with old Apache friends like Fargue and 'my poor Sordes' already engaged in the war, so distressed him that he ran a fever for two days. His patriotic fervour increased daily. 'To think that they have just destroyed Reims Cathedral!' he wrote to Maurice Delage on 21 September, 'and to think too that some apparent physical weakness will have prevented me from experiencing the splendid moments of this holy war, from having taken part in the most grandiose and the most noble action since man came into existence (including even the Revolution)!' The most he could do was help look after wounded soldiers in an emergency hospital at the St-Jean-de-Luz Casino. After another failed medical examination, this one specially arranged for those like him who had been exempted, his frustration turned to bitterness. 'To see some action do I have to wait for a couple of German uhlans to turn up in the non-existent garden of my unbuilt villa in St-Jean-de-Luz?' he asked, alluding with terrible irony to the fate of Albéric Magnard, a composer colleague who had recently died defending his villa at Baron from advancing German soldiers. 'Well, like poor Magnard, I've written a trio: at least it's a start.'

When Ravel returned to Paris in December it was partly to bring some political influence to bear on his application to enlist and partly to attend the rehearsals for the first performance of the Trio. Far

Maurice Ravel after a swim in the sea at St-Jean-de-Luz, as sketched by Alexandre Benois in July 1914

St-Jean-de-Luz as seen by
the British artist Romilly
Fedden in 1921

from being distracted from composition by the outbreak of war and
everything associated with it, he had 'never worked with a crazier,
more heroic passion,' he told Cipa Godebski. 'Yes, I am working,' he
had written to Maurice Delage from St-Jean-de-Luz, 'with the cer-
tainty, the lucidity of a madman. But sometimes depression is at
work as well and suddenly there I am sobbing over my sharps and
flats. Naturally, when I go down and see my mother I have to look
calm, cheerful even ... Can I go on like this?' There was no time for
bathing now: 'I have worked for a whole month from morning till
evening without even taking time off for a swim in the sea,' he told
Ida Godebska on 8 September. 'I wanted to finish my Trio, which,'
he added ominously, 'I have been treating like a posthumous work –
which doesn't mean that I have been lavishing genius on it but that
the manuscript and the notes that go with it are set out in such a way
that anyone else could correct the proofs.' Three weeks later he was
able to tell both his publisher Jacques Durand and Mme Kahn-Casella
that the Trio was finished.

No one aware of the extremes of Ravel's feelings in the summer of 1914 – feelings which he expressed in his letters with uncharacteristic candour – could doubt that the music he was writing at the time would be affected by them. If there is evidence anywhere in Ravel's music of the composer 'sobbing over the sharps and flats' it is in the third movement, the grieving *Passacaille*, of the Piano Trio. It is true that there is no documentary evidence of when he wrote each of the four movements or even that he approached them in the order in which they appear in the score. But it is reasonable to assume, from what we know of the slow progress of the work in the five months up to the end of July and the acceleration inspired by the outbreak of war – 'I did five months work in five weeks: I wanted to finish my trio before enlisting,' he told Roland-Manuel on 26 September – that no more than half the work was written before 1 August. And if two of the four movements were written after 1 August it is more likely to have been the last two than the first. The manuscript of the Trio is actually signed and dated 'St-Jean-de-Luz, 3 April–7 August 1914,' which would suggest that the work was all but complete by the end of July. But the evidence of the letters which were written at the time – and which, though addressed to different correspondents, are all consistent with each other – indicates that the manuscript is a month out with both dates, giving the impression (for whatever reason) that the work was written in four months rather than six.

Bearing in mind Ravel's passionate interest in the music of the Basque country when, with *Zazpiac bat* still very much on his mind, he started work on the Trio early in March 1914, the probability is that the opening *Modéré* was written first. The composer declared only the first theme to be 'Basque in colour' but, since its Dorian mode and the lilting rhythm of its charmingly irregular metre are nearly always there in one form or another, he could have applied that description to the whole movement. Whether or not those harmonic and rhythmic characteristics are actually and authentically Basque is not a question of the first importance. The point is that Ravel thought they were. The first theme could be a mature version, metrical disorder now rationalized into a repeated asymmetrical pattern, of that of the one-movement Violin Sonata written in 1897, before the Ravel family rediscovered the Basque country. They might both, on the other hand, be related to the songs his mother sang to him in his childhood.

The tenderly affectionate second subject in the same mode and much the same rhythm could be derived from the same source. But, whether Basque in character or just generalized Spanish, the first movement is a magical inspiration. Hypnotic in the gently circling motion of its first theme, reminiscent in its sudden turbulence of the squalls which assail the not dissimilar rocking rhythm of *Une Barque sur l'océan* in *Miroirs*, atmospherically poetic in the distantly rumbling echoes of the opening phrase towards the end, it draws a few last impressionistic features over its formal structure.

The first movement did not take him very long to write. What he found so frustrating that at one point it 'disgusted' him was, no doubt, a long struggle with the problems he set himself in the second movement. This too has parallels in an earlier work, in the impetuous repeated notes and the surging dance rhythms in 'Scarbo', the romantic motivation of which contrasts most significantly with the formal manoeuvres undertaken here. The extent of Ravel's technical ambition is indicated by the title of the movement, 'Pantoum'. A complex Malaysian verse form, the pantoum is difficult enough a challenge for a poet let alone a musician. Essentially, it requires two distinct ideas or themes which are to be treated in strict alternation and in such a way that they make sense both in themselves and in combination with the other. Ravel's musical solution to the problem is as masterful as Baudelaire's literary solution in 'Harmonie du soir'. With little or no transition he juxtaposes a few bars of playful staccato material with a floating legato Spanish-style dance tune and sustains the alternating pattern while both developing the two themes and, in the middle section, miraculously projecting a new melody in longer note values and a broader metre against continuing pantoum activity in the background.

When Ravel said of his Piano Trio, 'It's just Saint-Saëns', he was obviously exaggerating the extent of his debt to that composer, whose brilliantly successful Piano Trio in F he consulted primarily for guidance in the notoriously awkward business of balancing and blending piano and solo strings. But, just as the ingenious organization of the material in the Scherzo of the Saint-Saëns Trio might have challenged Ravel to display his structural virtuosity in the 'Pantoum', something in the nature and in the treatment of the main theme in the *Andante* of that work might have stimulated him to think in terms of a

passacaglia for his own slow movement. Nowhere in either of the
Saint-Saëns piano trios, however, is there a movement as deeply felt as
Ravel's 'Passacaille'. Although it is not a strict passacaglia, in that the
main requirement of the constant repetition of the theme is not
actually fulfilled, it preserves the cyclic inevitability associated with
that form while at the same time progressively increasing the harmonic intensity until it reaches a climax of anguish at the very centre
of the construction. Introduced at the very bottom of the piano, the
passacaglia theme rises as it develops in textural complexity to reach
its highest pitch at that same central apex before subsiding to the
gloom from which it emerged – at which point, with a simple change
of harmony, light breaks in at the beginning of the last movement.

The 'Final', which begins with an inversion of the three-note motif
which has opened all three of the previous movements, is clearly
intended as the emotional antithesis of the 'Passacaille'. It too has an
inexorability about it as its two themes, characteristically Basque in
their quintuple and septuple metres respectively, press on towards
a briefly expansive climax in radiant harmonies on the piano and
excited trills on violin and cello. But that is not all. The process starts
again, this time urged on by fanfare figures in all registers of an extravagantly written piano part, to achieve a triumph so comprehensively
joyful that the sonorities it requires exceed the bounds of chamber
music. Ravel, we are told by the violinist Hélène Jourdan-Morhange,
was always frustrated by instrumentalists who could not get this
concluding section to sound 'trumpet' enough in performance.

It is dangerous to attempt to deduce a composer's politics from his
instrumental music. In August 1914, on the other hand, France was
led by a government of 'sacred union', in which party politics were
transcended by patriotism, and it is surely not reading too much into
the splendidly overwrought finale of the Trio to conclude that Ravel
was inspired by that kind of idealism. He might also have shared the
illusion of military leaders like Foch and Joffre that a spirited counter-
attack by gallant French soldiers would have the war over and won
within a matter of weeks. That Ravel could have entertained dreams
of military glory and could even have reflected them in his music is a
notion incompatible with the conventional view of the composer as a
dry little man who kept his emotions, if any, firmly to himself. But the

documentary evidence of his patriotic fervour in the early days of
what he called 'this holy war' is incontrovertible and the occasional
glimpse of him at this time is most revealing.

The society portrait painter Jacques-Émile Blanche remembered
going to an exhibition at the Galérie Druet one day during the war
and finding himself 'face to face with a young airman in a rather droll
outfit. It was Maurice Ravel. He told me how he had become a
bombardier … He was positively lyrical in his passion for his new
profession.' Blanche was not the most reliable of witnesses and his
attitude to Ravel was at best equivocal but the episode is too bizarre to
have been invented. Besides, it is corroborated by another glimpse of
Ravel the postulant airman, this one offered by Roland-Manuel who
recalled Ravel visiting him in his barracks on 27 February 1915, the day
before his company was due to be sent to the Dardanelles: 'When you
come back,' Ravel told him, 'you will have to show me respect because
observers in the air force are ranked as officers … They can choose
their own uniforms. I rather fancy that of the Military Riding School
at Saumur.' Clearly, Ravel was so confident of being invited to join
the most dangerous and most romantic branch of the armed forces –
as observer or bombardier, he argued, his militarily insufficient weight
would be a positive advantage – that he had bought his officer's
uniform in anticipation.

When he eventually was allowed to enlist, in March 1915, it was as
a private soldier in the artillery. But he still cherished his flying
ambitions. 'After eight months of string-pulling, I have at last got
myself accepted in the 13th Artillery Regiment,' he wrote to Vaughan
Williams, who had himself volunteered and was serving as a wagon
orderly in the Royal Army Medical Corps. 'Now,' Ravel added, 'I am
waiting for my appointment as an aeroplane bombardier, which I
have applied for and which cannot be long in coming.' He persisted
in what his brother called his 'mad ideas' until, a year later, he was
finally ruled out of flying on medical grounds. After that his 'Icarus
dreams', as he preferred to call them, were restricted to the intriguingly titled but unrealized (and probably never even started) musical
projects, *Dédale 39* and *Icare*.

In the prevailing patriotic atmosphere, while waiting to enlist after
he had finished the Piano Trio, Ravel felt that he could not go back to
La Cloche engloutie, his Gerhardt Hauptmann opera, or to *Wien*, his

Ravel in uniform at the home
of his 'War Godmother'
Mme Fernand Dreyfus

long-planned waltz-time tribute to Johann Strauss: both had national
associations he considered inappropriate at the time and, in the spirit
of the Franco-Belgian alliance, he thought for a while of going back to
an old operatic project based on Maeterlinck's *Intérieur*. While still in
St-Jean-de-Luz, however, he had started on a 'French suite' which,
inspired by the harpsichord music of the French Baroque masters, was
later to be called *Le Tombeau de Couperin*. It is another remarkable
example of the parallel thinking of Ravel and Debussy that the *musi-
cien français*, as Debussy now signed himself, was looking to the same
source of inspiration for the series of chamber sonatas he was to start
at Pourville in 1915.

Back in Paris in December, Ravel diverted his attention from the
French suite to a little song for unaccompanied four-part chorus,
'Trois Beaux Oiseaux du Paradis' ('Three Fine Birds from Paradise'),
for which he wrote not only the music but the words as well. Soon
after the successful first performance of the Trio at an SMI concert in
the Salle Gaveau on 28 January, he wrote two more pastiche
Renaissance chansons, 'Nicolette' and 'Ronde', to go with it. To judge
by the amusingly colourful scoring, the resourceful use of words and
the cleverly mock-archaic style of both text and music, Ravel enjoyed
writing the *Trois Chansons*. But, while they cannot be compared in
quality to Debussy's *Trois Chansons de Charles d'Orléans*, they
represent more than a pleasant way of passing the time. 'Trois Beaux
Oiseaux du Paradis', which is presented in the published score as a
kind of slow movement between the two burlesques, is a touching
dialogue between a solo soprano and three other soloists representing
respectively the blue, white and red birds which bring her symbolic
messages from her 'sweetheart gone to war': the last one chills her
heart. It is not insignificant, bearing in mind Ravel's military
ambitions, that 'Trois Beaux Oiseaux du Paradis' is dedicated to the
music-loving politician Paul Painlevé – pioneer pilot and, for two
months before the advent of Georges Clemenceau, prime minister.
'Ronde' is dedicated with admirable political tact to Clemenceau's
Hungarian-born sister-in-law, Sophie Clemenceau, and 'Nicolette' to
Tristan Klingsor, who also had friends in high places.

By means of no little intrigue and a discreetly mistaken measure-
ment – he was 1.65 m in height when he went into the army and
1.61 m when he came out – Ravel was passed fit for military service on

10 March 1915 and officially assigned to the army on 17 April. But it was only after he had completed his training as a driver in Paris – friends reported seeing him enveloped in his blue uniform driving his lorry in a convoy down the Champs-Elysées – that, in March 1916, he was sent to the war zone at Verdun. If he had any glorious illusions left by then he lost them as soon as he saw for himself what destruction and carnage was involved in defending this border fortress on the Western Front. At first he was well out of the range of enemy shells, though constantly under the threat of Zeppelin raids, and it was probably not until he was sent near to the front line to retrieve an abandoned vehicle that he began to understand the reality of the situation: 'Nothing unpleasant happened to me,' he wrote to Jean Marnold on 4 April.

Driver Ravel in helmet and goatskin with damaged wheel on the Western front near Verdun

I didn't need my helmet and my gas mask stayed in my pocket. I saw a hallucinatory thing: a nightmare town, horribly deserted and silent … It was agonizing to be alone in the middle of this town sleeping its sinister sleep under the brilliant light of a lovely summer's day. I will no doubt see more frightful, more repugnant things than that, but I don't think I will ever experience anything deeper, stranger than this mute sort of terror.

He did, in fact, see worse things and had worse experiences, many of which he described in a series of vividly written letters to Mme Fernand Dreyfus, Roland-Manuel's stepmother, who had 'adopted' him under a 'War Godmother' scheme and whose moral support at this time was even more valuable than her food parcels: his own mother was not a fluent correspondent and, anyway, he could tell her nothing that might alarm her. He did not, on the other hand, see very much active service. Certainly, in May he was regularly taking part in dangerous missions driving day and night, without lights, on bad roads with loads far too heavy for his lorry. 'In spite of that,' he wrote to an officer who had befriended him,

you can't drive slowly because you are within range of the mortars … One of them, an Austrian 130, exploded so near to me that it threw its powder in my face. Adélaïde and I – Adélaïde is my lorry – escaped the shrapnel, but the poor thing couldn't go on and, having almost let me down in a danger zone … she was so much in despair that she lost one of

her wheels in a forest where I had to play at Robinson Crusoe for ten days,
waiting for somebody to retrieve us.

More often than not, in fact, his lorry was in repair and the
enforced idleness – as he waited, for literally weeks on end, for spare
parts to arrive – combined with the stress of what he had been
through before to plunge him into a state of lassitude and dejection.

He did, however, find the time and the energy to reject the over-
tures of the National League for the Defence of French Music
(whose honorary presidents included Saint-Saëns, D'Indy and other
composers associated with the Société Nationale) and to refute the
argument that German and Austrian music should be banned from
public performance in France. 'It is of little importance to me that
Monsieur Schoenberg, for example, is of Austrian nationality. He is
still a high-quality musician whose very interesting discoveries have
had a beneficial influence on certain allied composers, even some of
our own. I am delighted, moreover, that Messieurs Bartók, Kodály
and their disciples are Hungarian and that they show it in their music
with such zest.' The threat he received in reply, that his attitude could
lead to his own music being banned, did not worry him in the least:
as a serving soldier, he occupied the moral high ground and, besides,
his colleagues in the SMI were on his side.

He was more worried about his health – in one last effort to get
into the air force, he was told he had a hypertrophy of the heart –
but, as he wrote to Mme Dreyfus in May 1916, 'Only one thing really
makes me suffer, and that is not being able to embrace my poor
Maman … and one other thing: music. I thought I had forgotten it.
In the last few days it has come back, like a tyrant. I can think of
nothing else. I'm sure I would have been in a really productive period.'
A few days later he wrote to Florent Schmit, 'I'm brimming over with
inspiration, to the point that I'll explode if peace doesn't come soon
to lift the lid.' Moved by Gérard de Nerval's *Popular Songs and Ballads
of the Valois*, he asked Marnold in Paris to send him anything he could
find about the folk-song of the region. In his billet in the country,
where he amused his landlady's children by making paper chickens
and moulding ducklings out of crumbs of bread, he started notating
birdsong as material for a new piece. Nothing came of these ideas: as
he said, 'The artist is not compatible with the warrior.'

When, after a short leave in Paris in August, he was posted to
Châlons-sur-Marne, his life as a warrior was virtually over. He immediately went down with dysentery and at the end of September had
to undergo an operation for it. Recovering well from that, he took the
opportunity during his recuperation to extend his reading and found
particular pleasure in Alain-Fournier's *Le Grand Meaulnes*, which so
excited him that he toyed for a while with the idea of basing a piano
concerto on it. But when he went home to Paris on sick leave all such
ideas were forgotten: having kept all news of his illness from his
mother, he discovered the terrible irony that his friends had also been
concealing the true state of her health from him.

In the presence of her two sons, Mme Ravel died at her home in
the avenue Carnot on 5 January 1917. The effect of that loss, for which
he never ceased to grieve, cannot be overestimated. It must have
been in a state of shock that only six days later he was persuaded by

A last photograph of Mme
Ravel, the composer's
mother, who died in 1917

Diaghilev, who had just arrived in Paris from Italy, to write a ballet on
a scenario by the Italian futurist poet Francisco Cangiullo. Certainly,
although he wrote from the Dreyfus address on the boulevard de
Courcelles to confirm his agreement, the project was never heard of
again. He returned to his duties at Châlons in February in relatively
good health but in a profoundly depressed state of mind. 'Morally,'
he wrote to Mme Dreyfus on 9 February, 'it's frightful … it is such a
short time since I was writing to her and receiving her poor letters,
which saddened me … and yet were such a great joy to me … I didn't
know it would come so quickly. Now I have this horrible despair, the
same obsessive thoughts.' In March he fell ill again, this time with
frostbite to his feet, and, although he had recovered from that within
a few weeks, after a posting to Versailles – which seemed to give him
plenty of opportunity to visit Paris – the French army decided it could
dispense with the services of its artist-warrior. He was formally given
his 'temporary discharge' on 1 June 1917.

8

Ravel with two dragonflies
in costumes designed by
Steinhof for the Vienna
production of L'*Enfant et les
Sortilèges* in 1929

*I am seeing no one but my frogs, my negroes,
my shepherdesses and other insects.*

Maurice Ravel at work
on *L'Enfant et les Sortilèges*

Recovery 1917–25

For four years after the death of his mother Ravel was virtually
homeless. The apartment in avenue Carnot held too many memories
for Maurice and Edouard to stay there and neither had the will to set
up house on his own. Edouard made himself at home with his good
friends and business associates, the Bonnets, who owned the motor
spare-parts factory which he managed in Levallois; years later, on the
death of M. Bonnet, Edouard was to marry his widow, Angèle. As for
Maurice, he at first found refuge with his War Godmother, Mme
Fernand Dreyfus, just off the boulevard de Courcelles and then, after
his discharge from the army, in the Dreyfus family's country house at
Lyons-la-Forêt near Rouen.

Normandy was a long way from his pre-war refuge in the Basque
country. But if he had gone back there at this time he would have
had to face not only the grievous absence of his mother but also the
awkward presence of Claude Debussy and Emma Bardac: suffering
agonies from the illness that was to kill him a few months later, and
reluctantly coaching an insistent Marguerite Long in his piano
Études, Debussy was spending his last summer at the Chalet Habas
in St-Jean-de-Luz. Ravel, though in a pitiable state himself, at least
had the power to create and, in the delightful surroundings of the
Lyons Forest, he was immediately able to start work again.

The creative paralysis was to come later. For the present, as he
wrote to Jacques Durand on 7 July 1917, he was in relatively good
health: 'I don't know if I'm putting on any weight but I'm not cough-
ing any more.' He was also making progress with *Le Tombeau de
Couperin*: 'The menuet and the rigaudon are finished. The rest is
taking shape.' What enabled him to start composing again so quickly
was that he had been thinking about the work for three years by now,
having made a start on it even before October 1914 when he wrote
from St-Jean-de-Luz to Roland-Manuel to tell him that he had begun
two piano pieces: '1° a French suite – no, it's not what you think:
the *Marseillaise* will not be featured in it, and there will be a forlane,

a gigue, no tango however. – 2° a *Nuit romantique*, with spleen, infernal hunt, accursed nun etc.' The unlikely sounding 'Romantic Night', of which only a one-page sketch survives, was abandoned – but not as quickly as one might imagine. The 'French suite', which was no less patriotic for not having the *Marseillaise* in it, must have developed in his mind during those periods when music returned 'like a tyrant' to obsess him while serving at Verdun. Although it was more than just a matter of writing it down when he settled in at Lyons-la-Forêt in June 1917, he did have the six movements finished before the end of November.

How much of *Le Tombeau de Couperin* was written at St-Jean-de-Luz before the composer enlisted – the manuscript is dated 'July 1914, June–November 1917' – is not at all clear. The probability is that it began as a diversion when work on the Trio was particularly difficult, as we know it was in July 1914. We also know that the composer was amused by Pius X's recent attack on the tango, which was considered morally offensive, and by the somewhat absurd Papal efforts to revive in its place the forlana or furlana, a supposedly innocent dance associated with Venice in the seventeenth and eighteenth centuries. That is what is behind Ravel's allusions to the forlane (the French form of the forlana) and the tango in his letter to Roland-Manuel. He was fascinated also by an article on the forlane in the April 1914 issue of the *Revue musicale* which was illustrated by the *Forlane-Rondeau* from François Couperin's fourth *Concert royal*. In a letter to Cipa (undated, unfortunately) he wrote, 'I'm working on something for the Pope. You know that this august personage has just launched a new dance, the forlane. I am transcribing one by Couperin … I'm going to see to it,' he added, 'that it is danced at the Vatican by Mistinguett and Colette Willy *en travesti*.'

It was no doubt in a similarly satirical frame of mind that Ravel conceived the bizarre idea of his *Nuit romantique*. And it was surely with that project still in mind – and not in preparation for *Le Tombeau de Couperin*, as is generally but unconvincingly assumed – that shortly after his arrival at Lyon-la-Forêt he asked his friend Lucien Garban to send him Liszt's *Études transcendantes*, *Mazeppa* and *Feux follets*. This was just the kind of material he would need to look at if he was going to write 'infernal hunt' and 'accursed nun' music. If he consulted Liszt for *Le Tombeau de Couperin*, which was intended as a tribute to Couperin and 'eighteenth-century French music in general', it could only have been to determine what to avoid. Where he did indulge himself in pianistic virtuoso effect, at the end of the *Toccata* last movement, Liszt was not in his opinion the immediate source of the inspiration: 'It's pure Saint-Saëns,' he used to say.

In the melancholy circumstances of 1917 *Le Tombeau de Couperin* proved to be a more viable project than a satirical comment on the romantic artist's enthralment to nocturnal manifestations of the supernatural. It is true that the initial inspiration for the *Forlane*, conceived while he was 'working on something for the Pope' in St-Jean-de-Luz in the summer of 1914, was also satirical. But by the time he returned to the suite in 1917 it had acquired its Baroque-style title – in this context a *tombeau*, literally a 'tomb', is a form of artistic tribute to a revered predecessor – and he was probably already thinking in terms of making it a memorial to friends who had died in the war: one of them, Jean Dreyfus, was the stepbrother of Roland-Manuel and the stepson of the Mme Dreyfus in whose house he was staying at the time.

Arriving at Lyons-la-Forêt at the end of June with the *Forlane* complete perhaps and the *Rigaudon* and *Menuet* so well sketched that he was able to dispose of them by the time he wrote to Durand with news of his progress less than two weeks later, he would then have

Lucien Garban, pictured here with Ravel (right) and Mme Garban at Lyons-la-Forêt in 1922, worked on the publication of Ravel's scores at Durand and was one of the composer's closest friends.

turned to the non-dance movements, the *Prélude*, the *Fugue* and the *Toccata*. Apart from the fact that he was able to write them at all, the extraordinary thing about these three pieces is that there is nothing overtly sorrowful in them. And, until the end of the *Toccata*, there is no kind of joy in them either. There is a peculiar emotional numbness about them, as though the composer were trying to protect himself from feeling too much. The effect is achieved partly by the use of modal harmonies, excluding the conventional emotional symbolism of major and minor keys, and partly by limiting expressive potential through the discipline of strictly applied rhythmic or contrapuntal patterns, often according to Baroque precedent. Except in the very last line, there is not one bar in the *Prélude* which does not repeat the triplet figuration heard at the beginning. The *Fugue* is a highly ingenious example of three-part writing, of subject and counter-subject treated according to the standard academic procedures but with every appearance of spontaneity and with deceptive ease. The *Toccata* is no less thorough than the *Prélude* in repeating the same rhythmic figure from beginning to end.

They are by no means dry pieces: the melodic charm of the *Prélude*, heightened by graceful harpsichord-style decoration, and the lyrical phrases floating on the turbulence of the *Toccata* are irresistible evidence of that. They are not inexpressive either: there is a gently rueful quality in the harmonies of the *Prélude* and there is a hint of little-boy-lost, *Petit Poucet* pathos about the *Fugue* in spite of the sense of direction implicit in the form of the piece. But these three movements of *Le Tombeau de Couperin* are different in kind from the other three, and not only because the latter are dances and the former are not. The satirical inspiration behind the *Forlane* is evident even in a version faithfully developed, at least in terms of its 6/8 metre and its rondo structure, from a transcription of a Couperin original. The rhythm of the forlane might not be as seductive as that of the tango but, Ravel wittily suggests, there is ample opportunity for a variety of illicit thrills in the harmonies and for flirtatious episodes between the entries of the wistful main theme. The *Rigaudon* is a cheerfully robust interpretation of an old Provençal dance, with echoes of Chabrier both in the outer sections and in the exquisite combination of primitive rhythms and sophisticated harmonies in the middle section. The *Menuet* is the last and best example of its kind in Ravel's piano music. It is also the most emotional piece in the suite, a subtle melancholy colouring the elegant line and clear texture of the minuet and, in the central *Musette*, an outspoken anguish mounting in chromatic progressions in the right hand over a two-note drone in the left.

If anything of the discarded *Nuit romantique* spilled over into *Le Tombeau de Couperin* it was in the *Toccata* finale, where there is something disturbingly obsessive in its tenacious ostinato rhythms and something dangerously excessive in the paroxysm of Scarbo-like laughter at the end. This movement is dedicated to the memory of Captain Joseph de Marliave, music-loving husband of the pianist Marguerite Long. It was she who was to give the first performance of the work in 1919 and who was much later to defend Ravel against the charge of impropriety in commemorating the dead with such unfuneral music. 'The dead are unhappy enough as they are,' she said. 'Is it necessary to dedicate laments to them for ever? When a musician of genius gives them the best of himself and at the same time something they would have enjoyed, isn't that the most moving tribute he can make?' In this light the *Rigaudon* dedicated to two friends from St-Jean-de-Luz, the brothers Pierre and Pascal Gaudin, who were killed by the same shell on their first day at the Front, assumes an extra dimension of meaning. So too, to complete the roll of honour, do the *Prélude* dedicated to Lieutenant Jacques Charlot, who worked on Ravel's music at Durand, the *Fugue* dedicated to Lieutenant Jean Cruppi, son of the Mme Cruppi who had done so much to help him in getting *L'Heure espagnole* staged at the Opéra-Comique, the *Forlane* dedicated to another friend from St-Jean-de-Luz, Lieutenant Gabriel Deluc, and the *Menuet* dedicated to Jean Dreyfus.

Le Tombeau de Couperin was to be Ravel's last work of any import-ance for nearly three years. He was creative enough to design his own title page for the score – a cinerary urn in his favourite late eighteenth-century manner – but the will to compose which, miraculously, had sustained him for six months at Lyons-la-Forêt deserted him on his return to Paris. He was now living with his brother and the Bonnets in their villa in St-Cloud, in bourgeois comfort no doubt but also in full awareness of the proximity of enemy forces who were inflicting bombs from aircraft and shells from long-range 'big Bertha' weapons on the capital itself. The only original work he was able to complete in 1918 was a fifteen-bar-long *Frontispice* for two pianos and not four but, eccentrically enough, five hands. Written as a frontispiece for Riciotto Canudo's *Poème du Vardar*, a collection of poems inspired by the author's recent experience as a soldier in the Vardar, it was clearly not intended for performance: it is a collage of disparate strands of raw melodic material intended as much for the eye as the Picasso portrait of the author which was published in the same volume. Apart from that visionary little essay in surrealism, the only other work he could manage at this time, as in similar circumstances in 1908 and 1912, was orchestration: the masterly version of *Alborada del gracioso*, which fulfils a dramatic potential only partially realized in the piano original in *Miroirs*, dates from precisely this time.

Ravel's great misfortune in 1918 was that, while still depressed by the loss of his mother and stressed by the continuing hostilities, his health – severely undermined by war-service conditions which he had obviously not been fit to meet – was progressively and seriously failing. Writing to Marguerite Long in an effort to get her to give the first performance of *Le Tombeau de Couperin* in St-Jean-de-Luz, where she was spending the summer again, he told her, 'I have had some vile moments: I even thought at one time that I would never work again. I have been feeling better about that for a few days but I'm still fairly distressed, and I'm also making the mistake of living in wartime.' That was in early July, shortly after he had managed at least to write the *Frontispice* for Canudo. In September, clearly worried that he might have succumbed to the infection ravaging Europe at the time, he informed Mme Dreyfus that he had been 'terribly out of sorts recently. Spanish flu? I don't know. Five days of fever, with no other troubles. But it has left me in an unbelievable state of lassitude and weakness.' Two months later he told Alfredo Casella that he couldn't see himself doing anything more than 'getting from my bed to a chaise longue … Writing these few lines is going to make my temperature rise.' In fact, on the orders of his new doctor, Raymond Geiger – Dr Bonniot had retired by now – he was taking his temperature at least twice a day and was forbidden to work: 'You can imagine how much that depresses me,' he told Casella. It looks from the symptoms he mentions and his reference to his 'wretched right lung' as if he was suffering from the beginnings of tuberculosis. He does not use the word himself, except in relation to the 'tubercular ganglions' which were also worrying him, but the sun-and-mountain-air treatment recommended by Dr Geiger seems to confirm that tuberculosis was his diagnosis.

Certainly, within the first week of January 1919 – less than two months after the armistice that officially ended the war – he was installed in the Hôtel du Mont Blanc in Megève, 1,100 metres up in the Alps of Haute Savoie, and he would be staying for three months. He was not very happy there. He liked the snow, the sun and the view but he did not like the isolation – Megève at that time was by no means the popular resort it is now – and, as his health failed to improve, he was worried by the thought that he might have to move to an ever higher altitude. He also disliked the enforced idleness. He did a little tobogganning but when the local doctor made his next weekly visit he was forbidden to do even that. Worst of all, he was totally incapable of working. At first he told himself that it was because the piano in his room was intolerably flat. By the end of the month, however, he was confessing to Georgette Marnold, daughter of Jean Marnold and new-found confidante, his fear that 'perhaps I will never work again.' But after weeks of complaining about his insomnia and his cough and his erratic temperature, he did begin to feel better. Leading what he jokingly called 'sana life' – without, apparently, making the connection between sanatorium and tuber-

A postcard from Ravel at Megève – 'beautiful view, terribly cold' – to Mme de Saint-Marceaux in Paris

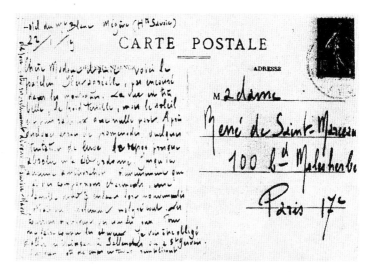

culosis – he was smoking less, putting on weight and thinking about work in more positive terms.

The turning point was a letter he wrote on 20 February to his friend Jacques Rouché, director of the Opéra, asking him to put him in touch with Colette de Jouvenel, whose address he had lost. Colette, long since divorced from Henri Gauthier-Villars and now married to Henry de Jouvenel, had been asked by Rouché in 1916 to write a 'fairy-tale ballet' for the Opéra. 'I still don't understand,' she recalled in 1939,

> *since I write so slowly and painfully, how I was able to deliver it within a week. He liked my little poem and suggested various composers whose names I received as politely as I could. 'But,' asked Rouché after a silence, 'what if I were to suggest Ravel?' I loudly dropped my politeness and couldn't conceal my enthusiasm. 'There is no point in hiding the possibility,' Rouché added, 'that it could take a long time, assuming that he accepts.' He accepted. It did take a long time.*

Colette, at the time of writing *L'Enfant et les Sortilèges*, photographed by Henri Manuel in the 1920s

L'Enfant et les Sortilèges, as the 'fairy-tale ballet' eventually came to be known, would not be ready for performance until as long as nine years later. If anyone wrote more slowly and more painfully than Colette, even at the best of times, it was Ravel. And these were obviously not the best of times. The one situation less favourable for thinking about writing a major stage work would have been when he was on active service at the Western Front, which was just when Rouché, not very cleverly, sent Colette's libretto to him. Predictably, it failed to reach him. Acquiring another copy in 1918, he took it with him to Megève and was getting seriously interested in it at the same time, it seems, as Colette was finally giving up hope of ever hearing from him about it. She expressed her feelings to Rouché who then communicated them to Ravel and, at last, elicited his request for her address. Ravel wanted to tell her about various suggestions he had to make for what he called their *opéra-dansé* – quite specific suggestions, as it turned out when, a week later, he wrote to Colette herself with sincere apologies and with the surely no less sincere promise that he would be getting on with it on his return to Paris at the beginning of April. 'In fact,' he said, 'I'm working on it already: I'm taking notes – without writing a single one – and I'm even thinking of a few changes … Don't worry: I don't mean cuts – on the contrary.'

Although Colette was more than willing to add any number of lines to her libretto, Ravel did not immediately turn his attention to the project on his return to the Bonnet villa in St-Cloud. Once again, he set out to ease himself into composition by means of the always congenial exercise of orchestration. On commission from Diaghilev he made an affectionate arrangement of Chabrier's *Menuet pompeux* for the Ballets Russes and, at the request of his publisher, he made orchestral versions of four movements – *Prélude, Forlane, Menuet, Rigaudon* – from *Le Tombeau de Couperin*. But he was still far from being himself. Edouard thought that his brother was living it up too much in Paris, now that he had been set free from his isolated station in the Alps, and it does seem highly uncharacteristic of Maurice Ravel to end a letter, as he did in May 1919, with the announcement that he was going out to a banquet and would 'come back drunk' – even though he did indicate that this was to be a last fling before settling down to a summer of hard work.

There had been distractions of course. On 11 April – Marguerite Long having by now regained her confidence after abandoning the piano on the death of her husband in 1914 – he had at last secured the first performance of *Le Tombeau de Couperin* at an SMI concert in the Salle Gaveau. It was Ravel's first public appearance since the end of the war and since the death of Debussy. He was warmly received both for his new status as the leading French composer of the day and for the quality of the new work, which was immediately encored. Then there were the rehearsals for the first performance of the orchestral version of *Alborada del gracioso* on 17 May. None of this restored his spirits, which were further depressed by the sudden death of his aunt in Geneva and his efforts to sort out the affairs of his distressed Uncle Edouard. He was pleased to hear about a remarkably popular production of *L'Heure espagnole* at Covent Garden – 'seventeen curtain calls … the greatest success in the lyric theatre for thirty years' – but showed little interest in going to see it. As he wrote to Vaughan Williams in September, although his winter stay in the mountains had done his health a lot of good, 'I now have to look after my morale, and I don't know how to go about it.' At much the same time he heard of the death of the mother of his Spanish friend and fellow composer Manuel de Falla: 'It is a terrible thing that has happened to us,' he wrote in heartfelt commiseration. 'From that moment life is transformed. You can still feel joys, emotions, but not in the same way any more; it's a bit like when you haven't slept or when you have a fever … I haven't been able to get back to work … Try to be stronger than me, my dear friend.'

What saved Ravel from what might well have been collapse at this point was a combination of two complementary circumstances. One was the generosity of his friend Ferdinand Hérold who, far from being embittered by the composer's abandonment of his libretto for *La Cloche engloutie*, was deeply concerned by the state both of his health and of his mind. When Ravel told Hérold and his wife that he needed 'to get away from the city and the noise and to escape somewhere, anywhere, as long he would be alone and could work out his creative thinking,' they offered him the use of an old family house in Lapras, a village at the bottom of a valley near Lamastre in Ardèche, 570 kilometres southeast of Paris. It was, they assured him, good for work and for rest and no one would disturb him. He accepted readily and, having been taken there and settled in by Hérold, he stayed at Lapras in complete solitude for most of the winter and part of the following spring.

The other heaven-sent intervention was a commission from Diaghilev. It is not certain exactly when the Russian impresario asked Ravel to write another ballet score for him but it is more than likely – since Ravel was clearly not Diaghilev's favourite composer – that the idea derived in the first place from Misia Edwards, the long-intended dedicatee of the score which was now about to be written at last. As long ago as 1906 Ravel had told Misia that he was thinking of making a start on '*Vienne*, which is destined for you, as you know.' It was intended at that time to be 'a grand waltz, a kind of homage to the memory of the great Strauss, not Richard, the other – Johann,' as he described it to Jean Marnold: 'You know how much I like those wonderful rhythms.' *Vienne*, or *Wien* as he more often thought of it, survived as a viable project until 1914 when a work named after the capital of Austria struck him as being 'inappropriate to the demands of the time'. But then, in the refreshingly positive letter written from Megève to Jacques Rouché on 20 February 1919, it surfaced again, this time under what would be its definitive title: 'I am also thinking of *La Valse*, the choreographic poem which I have mentioned to you before.' It was the same work – he was still calling it *Wien* from time to time even in 1919 – but, significantly, whereas it had once been a 'symphonic poem' it was now a 'choreographic poem'. By the time he left Paris he had a firm commission and the prospect of a production the following season.

Soon after his arrival at Lapras, when he had finished off the orchestral version of the *Deux Mélodies hébraïques* and dispatched it to Durand, he cheerfully told Georgette Marnold that he had at last found his vocation: 'I was born to be a hermit.' As the new year approached, however, he was not so happy. Christmas passed unnoticed but he was dreading New Year's Eve which, he told Ida,

> *is going to be sinister. I'm thinking of the ones we used to have in our charming apartment in avenue Carnot where I was so happy. I'm thinking it will soon be three years since she went and that my despair increases every day. I'm thinking about it even more since I have got back to work again and that I no longer have that dear silent presence enveloping me with her infinite tenderness – which, I see more clearly than ever, was my only reason for living.*

The consolation was that *La Valse* was actually in progress: 'I have at last been able to get started,' he had told Roland-Manuel on 22 December, 'and am now in top gear.' On 31 December he allowed himself a seasonal indulgence by starting on the orchestration, even though the piano score was probably only half finished. A week later he was still 'waltzing frantically' and by the middle of January he was able to announce to Ida that he would have it finished before the end of the month: 'I have written to Misia that I shall then be able to let Diaghilev hear it, although I would rather wait until the middle of February.' After completing the solo-piano version only a week or so later than predicted, he turned to the two-piano version and filled in the final details of the orchestral score (which is actually dated 'Lapras, December 1919–March 1920') on 12 April. For a composer who had written nothing new since 1914 except, at the most, three movements of *Le Tombeau de Couperin* it was a miraculous recovery.

The one serious intrusion on Ravel's seclusion at Lapras was the announcement in the *Journal officiel* of 15 January 1920 and the newspapers of the following day that he had been made a Chevalier of the Légion d'honneur. Far from being grateful for what was one of the greatest honours the French nation could bestow, he was horrified, not least because he had not given his consent to it but above all because he did not want it. Whatever the cause of the problem – administrative incompetence, delays in the post between Paris and Lapras, Ravel's failure to respond to the official invitation in good time (the documents did not arrive until 12 January) – it inevitably resulted in his rejection of the honour becoming public knowledge. It cost him not only a few sleepless nights and lost composition time but also, when the news came out in April, the embarrassment of another 'affaire Ravel', although in this case he was well out of the way of the press and it was his brother in Paris who had to speak for him. Edouard duly alluded to the relevant passage from Baudelaire's *Mon coeur mis à nu*: 'If a man has merit, what is the point of decorating him? If he has none he can be decorated because it will give him distinction.' There were personal reasons, too, he said, stimulating even more speculation. The most convincing explanation, based on Manuel Rosenthal's not entirely reliable memories of his teacher, is that Ravel felt badly let down by a breach of trust on the part of the politicians whose help he had sought in his efforts to enlist in 1915: though sworn to secrecy, they had let the news leak out in such a way that his mother got to know about it before he was ready to tell her. 'That,' he is quoted as saying, 'I was unable to forgive and that is why I refused the distinction.'

'Ravel rejects the Légion d'honneur,' wrote Erik Satie in the avant-garde journal *Le Coq* in May 1920, 'but all his music accepts it.' Although Ravel was to forgive Satie for this jibe, as for many others, he cannot have failed to register the message that suddenly, in the light of the post-war Parisian aesthetic, he was considered seriously old-fashioned. Satie, on the other hand – after decades of obscurity, during which Ravel had been one of his few consistent supporters – was in the ascendant and there was little he would not do or not say to enhance his new-found reputation. As the composer of *Parade*, he certainly deserved his notoriety: his wonderfully mischievous music-hall score had been at least as effective as Cocteau's fairground scenario and Picasso's cubist designs in securing a very satisfactory wartime scandal for Diaghilev and his company. For the same reason he was

Erik Satie photographed by the sculptor Constantin Brancusi in about 1923

well qualified to act as figurehead to the disparate group of young
composers arbitrarily labelled in the press as 'Les Six' and identified as
the avant-garde opposition – under the intellectually dubious but
politically effective leadership of Jean Cocteau – to both Wagnerian
'fog' and the 'misty haze' of impressionism. It was unfortunate, however, that to preserve his position on Ravel's return to the musical
scene after the war Satie did all he could to turn his young colleagues
– and with particular success as far as Georges Auric and Francis
Poulenc were concerned – against the composer he now called the
'ring-leader of the sub-Debussyists'.

Ravel can have been only vaguely aware of these undercurrents
when, in April 1920, he returned from Lapras to undertake the task of
introducing *La Valse* to Diaghilev and his colleagues in Paris. So, on
his arrival at Misia's apartment to present the audition, he probably
sensed nothing at all ominous in finding something of the new order
already in place: among those present – alongside the impresario and
his secretaries, his choreographer Leonide Massine, his favourite composer Igor Stravinsky and the pianist Marcelle Meyer – was Francis
Poulenc, the youngest and one of the most gifted of Les Six. As
Poulenc recalled the occasion,

> *Ravel arrived, his music under his arm, and Diaghilev said to him:
> 'Well, my dear Ravel, how nice to hear* La Valse.' *And Ravel played* La
> Valse, *with Marcelle Meyer, I think, perhaps not very well … Now, I
> knew Diaghilev very well at that time, and I'd seen his false teeth move,
> I'd seen his monocle move, I'd seen that he was very embarrassed, and*

Jean Cocteau and the
'Groupe des Six' in 1925 –
Cocteau, the writer and
artist, is at the piano; five of
the composers – Darius
Milhaud, Arthur Honegger,
Germaine Tailleferre,
Francis Poulenc and Louis
Durey – stand behind him;
the sixth, Georges Auric, is
represented in his absence
by a drawing by Cocteau.

*I'd seen that he didn't like it and that he was going to say 'No.' When
Ravel had finished, Diaghilev said to him something which I thought was
very true. He said, 'Ravel, it's a masterpiece, but it isn't a ballet. It's a
portrait of a ballet, a painting of a ballet…' But what was extraordinary
was that Stravinsky said not a word! Nothing! … I was staggered.*

So too, though he took good care to conceal it, was Ravel. From
that moment he would have nothing more to do with Diaghilev
and his once cordial relationship with Stravinsky would be reduced to
little more than a formality.

Diaghilev was right in some ways. *La Valse* is a masterpiece and it is
not so much a waltz as a painting of a waltz, or rather two paintings –
an impressionist and an expressionist side by side in the same frame.
Up to just over halfway through, it is *Wien* as Ravel might have
written it when he conceived the idea in 1906. Emerging out of the
darkness of the rumbling basses in the opening bars, a Viennese
concert waltz in as many as five different sections, each with its own
distinctive and seductive melodic material, is seen to take shape.
Fragmentary in form, with not one episode fully worked out and with
some themes presented at length while others are reduced to rhythmic
gestures, the structure is apparently held together only by the centri-
fugal force of the whirling rhythms. But then, at the height of a
brilliant episode of virtuoso figuration on trumpets and woodwind,
the light is extinguished and the dark rumblings are heard again. The
waltz is reassembled out of the same material but this time even more
fragmentarily, in no orderly sequence and with increasing vehemence
as the rhythmic and harmonic excesses characteristic of the genre are
driven to extremes. This is *Wien* as Ravel could never have written it
before the war and as he had to write it in the light of his own all-too-
personal experience of what Viennese waltz-time culture had become.
The heavily percussive climax which finally explodes an essentially
civilized scene – the last two bars (in the orchestral version) shattering
the waltz rhythm itself – seems more violent than anything even in
The Rite of Spring.

Ravel disliked political interpretations of *La Valse*. He was always at
pains to point out that it was written for the stage and had nothing to
do with either dancing on a volcano at the end of the Second Empire
or the pitiable state of Vienna after the war. But speculation as to what

really inspired the work was never likely to be silenced by the scenario
he published in the score: 'Clouds whirl about. Occasionally they part
to allow a glimpse of waltzing couples. As they gradually evaporate
one can discern a gigantic hall, filled by a crowd of dancers in motion.
The stage gradually brightens. The glow of the chandeliers breaks out
fortissimo. An Imperial Court about 1855.' It sets the scene but that
is as far as it goes. It does not begin to take into account what Ravel
himself recognized as the 'fantastic and fatal' element in the score, the
explosive catastrophe which ultimately sets *La Valse* apart as one of
the most frightening of all artistic products of World War I.

    Although Ravel surely knew that he was not really 'born to be a
hermit', he did realize during the course of his stay at Lapras that he
would be in a better position to work in future if he were to move
out of Paris to live by himself. In March 1920 he had already asked
Georgette Marnold to look out for 'some old place at least thirty kilometres from Paris' and he eventually found what he wanted in the
handsome little town of Montfort l'Amaury, the ancient citadel of
Simon de Montfort on the edge of the forest of Rambouillet. In the
meantime, he had to resort once again to the hospitality of friends –
this time Pierre and Pierrette Haour, who owned an elegant château,
La Bijeannette, at Châteauneuf-en-Thymerais, not so very far from
where he would later settle in the Ile-de-France. As though to confirm
the wisdom of his decision to move into the country, he found
conditions at La Bijeannette so conducive to work that between May
and September 1920 he was able not only to complete a Duo for
violin and cello (later to become the opening *Allegro* of a four-
movement Sonata) but also to make a good start on *L'Enfant et les
Sortilèges*. Aware perhaps of Kodály's example, he had been thinking
about the Duo for some time and he was moved to get on with it
now by a request from Henry Prunières, editor of the *Revue musicale*,
who was to issue a special number, a *Tombeau de Claude Debussy*
(December 1920), featuring musical tributes from several leading composers of the day – including Bartók, Dukas, Falla, Goossens,
Malipiero, Roussel, Satie, Schmitt and Stravinsky.

    One thing he had meant and failed to do at La Bijeannette was to
practise the piano – his failing keyboard technique being a recurring
source of concern for him – in preparation for his first visit to Vienna
in October. On what amounted to a cultural mission sponsored by

the French Embassy, he was to take part in performances of his songs, attend a Vienna Symphony Orchestra concert of his orchestral music and, with Alfredo Casella as his partner, introduce the two-piano version of *La Valse* at Schoenberg's Society for Private Musical Performances. The first performance of the orchestral version of *La Valse* took place in Paris two months later, bringing Ravel another popular triumph to follow the success of a ballet version of *Le Tombeau de Couperin* introduced by the Swedish Ballet at the Théâtre des Champs-Elysées in November. Satie and Cocteau's young avant garde might have been of a different opinion, but as far as the general public was concerned Ravel had by now recovered the position he occupied before the war.

He was unable to consolidate it with a new work for some time, however. The violin and cello Duo written for the *Revue musicale* was performed together with the other Debussy memorial tributes at an SMI concert in January 1921 but, though this short *Allegro* was certainly adequate for its immediate purpose, for Ravel it was only the first movement of what was going to prove to be an exceptionally problematic work in four movements. Moreover, although the move to Montfort l'Amaury would eventually prove well worthwhile in terms of the peace and quiet he needed for his work, it was not at all easy at first. The town – forty-five kilometres from Paris or an hour by train from Les Invalides and ten minutes by horse-drawn coach from the station which served both Montfort and the neighbouring

Right, Le Belvédère from the road leading up the hill out of Montfort l'Amaury; *above,* the composer's studio at Le Belvédère with the portrait of his mother hanging on the wall next to the piano

community of Méré – was well placed in relation to the capital. The house – Le Belvédère, built in 1907 on a hill above the village and overlooking the wooded countryside beyond – was desirable at least for the splendid view from the balcony at the back and, under the fanciful Basque-style conical tower, a certain turn-of-the-century Gothic charm in its external features. Constructed out of inferior materials, however, and awkwardly designed to fit the sloping site, it was both damp and inconvenient, not least in that there was no interior communication between the upper floor on street-level at the front and the lower floor at the back, which could be approached only by way of the little garden.

Although the purchase of Le Belvédère – aided by a legacy from his Swiss Uncle Edouard, whose pastel portrait of the composer's mother was to hang in pride of place in the studio – was apparently not concluded until April 1921, Ravel had access to the house at least two months earlier. In February he wrote from Montfort to the directors of the Théâtre de la Monnaie in Brussels, thanking them for what he described as 'a perfect presentation' of *L'Heure espagnole* in January and apologizing for the delay: 'I am camping in a corner of the house, trying to speed up the activity of masons, painters, joiners etc; shuttling between Montfort and Paris, the days go past at an alarming rate.' An additional wing would be built on and existing rooms subdivided to make a total of twelve where there had originally been four. The salon, the Japanese salon, the dining room, the studio, the library, the garden-level bedroom: all these were designed, elaborately furnished with the appropriate ornaments, and to some extent decorated by Ravel himself. At the same time he had to see to new productions of *Daphnis et Chloé* at the Opéra in June and of *L'Heure espagnole* in the same theatre in December and, between the two, find the courage to make his first visit to St-Jean-de-Luz since the death of his mother. Not surprisingly in these circumstances, little progress was made on the Sonata for violin and cello.

One of the problems with the Sonata was that, in response partly to the new post-war aesthetic, he was setting out in a different direction. 'I believe that this Sonata,' he says in the autobiographical sketch, 'marks a turning point in the evolution of my career. Economy of texture is here pushed to the extreme. Renunciation of harmonic charm; an increasingly marked reaction in favour of melody.' It was

the most formidable challenge he had ever set himself. 'This devil of
a duo is giving me a lot of trouble,' he wrote to Roland-Manuel in
October 1921. By January 1922 he was so impatient with his progress
on it that he was determined to confine himself to Montfort until it
was finished. At the beginning of February he wrote to Calvocoressi:
'The duo was finished. Then I realized that the scherzo was much
too extended and, moreover, a mess. I am starting it again from the
beginning.' A month later it was really finished and the first performance, to be given by his violinist friend Hélène Jourdan-Morhange
and the cellist Maurice Maréchal, was scheduled for 6 April. 'It looks
nothing much, this thing for two instruments: there is almost a year
and a half's hard labour in it,' he told Calvocoressi. 'In that time,'
he went on, comparing his productivity to that of a notoriously prolific member of Les Six, 'Milhaud would have been able to produce
four symphonies, five quartets and several settings of Paul Claudel.'

If there were any implications in that remark about the superior
quality of the 'nothing much' it had taken him so long to complete,
they were not unjustified. The duo Sonata is a great achievement
of ingenuity and will-power against extreme technical odds. The
paradox at the heart of it is the way the two instruments so willingly
collaborate without actually merging their harmonic identities. So
there is a tension between them – varying in abrasiveness according
to the nature of the material – even in the *Allegro* first movement,
where they exchange ideas most freely and graciously. The second
movement, the scherzo which was completely rewritten in February
1922 and which draws for its primitive colour effects on Bartók's
most recent developments in string scoring, makes a special point of
the harmonic divergence by awarding the two instruments frankly
different key signatures – in competition perhaps with the self-conscious but comparatively mild bitonal language of that same Darius
Milhaud. In compensation the slow movement is a profoundly
thoughtful conversation, rising melodiously from the lower register
of the cello to an accelerated central climax and returning to the
initial idea without once resorting to the conventional contrapuntal
procedures the linear material seems to invite. Both the central
movements make more or less subtle thematic allusions to the opening *Allegro*. The last movement, based on a militant fanfare motif,
seals the cyclic unity in an attractively lyrical episode referring back to

the first movement and then marches on to a climax of melodic aggregations scored for what sounds like four instruments rather than two.

The eighteen months Ravel spent on the Sonata for violin and cello, though not the most prolific of his career, were infinitely more productive than the next eighteen months or, indeed, the next two years. There was no end of external reasons for not getting on with composing. One was that his growing fame brought with it numerous invitations to attend Ravel festivals, to take part in Ravel recitals, to conduct Ravel scores at orchestral concerts – not only in France but throughout Western Europe. He was particularly appreciated in London, where he regularly stayed with the Hardings – Mrs Harding being the Swedish-born soprano Louise Alva – at 14 Holland Park. By the end of 1924 he had carried out professional engagements of one kind or another also in Amsterdam, Milan, Brussels, Barcelona and Madrid and had turned down more than one invitation to tour the USA. 'I haven't yet despaired of getting back to work,' he told one American contact, 'and no matter how flattering the success might be it doesn't seem to me worth the three or four months.' But there were still all kinds of things getting in the way – the installation of central heating at Le Belvédère, the construction of an internal staircase, an infected foot, two fingers injured by a folding chair, influenza, insomnia …

Moreover, in spite of the move to Montfort l'Amaury, his social life in Paris was still flourishing. He had a room permanently reserved in the Hôtel d'Athènes, just across the road from the Godebskis' apart-ment in rue d'Athènes, and visits which were meant to last a few days were frequently extended to a few weeks. As an insomniac, he enjoyed the night life of the capital and was particularly attracted to the Grand Écart in Montmartre or better still, in spite of its asso-ciations with Cocteau and the less friendly members of Les Six, the Boeuf sur le toit on the fashionable rue Boissy d'Anglas – a trendy meeting place for intellectuals and for musicians as willing to hear jazz and American popular music as Bach or Milhaud performed by the brilliant two-piano partnership of Wiener and Doucet. On his Sundays in Paris he would visit the Clemenceau salon in the afternoon and the Godebskis in the evening. On his Sundays in Montfort, now that he had found an excellent and faithful housekeeper in

Mme Révelot, he did his own entertaining, inviting his friends from Paris for lunch, regaling them with cocktails of his own devising, taking them for a walk in the forest in the afternoon and joining them for dinner at the Relais in Rambouillet.

Had he been inspired to work he would not, of course, have been so easily distracted. But there was no such inspiration, as he rather surprisingly admitted to a reporter who asked him in January 1923 what he was working on: 'I'm not working. I'm depressed. Perhaps I'll never do anything again.' The most he had been able to do since the Sonata for violin and cello was orchestration and the 'tailoring' of another short piece for a special issue, a tribute to Gabriel Fauré, of the *Revue musicale*. A classic of its kind, his orchestral version of Mussorgsky's *Pictures at an Exhibition* had been commissioned by Serge Koussevitsky and completed in the summer of 1922, mainly in the Dreyfus house at Lyons-la-Forêt. Before the end of the year he had also orchestrated two Debussy piano pieces, the Chabrier-inspired *Tarentelle styrienne* (the title of which he abbreviated to *Danse*) and the *Sarabande* from *Pour le piano*, both at the request of their publisher, Jean Jobert. The *Berceuse sur le nom de Gabriel Fauré*, which did double duty as a present for the recently born son of the Roland-Manuels and as a tribute to his old composition teacher, was written in a single day at Lyons-la-Forêt. Based on a theme of twelve notes derived, in the usual arbitrary way, from the twelve letters of the name of Gabriel Fauré, it is an engagingly tender lullaby simply scored for muted violin with a piano part so affectionately and yet so imaginatively harmonized that it seems to anticipate Messiaen at one point.

Ravel's use of the violin in *Berceuse sur le nom de Gabriel Fauré* is significant; it is significant too that the violinist in the first performance of the *Berceuse*, at an SMI concert in December 1922, was again Hélène Jourdan-Morhange. The composer had first met the violinist after she had played in a hastily prepared wartime performance of the Trio with the pianist E. Robert Schmitz and the cellist Félix Delgrange. Her husband, the painter Jacques Jourdan, had been killed in the war and, although she eventually married another painter, Jean-Luc Moreau, she became the closest of Ravel's female friends. She was close in the geographical sense, too: she and Moreau had a cottage at Les Mesnuls, which was within easy walking distance of both Le Belvédère at Montfort l'Amaury and Colette's house La Gerbière at

Méré. At one point he thought about writing a concerto for her and it is almost certainly with her in mind – since he eventually dedicated the work to her – that he conceived the idea of writing a Violin Sonata in 1923. Sadly, because of what has been variously described as 'rheumatism' and 'motor cramps', she had to abandon her performing career at about this time – which is possibly one reason why it took Ravel so long to complete the sonata.

There was, however, another, younger violinist in Ravel's life, the Hungarian Jelly d'Arányi – niece of Joseph Joachim, pupil of Jenö Hubay, specially favoured interpreter of Béla Bartók – whom he first met when she played Bartók's First Violin Sonata with the composer at the piano in Paris in April 1922. He met her again in London three months later. She and Hans Kindler performed the Sonata for violin and cello at a private musical evening – probably at the Hardings in Holland Park – and she entertained Ravel for half the night afterwards with an apparently inexhaustible repertoire of Hungarian gypsy melodies. That was the initial inspiration of *Tzigane*, the concert rhapsody which he would dedicate to Jelly d'Arányi. It would take him nearly two years to complete it.

An advertisement for the concert featuring the first performance of *Tzigane* in London in 1924. The image of Ravel at the piano is taken from a 1911 drawing by Achille Ouvré.

In 1923 Ravel wrote nothing except a few bars of connecting material for a ballet at the Opéra-Comique, *Le Portrait de l'Infante*, the score of which was compiled from *Pavane pour une Infante défunte*, *Alborada del gracioso* and the *Rapsodie espagnole*. In December he announced that he was 'immersed in work' but all that came of it, at the beginning of 1924, was an orchestral version of the Yiddish song 'Mejerke mein Suhn' from the *Chants populaires* of 1910 and another little piece for another special number of the *Revue musicale*. As he wrote to Falla in January 1924, 'I thought I would finish my Violin Sonata towards the beginning of February. I have just abandoned it … my depression is worse than ever. All I can do is set an epitaph by Ronsard, which corresponds pretty well with my present state of mind.' Several composers had been invited to provide settings of Ronsard texts for a quatercentenary tribute to be published by the *Revue musicale* in April 1924, among them Gabriel Fauré. At the age of seventy-eight, naturally enough, Fauré considered Ronsard's dying farewell to his soul – 'Follow your fortune; do not disturb my rest; I am sleeping' – an eminently suitable subject. On finding that Ravel had already set the same text, he dropped the idea, wondering perhaps what had moved his so much younger colleague to make such a macabre choice. Ravel's 'Ronsard à son âme' ('Ronsard to his Soul'), with its skeletal piano accompaniment of archaic bare fifths sustained throughout, is a chilling experience. Later the composer would refer to it, with characteristic irony, as the only one of his songs he could accompany with his left hand while smoking a cigarette with his right. When he wrote it, on the other hand, he treated it almost as though it were his own epitaph.

Tzigane is another disturbing experience, though for quite different reasons. Hélène Jourdan-Morhange having by now abandoned her career as a violinist, Ravel had promised the first performance of the Violin Sonata – which was to take place in London in April 1924 – to Jelly d'Arányi. He continued to agonize over the sonata for the first two months of 1924 and then, in March, he put it to one side and turned instead to *Tzigane* – which, he told d'Arányi, 'I am writing specially for you, which will be dedicated to you and which will replace in the London programme the sonata which I have temporarily abandoned.' He asked Lucien Garban at Durand to send Liszt's *Hungarian Rhapsodies* to Montfort and Jourdan-Morhange to bring

Hélène Jourdan-Morhange with the formally dressed Ravel and Viñes on the beach at St-Jean-de-Luz

Paganini's *Twenty-four Caprices* and her violin as well. *Tzigane* was a piece he knew he could manage, even if only at the last minute, because it is basically pastiche. A brilliant exercise in virtuoso scoring and an impressively stylish celebration of Hungarian gypsy melody, *Tzigane* is nothing more than that, nothing more than similarly sensational scores by Saint-Saëns or Sarasate.

Even Jourdan-Morhange, who generously sympathized with 'poor Jelly d'Arányi' in having only two days to prepare the piece, confessed that *Tzigane* was the one work of his in which she could find 'nothing of the essential Ravel'. What is characteristic about it is that it is a response to a formidable technical challenge. More Hungarian and more rhapsodic than most Hungarian rhapsodies, it takes considerable risks, not the least of them being a slow introduction for unaccompanied violin lasting as long as the dangerously and excitingly acrobatic quicker section which follows. On its first performance in Paris, in an effort to make *Tzigane* sound even more Hungarian, Ravel got the pianist to make use of the *luthéal,* a recently invented and almost immediately obsolete keyboard attachment which, apparently, could make the piano sound like a cimbalom. '*Tzigane* is quite the most artificial thing Ravel has ever put his name to ... a great success of course with the ladies with lorgnettes and the gentlemen with paunches,' Henri Sauguet reported to his young composer colleague Francis Poulenc the following day.

The popular success of *Tzigane* was an important factor in encouraging Ravel in his work on *L'Enfant et les Sortilèges*. More encouraging still, in a sense, was a visit out of the blue from Raoul Gunsbourg, director of Monte Carlo Opera. As the composer described it, 'Gunsbourg fell on my home like a bomb; bombs didn't surprise me any more. Gunsbourg surprised me: "Your *Heure espagnole*," he told me, "was a triumph at Monte Carlo. Give me something else, quickly!" And that's how I at last finished *L'Enfant et les Sortilèges*.' The arrangement was that Ravel would deliver the score by the end of the year and that the work would be given its first performance in the Salle Garnier at Monte Carlo in March 1925. He had to resort to his hermit way of life to do it: 'I am seeing no one but my frogs, my negroes, my shepherdesses and other insects.' He even missed Jelly d'Aranyi's first performance of the orchestral version of *Tzigane* in November. But, though he was still revising the score in the Hôtel de Paris in Monte Carlo four months later, it was finished on time.

Sidonie-Gabrielle Colette – whose version of the Daphnis and Chloe story in her novel *Le Blé en herbe* is as sensual as Ravel's is chaste – was not the most likely collaborator. When they agreed to work together they had known each other for twenty years and had never particularly liked each other. The music-hall career she had adopted after her divorce from Gauthier-Villars – the high point of which was a scandalous double act with 'Missy' at the Moulin Rouge in 1907 – amused Ravel but did nothing to encourage him to take her seriously. After her marriage in 1912 to the editor of *Le Matin*, Henry de Jouvenel, although the scandals did not stop, her status as a writer was much enhanced. Reading her libretto six or seven years later he must have realized that they had more in common than he thought, including not only a love of animals but a feeling for the personality of inanimate objects too. She in her turn must have known that no one was better equipped to set to music her cats and her squirrels, her chairs and her grandfather clock, than the composer of the *Histoires naturelles*. If they approached the work from different directions – Colette as a mother of a child who needs her, Ravel as a child who needs a mother – the symbiosis was no less effective for that.

Adjustments had to be made of course. Ravel could not accept Colette's original title *Ballet pour ma fille* ('Ballet for my Daughter')

simply because, as he said, he had no daughter. So they agreed on
L'Enfant et les Sortilèges ('The Child and the Magic Spells') which is
both accurate as a description of the subject matter of the work and
strictly neutral in any difference of opinion as to whether it is opera or
ballet. A *Fantaisie lyrique en deux parties* ('Lyric Fantasy in Two Parts')
according to the title page, it has more singing in it than Colette
originally provided for and at the same time such a significant dance
element that Gunsbourg appointed the promising young
choreographer George Balanchine as ballet master for the original
production. Apart from requiring additional material – 'Couldn't the
squirrel's part be extended?' the composer asked his librettist, 'Just
imagine what a squirrel could say about the forest and how that would
sound in music!' – Ravel probably made fewer changes than is
generally assumed. The only one we know about followed a letter
from Ravel to Colette specifically requesting her to change the
Limoges porcelain featured in one scene to black Wedgwood, so that a
ragtime could be introduced at this point. 'But certainly a ragtime!'
Colette replied. 'By all means negroes in Wedgwood! Let's have a real
gust of music-hall wind blowing away the dust of the Opéra!'

Clearly, Colette was well disposed towards the new musical aesthetic associated with Cocteau, Satie and Les Six. If Ravel wanted to
demonstrate that, while drawing on the popular sources they claimed
as their own, he could outshine all of them put together, *L'Enfant et
les Sortilèges* was the opportunity to do it. Once the dramatic situation
is established, the first part alone offers no fewer than nine separate
numbers which he could set in as many different styles. As he told
Roland-Manuel when he was working on this part of the score at La
Bijeannette in 1920, it would be 'distinguished by a mixture of styles.
It will be severely criticized but that won't bother Colette and I don't
care a damn.' Melody would be the main thing and, in what he later
described as 'the spirit of the American musical', the voice would
dominate the orchestra which 'without renouncing virtuosity' would
nevertheless remain in the background.

First he had to set the scene. A pair of oboes, whose bleak
harmonies and uncertain metre are even more suggestive of loneliness
and aimlessness than the opening of *Petit Poucet* in *Ma Mère l'Oye*,
introduce the Child, a boy of six or seven, who refuses to do his
homework and who, on the entry of his Mother, is not only unre-

pentant but also offensive enough to stick out his tongue at her.
Sentenced to solitary confinement with only dry bread and
unsweetened tea until dinner time, he explodes into an orgy of
destruction. To the accompaniment of cacophonous bitonal
harmonies on the piano and in the orchestra, he shatters his teapot
and teacup, opens his squirrel's cage to stab the animal with a pen,
pulls the cat's tail, knocks the kettle into the fire, lacerates a wall
hanging with the poker, swings on the pendulum of the clock, and
tears up a pile of books.

For the rest of the first scene the Child is haunted by the objects
and creatures he has so wantonly abused. An armchair and a Louis XV
bergère chair courteously withdraw their services and those of their
furniture colleagues in a surreal minuet. The grandfather clock
deprived of its pendulum runs out of step in an accelerated march.
The black Wedgwood teapot sings a grotesquely aggressive ragtime in
franglais; the china cup sings a pentatonic foxtrot in spoof Chinese;
and the two are put together in riotous music-hall polyphony: tea for
two, as Ravel would have known it from his favourite popular song,
was never like this. Lamenting the loss of his china teacup, the Child
is threatened by the fire in a brilliant coloratura aria which finally
burns itself out. The shepherds and shepherdesses depicted on the
lacerated tapestry sadly take their leave of each other in a charming
pastoral chorus accompanied by an ostinato drum rhythm, drone
harmonies and rustic woodwind sounds Stravinsky would later recall
in *The Rake's Progress*.

The heart of the first scene is a sentimental episode with the
golden-haired Princess from the torn-up picture book. She magically
materializes in harp arpeggios to sing to the Child a tenderly intimate aria accompanied only by solo flute and, in spite of his heroic
efforts to save her, she just as magically dematerializes. The Child's
reaction is his one song in the whole work, a short but touchingly
regretful aria inspired, Ravel confessed, by *Adieu, notre petite table* in
Massenet's *Manon*. There is an antecedent for the crazy polka sung by
a wildly inaccurate arithmetic and a chorus of dancing Figures in a
similar passage for the tutor in Chabrier's *Une Education manquée*.
But, although there are other cat duets, there is nothing like the erotic
feline encounter conceived here by Colette – one of whose more
celebrated music-hall roles was the *Chatte amoureuse* at the Ba-Ta-

Clan – and Ravel, who studied the language of his own Persians in loving detail.

The cats' quintuple-time waltz acts as a transition to the second scene which, as the slide-flute owl and the nightingale piccolo so poetically indicate, is set in the garden at night. Some of the music here, including the evocatively onomatopoeic chorus of tree frogs and the groaning trees, was retrieved from the score of the abandoned *Cloche engloutie*. The sequence of dance numbers continues. After the trees' complaint about the injuries inflicted by the Child earlier in the day, a dragonfly sings a café-concert waltz as a lament for the loss of its partner, caught in the Child's net and impaled to the wall. But the numbers are now more extended and they merge together in mounting dramatic tension. The waltz episode initiated by the dragonfly incorporates the song of the nightingale atmospherically combined with an echo of the chorus of tree frogs, a quicker episode for a similarly bereaved bat, a radiantly lyrical variation with a passage from *La Valse* ingeniously superimposed on it and, finally, the squirrel's passionately lilting hymn to freedom.

Calling for his Mother ('Maman') the lonely Child is attacked by the assembled animals in an increasingly ferocious dance reflecting his own destructive outburst in the first scene. But at the height of the violence, instead of looking after his own injuries the Child bandages the bleeding paw of a young squirrel. All is forgiven. The animals, stunned by his selflessness, do their best to help him by calling for 'Maman' and, as the lights go on in the house, join in a slow fugue in praise of his kindness. The Mother appears on a recall of the oboe melody from the beginning of the work and, with his arms out-stretched towards her – in what must be the least sensational and yet one of the most poignant closing cadences in opera – the Child utters a final 'Maman'.

'Thanks,' according to Ravel, 'to a marvellous orchestra, which likes the work,' to Vittorio de Sabata, 'a conductor such as I have never encountered before', to Marie-Thérèse Gauley as the Child, 'a ravishing voice', and to a cat duet 'which will never be better miaowed', the Monte Carlo production of *L'Enfant et les Sortilèges* was a great success. Arthur Honegger, the least critical of Les Six, found it 'astonishing'. Georges Auric, the most virulent of them, had to admit that Ravel had won.

9

Maurice Ravel at the piano
in his studio at Le Belvédère
in 1933

*I still have so much music in my head ... I
haven't said anything yet, and I have still so
much to say!*

Maurice Ravel

Decline 1925-37

Ravel bore no grudge against the radical young composers who had reacted so violently against him, against his music, and against 'ravelism' in general. In his fiftieth-birthday year, with the success of *L'Enfant et les Sortilèges* and the honour of a special number (April 1925) of the *Revue musicale* to sustain him, he was in the ascendant once more and well placed to take reprisals. To the astonishment even of those who knew him best, however, his instinct was not to retaliate but to encourage good composers whatever their attitude to him might be. When Cipa Godebski reproved him for cheering the first performance of *Salade* by Darius Milhaud – 'who spends his time dragging you through the mud' – Ravel replied, 'But he's right: that's what you must do when you're young!' When he wanted to congratulate Georges Auric on his ballet *Les Matelots* and Hélène Jourdan-Morhange remonstrated with him – 'How could you go and congratulate Auric after the article he's just written about you?' – his answer was: 'Why shouldn't I go and congratulate Auric. I like his ballet. He knocks Ravel? Well, he's right to knock Ravel; if he didn't knock Ravel, he'd imitate Ravel, and there's enough Ravel already!'

Fundamentally liberal and conciliatory though he was – he was reconciled even with Cocteau by 1922 – there were two people Ravel could not forgive. One was the critic of *Le Temps*, Pierre Lalo, whom he had attacked on several occasions in the past and was to attack again. The other was Diaghilev who had let Ravel down once too often when he rejected *La Valse* in 1920. Their next meeting took place five years later, as Serge Lifar, Diaghilev's favourite dancer at the time, most interestingly recalled:

> *In 1925, when Gunsbourg staged the first performance of* L'Enfant et les Sortilèges *with the collaboration of Diaghilev's dancers, they met at Monte Carlo. Diaghilev offered his hand to Ravel ... The latter refused to take it – which was something Diaghilev was hardly used to, since everyone always excused him everything – and even challenged him to a duel.*

*The engagement did not take place but I remember the painful moments
Diaghilev experienced at that time.*

Ravel was no doubt pained by the encounter too. But after the
success of his *Fantaisie lyrique* in Monte Carlo, his reputation was at a
premium and his morale was correspondingly high. As usual after
completing a large-scale score, he was slow to start on the next work.
The difference this time was that he attributed his inactivity not to
depression but to 'a colossal case of laziness'. He was even able to joke
about it: 'I feel ten years older – it's the same after every job,' he
told Lucien Garban in April 1925. 'Fortunately, I haven't produced
very much.'

He was procrastinating – 'I really intend to get on with it tomorrow' – over a particularly flattering commission from the
American patron, Elizabeth Sprague Coolidge, who sponsored a new
chamber work from a leading composer every year. What she wanted
from Ravel was a song cycle, the voice to be accompanied 'if possible'
by flute, cello and piano, the text to be chosen by the composer. In
turning to the poetry of Evariste Parny, an eighteenth-century disciple
of Jean-Jacques Rousseau, Ravel made an inspired and surprising
choice: the *Chansons madécasses* ('Madagascan Songs'), 'seem to me,'
he said in the autobiographical sketch, 'to introduce something
new, dramatic – indeed erotic – arising from the subject matter of
Parny's poems.'

Though not in fact collected from Madagascan natives as Parny
claimed, his prose-poems do have an appealing exoticism about them
and an interesting anti-colonial political sentiment too. Ravel had set
nothing like these texts since *Shéhérazade*, although in this case the
voluptuous element is confined strictly within the limits of chamber
music. 'It is a sort of quartet,' the composer said, 'where the voice is
the principal instrument. Simplicity dominates.' But, of course, he
was late with it and by the beginning of May he had completed only
one part of the cycle. 'Aoua!' was first performed as a separate item
in a private concert in the Hôtel Majestic in Paris. It was an incongruously civilized setting for a song fiercely proclaiming its revolutionary
message, 'Do not trust the whites!' Artistically, it proved to be highly
effective. Politically, it provoked a reaction which was unfortunate but,
at a time when French troops were dying in a campaign against the

Republic of the Rif, not unpredictable: as the song was about to be encored, a colleague of the composer got to his feet and called out, 'Monsieur Léon Moreau is leaving, not wanting to hear such words again while fighting is going on in Morocco.' Ravel, no doubt fully aware of the political implications of his song, somewhat disingenuously defended himself in the ensuing controversy by pointing out that the text was written before the Revolution and had nothing to do with the present situation.

Having had the delivery date for the complete cycle of Madagascan songs put off to somewhere nearer the end of the year, Ravel turned his attention to other things – including a trip to London in June to stay with the Hardings and, diplomatically, to attend a reception held by Mrs Coolidge. He thought about writing an operetta, got back to work on his long-planned Violin Sonata, and spent much time attempting to house-train a little dog he had adopted and affection-ately called Jazz. So, when the extended deadline approached, the songs were still not finished. He wrote to Mrs Coolidge on 19 December 1925:

> I did not leave Montfort all summer, hoping to finish the two Chansons madécasses *which I have promised you and a Sonata for violin and piano which I started nearly two years ago. I have had to abandon these projects: all this time has been taken up correcting the proofs of the orchestral score and directing the rehearsal of* L'Enfant et les Sortilèges *which the Opéra-Comique will be performing on 23 January. The next day I will be leaving for two months' travelling. You can imagine how sorry I am to have broken my word. Of course, this is only a delay, and as soon as I return ... I will really get back to work.*

In fact, the first night of *L'Enfant et les Sortilèges* at the Opéra-Comique was postponed until 1 February, which meant that Ravel had to miss it. By then he was on a train to Denmark, a week into a tour which had already taken him from Belgium to Germany and would continue to Norway, Sweden, England and Scotland. He was particularly well received in Copenhagen where he conducted Mozart's Symphony No. 40 in G minor, the one work in his repertoire neither written nor arranged by himself. In Oslo he admired the way people coped with the snow in 'all sorts of vehicles: trams, cars (with

chains), sleighs, skis …' In Stockholm he was impressed by a temperature of -18 and the charm of a frozen city with 'boats in the middle
of the ice'. In London he missed 'the snow, the sun and the skies
of Sweden' but was surprised by 'a delicious spring: crocuses in the
middle of the lawns, budding shrubs, nightingales. Tomorrow
morning I am leaving for Glasgow and Edinburgh' – where, in the last
week in February, he was even less likely to hear nightingales than
he was in London but where he enjoyed the romantic associations of
Scottish lochs 'enveloped in a fairy-tale atmosphere'. Returning to
Brussels at the beginning of March to see a production of *L'Enfant et
les Sortilèges* he was awarded the decoration of Chevalier de l'Ordre de
Léopold on the stage of La Monnaie.

At home in Montfort a few days later, he reviewed an impossible
situation: 'a sonata for violin and piano, half done, which my publisher is waiting for; two *Chansons madécasses* hardly begun; an
operetta of which the first note is not written and which has to be
ready by the beginning of next season.' Ten days later he was no
further ahead except that he had seen all the most successful operettas

A cat costume designed
by Paul Colin for the Paris
Opéra production of
L'Enfant et les Sortilèges
in 1939

in Paris. 'I have never heard so many of them in one go (professional duty!),' he told Louise Alvar. 'Now I am cloistered here at Le Belvédère – which I thought would make a better monastery than the casino at St-Jean-de-Luz.' By working all through April he did manage to complete the remaining *Chansons madécasses* in time for the rescheduled first performances of the whole cycle, with Jane Bathori as soloist, in the American Embassy in Rome on 8 May 1926 and at the Egmont Palace in Brussels a few days later. On its introduction to Paris at the Salle Érard on 13 June, in a programme consisting entirely of music commissioned by Mrs Coolidge, the work was greeted as a masterpiece.

When the *Chansons madécasses* were published by Durand later in the year they were illustrated by three woodblock-prints by Hélène Jourdan-Morhange's future husband, Jean-Luc Moreau. Stylistically, nothing could be less appropriate than these messy, murky post-Gauguin images of bare-breasted exotic maidens. Ravel's settings are full of light and, in 'Nahandove' and 'Il est doux' at least, they are most delicately coloured. His contrapuntal lines are so precisely and so sparingly drawn and his harmonies so economical, moreover, that they exclude conventional images of voluptuousness. The opening of 'Nahandove' for voice and cello is as cool as the opening of the first movement of the (still unfinished) Violin Sonata, which it closely resembles. The erotic element is obviously not excluded here – it is present in the lover's fond repetitions of the melodious name of Nahandove and the gentle sighs of the piccolo – but it is expressed mainly by quite other means than the sensuously curving lines and caressing instrumental textures of *Shéhérazade* and *Daphnis et Chloé*. The pulse quickens on the quietly percussive, discreetly urgent rhythm which is heard as Nahandove approaches and as the voice proclaims her arrival three times over in ever widening melodic intervals. The height of the physical intensity of their meeting coincides with the height of the complexity of the counterpoint, which briefly extends to five distinct parts. The erotic piccolo sound is recalled towards the end of the third song, 'Il est doux' ('It is sweet'), where the women dance to an exotically suggestive drumming in plucked harmonics on the cello and a dissonant strumming on the piano. The difference between the chaste flute solo at the beginning of 'Il est doux' and the seductive cadenza in 'La Flûte enchantée' in

Shéhérazade is an illuminating indication of the development in the composer's sensibility in the intervening twenty-three years.

Much the strongest of the three songs is the central 'Aoua!'. Ravel, who took it upon himself to add the dramatic opening war cry to Parny's text, was clearly more passionate about the anti-colonial sentiments expressed here than he was about the physical attractions of Nahandove and her companions. After the initial assault of the voice allied with violent dissonances on the piano, 'Aoua!' begins to take shape as a lament with a sorrowing flute trapped between the conflicting harmonies in the primitive rhythmic ostinato of the piano part. With an acceleration of the tempo and a succession of upward transpositions of the ostinato, indignation rises to a pitch of retaliative aggression. A second warning of 'Do not trust the whites!' precedes a newly militant tattoo of drum beats on the piano and belligerent dance rhythms on the flute presaging victory over tyranny.

The soloists in all the early performances of the *Chansons madécasses* were sopranos, either Jane Bathori or better still, in the composer's opinion, Madeleine Grey. Since then, like *Shéhérazade*, the cycle has nearly always been sung by women, although Parny's poems, unlike Klingsor's, are written from a distinctly masculine point of view. As far as Ravel was concerned, there was probably no more significance in his choice of soloists than that singers he knew and trusted were women.

The *Chansons madécasses* having been completed by the end of April and the operetta idea having been abandoned within a month after that, the one remaining project in the list of obligations Ravel had drawn up in March was the Violin Sonata. Perhaps because he had just had a telephone installed at Le Belvédère, and was consequently writing fewer letters, details of his activities during the rest of 1926 are scarce. There is no evidence that he did any kind of composition work between May and December. But he did continue to give concerts, the year ending with a short tour in Switzerland with brief stays in Berne and Basel and a longer one in Geneva where he took the opportunity to call on his cousin, Alfred Perrin, a violinist in the Alhambra music hall. At the same time he was negotiating with E. Robert Schmitz, French pianist and founder of Pro-Musica Incorporated, who had at last succeeding in persuading Ravel to think positively about undertaking a tour of the USA.

What finally concentrated his mind on the Violin Sonata was a deadline imposed by his publisher who was committed to promoting a concert of music by Durand composers in the Salle Érard on 30 May 1927. He was also under pressure from Marcelle Gerar, another of his faithful sopranos and a born organizer, who was hoping to present an all-Ravel concert a week earlier with the new sonata in the programme. There was no chance that the Violin Sonata would be ready for the 23rd. On the contrary, Ravel was afraid that it would be finished only just in time for George Enescu to sight-read it at the Durand concert on the 30th. Actually, although Enescu was not put in that position, it would not have worried him very much if he had been, as an incident recalled in Yehudi Menuhin's *Unfinished Journey* confirms. Enescu's eleven-year-old pupil was having a lesson with him in his apartment in the rue de Clichy when

> *Maurice Ravel suddenly burst into our midst, the ink still drying on a piano-and-violin sonata which he had brought along … Enescu, chivalrous man that he was, craved my indulgence … then, with Ravel at the piano, sight-read the complex work, pausing now and again for elucidation. Ravel would have let matters rest there, but Enescu suggested that they have one more run-through, whereupon he laid the manuscript to one side and played the entire work from memory.*

Though famed as one of the leading violinists of his generation, George Enescu was also a considerable composer and an excellent pianist.

At the concert, although he did not much like the jazzy idiom of the work, with the composer at the piano Enescu gave a famously successful first performance, ensuring that the Violin Sonata in G would have a far more brilliant future than the one-movement Violin Sonata in A minor he and Ravel had introduced thirty years earlier.

Press comment on the new sonata focused on the second movement. To offer a satirical ragtime allied with a Chinese foxtrot in the surreal context of *L'Enfant et les Sortilèges* was one thing; to present a blues as the slow movement of a chamber work was something else. Ravel was not attempting to provoke a scandal: recreating the blues in his own style was for him no different from his adoption of the minuet or the Viennese waltz. He had been enthusiastic about jazz since 1921 at the latest, when he commented to Georgette Marnold on the 'sometimes nerve-racking virtuosity' of the black musicians who performed it in the night clubs of Paris, and he was as likely to surprise a café violinist by asking him to play jazz as he was to delight a journalist by declaring that he preferred jazz to grand opera. The jazz element is not restricted to the slow movement, moreover.

The opening *Allegretto*, a fluently melodious pastorale, is an inspired rethinking of sonata form in terms of the differing capabilities of the violin and the piano. Up to a point about two-thirds of the way through, the thematic material passes from one instrument to the other without discrimination. When the piano reintroduces the first theme at the beginning of the recapitulation, however, the violin rises above it in a flight of legato melody which (though it actually emerges from an earlier suggestion low down in the left hand of the piano part) elevates the music to a new and sustained level of lyrical radiance. The stylistic peculiarity of the movement, which is romantic enough to recall the fervour of *Le Jardin féerique* at one point, is that it is consistently taunted by a mischievously percussive little figure from the same ragtime background as Debussy's *Minstrels*.

The second movement, explicitly headed *Blues*, is idiomatically highly sophisticated. It is so sophisticated in fact that in the middle section the piano introduces a theme which unmistakably anticipates 'I Got Rhythm' in George Gershwin's musical *Girl Crazy*, which would be staged on Broadway in 1930 – two years after the American composer heard Ravel play the Violin Sonata with Joseph Szigeti in New York. Opening with a pizzicato imitation of the banjo, which remains a consistent feature of the piece, *Blues* faithfully incorporates many of the characteristics of jazz at the time – the ambiguous harmonies, the provocative syncopations, the sensual melodic slides, the self-consciously casual ending on an unresolved dissonance – and yet it is still the Ravel of the Sonata for violin and cello and the *Chansons madécasses* with just a slight exaggeration of long familiar technical and expressive aspects of his style. It represents also, in spite of its intermittent charm, the Ravel who, ever since the war, was apt to find his music overwhelmed by violence.

The *Perpetuum mobile* – as we know from an account by Manuel Rosenthal, who had recently become the last pupil of what Ravel called the 'school of Montfort' – replaces an earlier finale which the composer bravely discarded. Watching it burn in the grate, he agreed with Rosenthal that it was 'ravishing' but explained that 'after that *Blues*, and because of the general form of the work, it didn't fit in with the rest.' The new last movement is exciting rather than ravishing. It fits in as a finale largely because of a precipitate momentum generated from the ragtime figure so prominent in the first movement and sustained throughout a perfectly proportioned construction. As the violin runs off in two-hundred consecutive bars of non-stop semiquavers, it is left to the piano to seal the unity of the work with more or less subtle backward allusions, most clearly and most passionately of all to the 'I Got Rhythm' tune from *Blues*.

The only other works completed in 1927 were a tiny song and a miniature fanfare. The song, 'Rêves' ('Dreams'), was written in February for a special number of *Feuilles libres* to be published in honour of Ravel's old friend, the journalist and poet Léon-Paul Fargue. Beginning with a playfully innocent melody accompanying a 'child running round marble statues' and including a finely calculated dissonance discreetly but persistently echoing the rumbling of the 'great organs' of a railway station, it is a sensitive setting of sixteen short lines by Fargue recalling fleeting images from a dream. The *Fanfare* – a delightful little march leading *wagneramente*, as it is mischievously marked in the score, to a massive stroke of the tam tam – was Ravel's contribution to *L'Éventail de Jeanne* ('Jeanne's Fan'), a tribute from no fewer than ten composers to Jeanne Dubost, celebrated hostess and director of a children's ballet school.

The ninety seconds of *Fanfare*, though high in small-scale quality, is not an impressive aggregate of new music for the seven months between the first performance of the Violin Sonata and the composer's departure for his tour of North America. The main reason for the inactivity is not to be found in the time spent in public engagements in Paris – where, most prestigiously, he and Stravinsky shared the conducting in the opening concert of the new Pleyel concert hall in the rue du Faubourg-Saint-Honoré – and in Amsterdam and London. It is not seriously attributable either to what he described as the 'dolce far niente' induced in him by his holiday in St-Jean-de Luz. Ravel's problem at this time, as so often before, was his precarious state of health. 'I am in a state of extreme fatigue,' he wrote in early December. 'I am in a rather bad way,' he told another correspondent a week later, adding gloomily that he had to undergo a 'rigorous treatment – injections of cytoserum, pituitary and adrenal extracts etc.' Two weeks later he embarked on the SS *France* from Le Havre for New York.

Probably not because of the stimulants he was given before he left but rather because of the stimulating atmosphere he found when he got there, Ravel survived his four-month tour of North America in the best of spirits and, for him, the best of health. When the boat docked in New York he was overwhelmed by reporters, photographers, film crews and caricaturists. At the Hotel Langdon, as the telephone went on ringing and as the interviews continued, 'every minute they were bringing baskets of flowers and the most delicious fruits in the world.' At an all-Ravel concert given by Koussevitsky and the Boston Symphony Orchestra in Carnegie Hall, he was overwhelmed by the enthusiasm of the audience: 'I had to appear on the stage,' he told his brother Edouard, '3,500 people all on their feet, a tremendous ovation, including whistling.' Following a crazy itinerary, he went from New York to Boston and back to New York; from New York to Chicago, Cleveland, San Francisco, Los Angeles, Seattle, Vancouver, Portland, Denver, Kansas City, Minneapolis, Chicago and back to New York; from New York to New Orleans, Houston, Phoenix, Buffalo and back to New York; from New York to Montreal and back to New York for the last time. What kept him going is that most of the travelling was done by overnight trains on which, far from suffering his usual insomnia, he found he could sleep all night and much of the day.

Ravel at the piano at his fifty-third birthday party in New York with his hostess Eva Gauthier just behind him and his admired colleague and friend George Gershwin on the far right of the picture. The other two guests are the conductor Oscar Fried (far left) and the composer Manoa Leide-Tedesco.

He was worried not so much by the distances he had to travel between the twenty-five centres he visited as by the abrupt changes of climate he had to put up with: 'Having been sweating in beach clothes in Los Angeles and finding spring everywhere since then, even in Canada, it's freezing cold again, storm and snow,' he wrote to Roland-Manuel on the train between Chicago and New York. The food worried him too. Although adequate supplies of Caporal cigarettes had been guaranteed him before he left, he missed the rare steaks he so much enjoyed at home: 'Dined the other day in Chicago with Mrs Rockefeller, millionairess. Hurried back to my hotel to have a beefsteak sent up to me.' But these were minor problems in comparison with such satisfactory experiences as being photographed with Douglas Fairbanks and Mary Pickford in the United Artists studio in Hollywood, making a pilgrimage to the Bronx home of Edgar Allan Poe, whom he described to a reporter as his 'greatest teacher in composition', and going to see the Grand Canyon – 'a ten-day excursion, six of them on the train, but that alone would have been worth the trouble of crossing the Ocean.'

As for the professional side of the tour, he was thrilled to conduct his own music with orchestras he considered 'the best anywhere' in concerts in New York, Boston, Chicago, Cleveland and San Francisco. Although he was emphatically not, as Serge Koussevitsky flatteringly described him, 'the greatest of French conductors', he was particularly pleased with his concerts in Cambridge and Boston. He was 'profoundly touched', he said, by the Boston Symphony Orchestra's 'conscientiousness in rendering exactly the spirit' of his music. He took less pride in his performance as a pianist in recitals in the smaller halls on the itinerary, although his technique apparently did improve as time went on. Joseph Szigeti, who played the Violin Sonata with the composer in New York, said that Ravel 'was somewhat nonchalant about his piano-playing', which is a nice way of putting it.

The Madison Avenue reception after the recital with Szigeti was attended by Fritz Kreisler, Edgard Varèse, Béla Bartók and, most interestingly for Ravel, George Gershwin. Ravel and Gershwin met several times in New York, listening to jazz together in Harlem and going to the same parties. At a dinner held by the soprano Eva Gautier to celebrate Ravel's fifty-third birthday, Gershwin played *Rhapsody in Blue* and 'The Man I Love' in such a way that, according to their hostess, Ravel was 'dumbfounded'. Although Ravel regarded him as 'a musician gifted with the most brilliant, the most seductive, perhaps the most profound of qualities', he resisted Gershwin's request for lessons in composition. 'I think you are making a mistake,' he is said to have told his American colleague. 'It is better to write good Gershwin than bad Ravel, which is what would happen if you worked with me … It is I who should be asking you for lessons to find out how to make so much money by writing music.'

Ravel came back from America with the very handsome sum of $27,000 in his pocket. When the SS *France* docked at Le Havre on 27 April, a reception party including his brother Edouard, Angèle Bonnet, the Delages, Marcelle Gerar and Hélène Jourdan-Morhange were there to greet him and present him with a bouquet. 'I wish you hadn't come,' he said with characteristic but not entirely tactful modesty. Pleased though he must have been to see them, he seems to have enjoyed more the little ceremony reserved for his arrival in Paris, where Manuel Rosenthal was waiting for him at the Gare Saint-Lazare. Having first of all satisfied his craving for the *boeuf mode en gelée* which he had been dreaming about for weeks, he said to his young pupil: 'Now you are going to come with me: for the first time in my life I am going to deposit money in my bank!'

On tour in America there had been no time for composition. Before leaving, Ravel had accepted a commission from the dancer Ida Rubinstein to orchestrate six pieces from Albéniz's *Iberia* for a Spanish ballet, provisionally called *Fandango*, which she was going to present at the Paris Opéra the following November. Fortunately, as it turned out in this case, Ravel made no early effort to get on with it. There were the usual distractions, including a special concert given in his honour by the SMI, and a very special event arranged for him by Marcelle Gerar at Montfort on 10 June. Gerar had introduced Ravel several months earlier to the sculptor and designer, Léon Leyritz, who had asked the composer's permission to model a bust of him. Ravel agreed, providing that he didn't have to sit for it. The stone sculpture, which Ravel later declared his 'best portrait', was duly produced from sketches made during rehearsals. In June it was ready for presentation and Gerar organized what she called a 'surprise garden party' for no fewer than forty people at Le Belvédère, where the bust would be ceremonially unveiled.

Maurice Ravel portrayed in stone by Léon Leyritz

The company – including composer colleagues Arthur Honegger, Jacques Ibert, Alexandre Tansman and Joaquín Nin as well as the regular circle of close friends – was hand-picked to be congenial. Honegger and Roland-Manuel volunteered to act as waiters and a grotesquely costumed and made-up René Kerdyck declaimed verses he had written for the unveiling. Ravel, who had been responsible for cocktails, was moved after lunch to borrow one lady's coat and another's hat and perform a dance *en travesti*. The threatened rain held off and, although the surprise element had been abandoned at an early stage in the planning, it was one of the happiest occasions in the composer's life. The one false note was struck by the unfortunate guest who began a song with the words, 'Little Ravel …' and then dried up on seeing the look on the face of a great artist who did not like to be reminded of his small stature. Port was taken at Rambouillet, dinner at Versailles and the 'Impromptu de Montfort', as it came to be called, ended in a night club at four in the

The 'Impromptu de Montfort' in the garden at Le Belvédère in June 1928: Ravel (with left arm raised) addresses a remark to Mme Kahn-Casella at the end of the table. Jane Bathori is to his left, the composer Joaquín Nin to his right and Cipa Godebski nearest the camera in the centre of the picture.

morning, with Ravel still engaged in earnest conversation with Léon-Paul Fargue.

A few days later, looking forward to combining a holiday in the Basque country with the pleasurable task of orchestrating the Albéniz piano pieces for Ida Rubinstein's *Fandango*, Ravel set off for St-Jean-de-Luz. Usually he went there by train but this time he was a passenger in the car of Joaquín Nin (father of a now more famous daughter, Anaïs Nin), which gave him the opportunity to make a diversion to Arcachon on the Atlantic coast southwest of Bordeaux. It was while passing the time at Arcachon that Nin casually asked Ravel what he was working on and, on being told about the *Fandango* project, had to break the news to him that the Spanish musician Enrique Arbós was already making arrangements from Albéniz's *Iberia* for a ballet called *Triana* and that he had exclusive rights to it. Ravel was at first inclined to brush the problem aside. 'I don't care a damn!' he said. 'Who is this Arbós anyway?' But when a telephone call to the publisher of *Iberia* confirmed that this was indeed the copyright situation and that absolutely nothing could be done about it, Ravel was furious. 'My holiday is ruined … These laws are idiotic … I need

Ida Rubinstein as the
Spanish dancer in *Boléro*

to work … Orchestrating *Iberia* was going to be such fun for me …
And what will Ida say? She'll be furious!' Having written in vain to
Albéniz's widow, Ravel returned to Paris in a panic to discuss the
situation with Ida Rubinstein, who naturally insisted that something
had to be done. But what – since he had set aside only enough
time for orchestration and since his own Spanish-style pieces had
already been used in one ballet or another – could he be reasonably
expected to do?

Exactly when Ravel conceived the desperately simple idea of what
eventually became *Boléro* is not clear but, if we are to trust the less
than reliable memory of his colleague and Ciboure resident Gustave
Samazeuilh, it was in St-Jean-de-Luz in that same summer. 'Before
going for our morning swim one day,' Samazeuilh recalled, 'I had the
delightful experience of seeing Ravel in a yellow dressing gown and
scarlet bathing cap playing the theme of *Boléro* with one finger and
saying to me, "Mme Rubinstein has commissioned a ballet from me.
Don't you think this tune has something insistent about it? I'm going
to try and repeat it a good few times without any development
while gradually building it up with my very best orchestration."' That
would have been in late July, when Ravel resumed his holiday after
his precipitous trip to Paris, or in early August. On 10 August he was
in Montfort determined to stay there and, he told Roland-Manuel,
'working like mad until mid October' – which was the deadline set by
his publisher.

Fandango was retitled *Boléro*, some time before the beginning of
October when, somewhat mysteriously, Ravel wrote to Roland-
Manuel about 'finishing a *Boléro* with the same material which you
have assured me Prokofiev used in *Le Pas d'acier*.' The only explanation of the reference to the Prokofiev ballet is that Roland-Manuel
must have accused Ravel – who had been present at the first performance of *Le Pas d'acier* in Paris in June 1927 – of imitating some feature
of the Russian composer's score. In fact, although the two works have
no actual material in common, there is a striking parallel between the
relentlessly repeated rhythmic patterns in *Boléro* and the industrial
ostinatos in the *Fabrika* ('Factory') section of *Le Pas d'acier* ('The Steel
Dance'). Ravel might have been irritated by his friend's angle of
approach, by way of Prokofiev, but Roland-Manuel had hit on an
important but generally underestimated aspect of *Boléro*.

The composer was slow to acknowledge the industrial element in it but when he did he insisted on it to the point of eccentricity.

Although Ravel apparently had no initial objection to Ida Rubinstein's concept of the ballet – according to which she would be the central figure, a flamenco dancer exciting the admiration and lust of drinkers in a bar as she works herself into a frenzy on a table top – he was not at all sure about it when he actually saw it: 'very successful presentation, but picturesque, which it shouldn't have been.' What he missed was the factory, the industrial element which Roland-Manuel had perceived in the score and which the composer had probably not been consciously aware of as he worked on it. Five years later he was to declare that 'my *Boléro* owes its inception to a factory' and that he 'would like to stage it with a vast industrial works in the background.' He knew exactly which factory too. 'There's the *Boléro* factory!' he said to his brother more than once as they were driving through the industrial suburb of Le Vésinet on the road between Paris and Montfort. Thanks to Edouard Ravel, who insisted on it in spite of objections from the conductor and choreographer, *Boléro* was finally presented as his late brother had envisaged it, and as Léon Leyritz not too picturesquely designed it, at the Opéra in 1941.

Though inspired by a professional emergency and though economical with creative effort to the point of parsimony, *Boléro* is absolutely fundamental Ravel. Only *L'Heure espagnole* represents as vividly the two sides of a musical personality formed, as the composer said, by 'the clicking and roaring of my father's machines' and 'the Spanish folk songs sung to me by my mother'. But in *L'Heure espagnole* they are in harmonious equilibrium, while in *Boléro* they are locked in conflict. The Spanish melodic element in *Boléro* is set against a rigorously mechanical rhythm sustained by the side drum at the same strict tempo and in basically unchanging harmonies for just as many repetitions as it takes until something has to give. The genius of the work is not so much its scoring – which is unfailingly entertaining in its variety and uniquely masterful in its graduated accumulation of colour – as in the judgement of the precise moment when the conflict can no longer go on: as the long-term crescendo reaches its height and the orchestration its maximum aggregation, the friction between melody and mechanism finally causes ignition, the tonality lifts off from C major to E major and, as it falls back, the edifice collapses.

Failure in equilibrium, which was turned to such dramatic artistic advantage in *Boléro*, was about to become an increasingly serious disadvantage for the composer in real life. Coincidentally, but not insignificantly, on the night of the triumphant first performance of *Boléro* at the Paris Opéra on 22 November 1928, Ravel suffered an ominous lapse in concentration in a recital he was giving in the French Embassy in Madrid. Amused to find himself congratulated as warmly as ever, he probably did not take the incident very seriously. He had no obvious need to be worried at this time. Only four weeks earlier he had been awarded an honorary Doctorate of Music by the University of Oxford where the public orator had announced (in academic Latin) that the composer of *Daphnis et Chloé* 'persuades all cultured people that Pan is not dead and that even now Mount Helicon is green.' Besides, he was enjoying his tour of Spain, giving concerts with Madeleine Grey and the violinist Claude Lévy on a busy but not too wearing itinerary covering nine centres in eighteen days. In Granada he happily renewed his friendship with Manuel de Falla; in Málaga, while not so happy about the gradual disappearance of the public as he continued to play, he did at least appreciate an audience 'which has the courage of its convictions'.

Maurice Ravel about to be presented by Professor Sir Hugh Allen for his honorary Doctorate of Music at Oxford in 1928

Far from worrying about his health at this time, and further still from thinking about conserving what was left of it, Ravel was contemplating nothing less ambitious than a world tour. He was also contemplating a large-scale opera to be based on Joseph Delteil's novel *Jeanne d'Arc*, a signed copy of which had been presented to him by the author in 1925. But for the heroic purpose of the world-wide procession he had mind – through Europe, North and South America and the Far East – he clearly needed a piano concerto. He had cherished at least two such projects in the past, the Basque rhapsody *Zazpiac bat*, which was well advanced before he abandoned it, and a fantasy inspired by Alain Fournier's *Le Grand Meaulnes*. The latest piano-concerto project was more realistic than either of those, not least because of his determination to go through with the world tour which depended on it. In December 1929, when Koussevitsky sought to commission the concerto and to obtain all American rights on it for the fiftieth anniversary season of the Boston Symphony Orchestra in 1930–31, the composer turned the conductor down. By then, when Ida Rubinstein no longer had exclusive rights on *Boléro* and the royalties on what was about to become a phenomenally popular work were beginning to pour in – the piano version sold out as soon as it was published – he could afford to reject such advances. But the real reason for not accepting Koussevitsky's terms was that, after giving the first performance in Boston, it would have been his intention to tour the concerto throughout the USA. In September 1930, when the work was still incomplete, he was persisting with the idea of touring it far and wide, although he was now saying, 'Providing I hold out.'

If he had not accepted a commission for another piano concerto in the first half of 1929 the world tour might well have happened. Unable as ever to resist a technical challenge, he had agreed to write a concerto for the Austrian pianist Paul Wittgenstein, who had lost his right arm in the war. Brother of the philosopher Ludwig Wittgenstein and clearly a musician of considerable character, he was now assembling a repertoire of piano works for left hand alone: he had already commissioned scores from Richard Strauss and Franz Schmidt and would later secure more from Sergey Prokofiev and Benjamin Britten. Ravel probably met Wittgenstein, and perhaps even heard him play one of his Strauss pieces, in March 1929 when he was in Vienna for the first performance in Austria of *L'Enfant et les Sortilèges*. Anyway, he was hard at work on the Concerto for left hand in the summer. 'I'm gestating a concerto: I'm at the vomiting stage,' he somewhat inelegantly wrote to Marie Gaudin, his Basque-country cousin, on 10 August.

Hastily excusing himself for having forgotten to send Marie the appropriate greetings on her Saint's Day, he asked her in the same letter to fix accommodation for him at 9 rue Tourasse, where he now preferred to stay when he was in St-Jean-de-Luz. 'You must know that we shall soon be seeing each other again: the Foujita posters must have warned you about the great Ravel event at Biarritz (200 francs a seat: I'm glad I don't have to pay to get in).' Whether Foujita got paid for his stylish poster design and whether the smart hotel in Biarritz got the hire fee for the hall where the concert was given on 11 September we do not know. We do know, on the other hand, that the organizer of the event absconded with the takings from the box office and that the performers, including Marcelle Gerar and Robert Casadesus, were recompensed out of the composer's own pocket.

There was a very much happier Ravel event in the Basque country eleven months later. On 24 August 1930, to celebrate the international fame of the composer who was born on the rue du Quai in Ciboure fifty-five years earlier, the name of that street was officially changed to quai Maurice Ravel and a plaque was mounted on the wall of No. 12 (now No. 27) to identify the house where he first saw the light of day. A special game of pelota was arranged to feature a star player whom Ravel much admired, a concert was given in the evening in the Hôtel du Palais in Biarritz by the composer with some of his favourite performers – Madeleine Grey, the pianist Robert Casadesus, the violinist Jacques Thibaud – and the evening ended with a gala dinner dance. Left with profits to donate to charity rather than with a hefty bill this time, Ravel gratefully signalled the 'complete success of this manifestation, which will surely be the most touching of my entire career.' At the same time he regretted losing a week he would otherwise have devoted to the left-hand Concerto, which was already overdue and would now not be ready for another month.

Another celebration, this one at Biarritz in 1930: Hélène Jourdan-Morhange, Jacques Thibaud and Ravel are on the left of the picture, Madeleine Grey on the far right.

Back at home in September, Ravel applied himself to his work 'without respite, or nearly: half an hour for each meal, an hour for a six km walk at the end of the day; five to six hours sleep.' One reason why he was in this situation was that he had spent much of the first

part of 1930 enjoying the success of *Boléro* and attempting to secure an authentic performing tradition for it. He conducted it in several concerts and the day after supervising a recording by Piero Coppola for the Gramophone company – insisting that the tempo should remain strictly the same throughout – he recorded it himself for Polydor. Prokofiev's comment on one of Ravel's early concert performances is revealing: 'Conducting was not one of Ravel's strong points but he directed the orchestra smoothly through this piece, wielding the baton with somewhat angular movements and almost surgical precision and skilfully restraining every attempt to accelerate the tempo.'

An unfortunate aspect of *Boléro* is that the tempo indicated by the metronome mark – though actually quicker than that of Ravel's own recording – is only half the speed of the authentic Spanish bolero. Joaquín Nin pointed this out to the composer when he received his copy of the score: 'That is not of the least importance' was the reply. In fact, as Ravel found out when Toscanini came to conduct the New York Philharmonic in *Boléro* at the Paris Opéra in May 1930 and took it 'at a ridiculous pace' the anomaly could be misleading. Notoriously, Ravel refused to acknowledge Toscanini's interpretation by declining to share the applause with him. He later attempted to explain to the conductor that his failure to stand had been misunderstood. Apparently, however, he had already remonstrated with him at the rehearsal and, infuriatingly no doubt, had been told, 'You don't know anything about your own music. This is the only way to make it work.' If Toscanini's 1938 recording is anything to go by, he persisted in that opinion.

Ravel had problems with another star performer when, in October or November, Paul Wittgenstein took delivery of his Concerto for the left hand. Invited to Montfort to hear Ravel play the solo part for him – with both hands – Wittgenstein did not appreciate what he heard. 'He was not an outstanding pianist,' he recalled, 'and I wasn't overwhelmed by the composition ... I suppose Ravel was disappointed, and I was sorry ... Only much later, after I'd studied the concerto for months, did I become fascinated by it and realize what a great work it was.' Perhaps because of that setback, or perhaps because he was heading for a breakdown anyway, Ravel had to abandon hope of completing the other concerto, the one he was writing for himself, by the end of the year. 'I hadn't anticipated the fatigue which has suddenly overtaken me,' he wrote on 5 December in reply to one of the several impresarios who were expecting to present the work, with the composer as soloist, during the current season. 'Threatened by terrible punishments – cerebral anaemia, neurasthenia, etc. – I have been ordered to rest and above all to sleep, a habit which I was beginning to lose. I will soon be able to start work again but with more moderation. I have to resign myself to the fact that the Concerto will not be ready for this season. I am sorry about it and I can only ask you to forgive me the feeble limitations on my productivity.'

Turning his attention to furnishing the little apartment which Léon Leyritz had designed for him in trendy art-deco style in Edouard's house in Levallois, Ravel did no more work on the Concerto until early February 1931. Even then he interrupted it to take part in an all-Ravel concert in aid of disabled war veterans in Brussels in March and to conduct *Boléro* and *La Valse* for Ida Rubinstein's troupe at Covent Garden in July. He was also wearing himself out practising studies by Chopin and Liszt to improve his technique in preparation for the tour – though by now a European rather than a world-wide tour – he still intended to undertake. Eventually, he had to recognize that the task was beyond him. 'My Concerto is finished,' he announced on 20 November, 'but I am far from being myself … I have been ordered complete rest and am being treated with injections of serum. I'll have to content myself with conducting Marguerite Long on 14 January.' He had delivered the score to the pianist on 11 November, both to her delight and to her consternation: 'I not only had to find my way round this forest of spidery notation but also to go through with my engagements at the end of the year and appear in several concerts.' She would not let him down.

Wittgenstein having by now reconciled himself to the score he had commissioned, it happened that the two piano concertos were both first performed in January 1932 – the one for left hand in Vienna, the other in Paris. They are as different from each other as two Ravel works of the same kind written at much the same time (though not, in fact, simultaneously) could be. They are not, on the other hand, as different as they are usually made out to be. Ravel went no further than to call one 'gay' and the other 'imposing'. Marguerite Long, on the other hand, found everything in the left-hand Concerto 'grandiose, monumental, on the scale of the flaming horizons, the monstrous holocausts where bodies burn and the Spirit sinks, vast herds of human beings grimacing with suffering and agony.' The description is absurd not only because Ravel had no more sense than anyone else in the 1930s of the Holocaust to come in the next decade but also because the music is nowhere near as grim as that. If there is a macabre element in the work it is far more likely to be retrospective, inspired perhaps by the thought that the war in which the pianist lost his right arm was the war in which France was fighting Austria, the war in which Ravel was, in a sense, fighting Wittgenstein.

The obvious difference between the Piano Concerto in G major and the Piano Concerto in D major for left hand is that while the former is characteristically bright in colour the latter is predominantly dark. This is a largely a technical matter: although the left hand covers most of the keyboard in the Concerto in D, it is necessarily based in the lower half. So that the piano would not seem freakish in this respect, Ravel had to favour the lower registers of the orchestra. It is for that rather than any sinister reason that the first theme arises from the shadowy nether regions, on double bassoon against quietly rumbling cellos and basses. Besides, Ravel liked to begin a work or movement in this way, as in *La Valse* above all. It is true that when the theme assumes its definitive shape it has something 'grandiose' about it. But, as we know from the not dissimilar motifs associated with the vainglorious peacock in *Histoires naturelles* and the strutting banker in *L'Heure espagnole*, the ceremonial dotted rhythms of the Baroque French overture might be imposing but not, to Ravel's ironic mind, deeply meaningful.

The composer's primary preoccupation in the Concerto in D was not prophecy or even reminiscence but the problems of making the left-hand pianist a complete soloist rather than half a soloist and of setting him in a context which would boast all the concerto attributes without demanding too much of his one-armed stamina. With the help of studies by Saint-Saëns, Alkan and Czerny among others, he devised a sleight of hand and sleight of sustaining pedal which would make left-hand textures sound no less interesting than two-hand textures. He also worked out a formal strategy according to which – as in Liszt's Sonata in B minor and Schoenberg's First Chamber Symphony but at half their length – slow-movement and scherzo or

finale elements would be incorporated in an integrated single-movement construction.

The structural economy is such that as soon as the double bassoon
introduces the main theme two horns reply to it with a second
subject, a syncopated blues tune, which is then combined with the
first in full orchestral ceremony. The entry of the piano, with a
cadenza of fanfares and wide-spread chords, is no less imposing.

Ravel's apartment, designed
for him in the latest art-deco
style by Léon Leyritz, in his
brother's house at Levallois

Even more ingenious in its scoring, the slow-movement element is an improvisation for piano alone, the left hand tracing a tenderly lyrical melody over its own arpeggio accompaniment. The longest section is the scherzo. The blues tune is developed against a relentlessly regular jazz-band rhythm; a bizarre jig-like variant with a hint of the 'Dies irae' in it is rapped out by the left hand; both themes come up against a side drum recalling its authority in *Boléro*. But for two cheerful interventions from the woodwind it would be alarming. The reprise of the opening section, extended by another masterly cadenza, restores stability and a brief recall of the scherzo summarily dismisses any sinister implications it might have had.

Of the two concertos, the composer's favourite was the one in G which he wrote for himself and considered 'more Ravel'. Certainly, it is unfailingly entertaining, inexhaustibly melodious and impeccably turned out. According to Gustave Samazeuilh, Ravel's Basque-country companion, the outer movements are based on folk tunes rescued from the abandoned rhapsody *Zazpiac bat*. Though accepted and elaborated on by others, his evidence is difficult to reconcile with Ravel's earlier rejection of those same tunes as unsuitable for a concert piece because they 'do not lend themselves to development'. It conflicts too with the fascinating testimony of Robert de Fragny, who recalled Ravel telling him that the brilliantly playful opening theme came to him 'on a train between Oxford and London' – which would have been in 1928, when he went to collect his honorary degree and was just starting work on the concerto.

The similarity between some of the melodic material and that of certain numbers of *L'Enfant et les Sortilèges* and parts of the Violin Sonata seems to confirm that it was, in fact, newly written for a work as up-to-date and as stylish in its way as the composer's art-deco apartment at Levallois. It is true that the soloist introduces the second subject with a little Spanish guitar-strumming but it is immediately displaced by a bit of blues on clarinet and trumpet and later by a slow foxtrot on the piano. The *Adagio assai* is in a world apart, sustained by the beauty of a self-renewing melody which flows so easily ... 'Flows so easily!' exclaimed Ravel when he heard Marguerite Long use those words, 'Flows so easily! I put it together bar by bar and I nearly died over it.' His slow-movement model was the *Larghetto* of Mozart's Clarinet Quintet. For the impetuous *Presto* finale he had to look no

Ravel with Marguerite Long
in Berlin in 1932

further than the first scene of *L'Enfant et les Sortilèges* – to the rage of
the Child, the out-of-control clock, the off-the-rails arithmetic –
and the 'nerve-racking virtuosity' of the jazz musicians he so
much admired.

Immediately after the triumphant first performance of the Piano
Concerto in G on 14 January 1932, Ravel and Marguerite Long took
the work on a three-month tour of Europe, visiting several smaller
cities as well as Brussels, Vienna, Bucharest, Budapest, Prague,
London, Warsaw, Berlin and Amsterdam. It was a challenging itinerary made all the more stressful, for his companion at least, by the
composer's absent-mindedness. 'He lost his luggage, his watch, his
rail ticket, my rail ticket and,' she recalled, 'he kept his letters in his
pocket, mine too' – this last habit almost provoking a diplomatic
incident in Poland when they failed to attend a prime-ministerial
reception to which they had been formally invited. None of this could
have been more distressing, however, than the experience of hearing
Paul Wittgenstein play the left-hand Concerto to a large gathering
at his home in Vienna. The Austrian pianist told Long that he had
made some 'adjustments' to the score but he did not, unfortunately,
warn the composer. Horrified by what he heard, Ravel walked up to
Wittgenstein after the performance and told him quite unequivocally,
'But that's not it at all!' Clearly, the pianist had a mind of his own.
When Ravel attempted to stop him playing the work in Paris,
Wittgenstein told him that 'performers must not be slaves!'
'Performers *are* slaves!' was Ravel's reply. Marguerite Long, who was
not known for her humility, would never have accepted that role but
she did play the Concerto in G more or less as the composer had
written it. Unfortunately for the Concerto in D, on the other hand,
Wittgenstein had sole rights on the score for six years. So, although
Ravel did consent to accompany Wittgenstein in the left-hand
Concerto in Paris in January 1933, it was not until March 1937 that
Jacques Février was free to give what the composer regarded as the
true first performance of the work.

After the European tour, which he had undertaken in defiance of
his doctor's orders, Ravel repaired to St-Jean-de-Luz for a long holiday.
By June he recovered enough strength to start work on what would
be his last composition. Three months later he regretted it. Excusing
himself, as so often, for a long delay in replying to a letter, he told
Jane Bathori on 15 September 1932 that he had been 'immersed in a

piece of work which I should never have undertaken and which has made me lose more than three months for nothing.' What had happened is that he had accepted a commission from a film company to write three songs to be sung by Chaliapin in Georg Pabst's version of *Don Quixote*, with the Russian bass in the title role. Ravel was not a great fan of Chaliapin but he admired the work of Paul Morand, who had written the words for the songs, and he liked the Cervantes story so much that he had long thought about writing an opera on the subject. Perhaps because Ravel was so slow in finishing the songs, Pabst turned instead to Jacques Ibert, who duly supplied suitable settings of texts by Ronsard and Arnoux. Ravel – who was never to be paid for his work, incidentally – was disappointed but, rather than abandon the cycle, he persisted with it and completed *Don Quichotte à Dulcinée* six months later.

Although the state of the composer's health is painfully evident from the handwriting in the manuscript, the music of *Don Quichotte à Dulcinée* ('Don Quixote to Dulcinea') betrays little or nothing of it. The settings are fairly simple, but so is the text. They are also, at least as far as the first and third of them are concerned, popular in tone, but this is cinema music. Though allied, because of its alternating bars of 6/8 and 3/4, to the quajira of Spanish folklore, 'Chanson romanesque' ('Romantic Song') is stylistically more like a sophisticated little number from a zarzuela. An extravagantly gallant declaration of love for Dulcinea, it is urbanely seductive in its lilting rhythms and piquant harmonies and tinged also by a gentle hint of pathos. In the same way, the 5/4 'Chanson épique' ('Epic Song') could be classified with the quintuple-time zortzico, although in its attitude of prayer and its church-organ harmonies it admits not the least suggestion of a Basque-country dance. 'Chanson à boire' ('Drinking Song'), an Arogonese jota as celebrated by generations of non-Spanish composers from Glinka to Chabrier, is an entertaining example of its kind, as attractive in its tipsy vocal line as in its characteristic cross-rhythms and the reckless bitonal gestures in the piano part.

It is appropriate that Ravel's composing career should end with an echo of *España*, the most famous work of 'the musician who,' Ravel had recently declared to Chabrier's heir, 'influenced me above all others.' It is bitterly ironic, on the other hand, that the last words he set are 'I drink to joy' because he was now condemned to four years of agony – not so much physical agony as the mental agony of being able to hear music in his head but not being able to write it down or play it or even, as time went on, describe it. His illness, the symptoms of which were described as 'ataxia' (the inability to co-ordinate voluntary movements) and 'aphasia' (the inability to express thought in words), had been developing quickly in recent months. It might have been accelerated by a traffic accident which, though his injuries were superficial, had a traumatic effect on him. It happened in Paris on 9 October 1932, when his taxi was in collision with another vehicle. 'It

A draft of a letter to Marie Gaudin dated 2 August 1933 and clearly showing the extent to which Ravel's faculties had declined by this time wasn't very serious,' he wrote to Manuel de Falla three months later, 'bruising of the thorax and some facial wounds. Even so, I haven't been able to do anything at all, apart from eating and sleeping. All I am suffering from now is an irrational terror of taxis, which I use only as a last resort.'

Getting back to work on *Don Quichotte à Dulcinée* in February 1933, he finished it only just in time. In the summer of the same year the extent of his illness was demonstrated to him in a most dramatic and alarming way. Bathing in the sea at St-Jean-de-Luz, he suddenly found that he could no longer swim – he could no longer co-ordinate the movements so long familiar to him – and had to be rescued from the water. He had the same problem with writing. A letter addressed to Marie Gaudin from Le Touquet, where he took refuge with friends later in the summer, is even more distressing for its erasures and its laborious handwriting than for its content.

You will not see me again at St-Jean this summer, alas! For quite a long time, in quite a bad way, I nevertheless continued to work, with no result, moreover. I had undertaken a pantomime: Morgiane, *which is to be performed at the Opéra in March. More and more off-colour, I went to see Vallery-Radot … Medication: a confusing heap of drugs, absolute rest, which is scarcely possible in my native country, too warm as well: the Northern beaches are more stimulating … In one month, all my symptoms have disappeared. Vallery would like to force me to stay here until the end of September, but as soon as I feel less dim I will try to escape and to work without tiring myself too much at Montfort.*

In fact, there were times when his health did seem to rally. In November, although it was to be his last appearance as a performer, he was even able to conduct *Boléro* and the Piano Concerto in G with Marguerite Long at the Concerts Pasdeloup. While he realized that he would never be able to write his *Jeanne d'Arc* opera – 'It's there in my head. I can hear it, but I'll never write it down' – he did not give up hope for *Morgiane*, a presumably short ballet for Ida Rubinstein to be based on the story of Ali-Baba in *The Thousand and One Nights* (the source of the *Shéhérazade* Overture and *Shéhérazade* songs he had written half a lifetime earlier). Perhaps he was encouraged by the way he had been able to collaborate with Manuel Rosenthal in creating

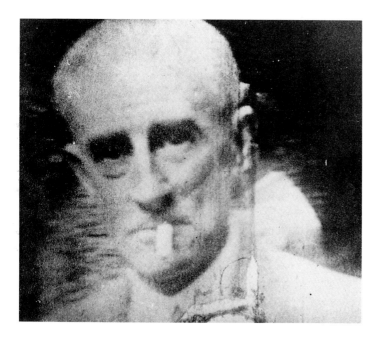

'Thin, as grey as a fog ...
the empty stare of a
ghost': a last photograph
of Maurice Ravel

an orchestral version of *Don Quichotte à Dulcinée*, which was
eventually first performed by Martial Singher and Paul Paray with the
Orchestre Colonne on 1 December 1934. But that and a similarly
fabricated orchestration of *Ronsard à son âme* was all that could be
managed in 1934.

One interesting aspect of these distressing last few years of Ravel's
life is the way his spirits could still be lifted and his co-ordination
improved by a change of scenery and a new situation. In the USA he
had thrived on his punishing itinerary and ever since then he had
been an obsessive traveller – partly because he enjoyed the glory of a
composer touring his own works, partly because it was an escape
from the toil of composition but more perhaps because every station,
every nearly-missed train, every unfamiliar city, every new concert
hall brought a fresh stimulus and, temporarily, his physical problems
diminished. A comment he made to his cousin in Geneva on his
extensive tour with Marguerite Long seems ironic at first sight but he
probably meant it sincerely: 'A grand tour of Europe really rested me,
my stay in my native country a little less, as ever.' Even now, in
March 1934, he was able to write to Marie Gaudin in a comparatively

unlaboured hand from a rest home at Mont Pèlerin near Vevey on Lake Geneva: 'Thanks to the stimulating air of the mountains I am starting to be able to write, more or less.'

In 1935, ostensibly to help him in his work on *Morgiane*, Ida Rubinstein paid for Ravel to visit North Africa with Léon Leyritz as his attentive companion. They left St-Jean-de-Luz in the middle of February, travelled through Spain at a leisurely pace and arrived in Morocco just over two weeks later. Writing from La Mamounia to Nelly Delage on 6 March, Leyritz reported in evident astonishment that Ravel was *'at this moment writing a letter to his brother*! All by himself! Slowly it is true; but it is a fact!' Three days later he wrote from the same hotel to Hélène Jourdan-Morhange with the news that 'Your dear "Ravelito" is working at this very moment … He has been humming me tunes from *Morgiane* and has been telling me about the kind of production he wants … It is true though that he is not yet capable of writing his music down.'

In spite of the hope expressed to Charles Koechlin at the funeral of Paul Dukas in May 1935 – 'I have notated a theme: I can still write music' – *Morgiane* progressed no further. The returns were rapidly diminishing. A last trip to Spain with Leyritz in the summer did nothing for him. A stay at another rest home near Lausanne in May 1936 seemed to cheer him up but his reserves were by now almost exhausted. He somehow coached Jacques Février in the left-hand Concerto at the beginning of 1937 and he continued to assist at recordings and to attend concerts. But the agony of not being able to write the music he could still hear in his mind proved too much for him. After a performance of *Daphnis et Chloé* in November he broke down in front of fellow-composer Louis Aubert and Hélène Jourdan-Morhange: 'I still have so much music in my head,' he sobbed, 'I haven't said anything yet, and I have still so much to say!' That was his last concert. Unable to write or read or express himself coherently, the most he could do now was listen to music on the radio and go for walks. One day he found his way from Montfort to the home of Hélène Jourdan-Morhange and Jean-Luc Moreau at Mesnuls, where Colette happened to be visiting. 'Thin, as grey as a fog, he still knew how to smile,' she recalled. 'On seeing me he said, "Ah, Colette …" in a natural tone of voice. But he scarcely made an effort to speak and, sitting with us there, he had the look of someone who was likely to

dissolve at any moment.' At home at Le Belvédère he would spend
long hours looking out of the window. On being asked what he was
doing he simply replied, 'I'm waiting.'

Those who knew him were aware that, without a miracle, this
Ravel 'with the empty stare of a ghost' would never recover. It was in
the hope of inducing the miracle that, although it was believed there
was no tumour, Edouard was persuaded to authorize brain surgery.
He was told, in layman's terms, that one hemisphere of his brother's
brain had atrophied and that the other could not compensate.
Without intervention there could be no hope for improvement in the
co-ordination of his movements or for any restoration of the other
affected faculties. Professor Clovis Vincent decided to operate because
it was better to try something – and if there were by any chance a
tumour he would find it – than to do nothing and leave the composer
in the miserable state he now found himself in. If he was also suffering
pain by now, as some sources indicate, the arguments in favour of an
operation would have been all the more convincing.

In the belief that he was going in for a test, Ravel was admitted to
a clinic in rue Boileau on 17 December and operated on, without
anaesthetic apparently, two days later. Although the surgeon did suc-
ceed in expanding the collapsed left hemisphere by injecting it with
serum, and although Ravel did wake up after the operation and ask
for his brother, he then fell into a coma and, without recovering
consciousness, died on 28 December 1937. The funeral took place
two days later, without religious ceremony, in the small cemetery at
Levallois-Perret where his father and mother were buried and where
his brother, his sole heir, would join him twenty-three years later.

Epilogue

It is not until you visit Ravel's home in Montfort l'Amaury – which is open to the public and preserved much as the composer left it in 1937 – that you realize not only how small he was but also how conscious he was of his shortcoming and how much it determined his personality and way of life. The rooms inside the building, which has something of a doll's house aspect to it even from the outside, are carefully scaled down to his size. In his own home at least he would be in proportion. No one else, unless he or she were more than a little below the average in height and width, could live there in any comfort. The feeling of exclusivity is intensified when you are in the garden-level bedroom contemplating the elegantly draped Louis-Philippe bed, which is on the same small scale as the rest of the house. Here, surely, is a clue to an obscure and much debated aspect of the composer's life and personality.

In Le Belvédère it becomes quite clear that Ravel did not expect to share his life, still less his bed, with anyone. He is said to have proposed marriage to Hélène Jourdan-Morhange, although she – who lived with the artist Jean-Luc Moreau for most of the time that Ravel knew her – mentions no such thing in her affectionate and revealing book on the composer, *Ravel et nous*, which was published eight years after his death. It could be that she was too modest to say anything about it and it is true that, while his letters to her are no more intimate than those to some of the other women in his life, he was very fond of her, not least perhaps because she was actually smaller than he was. The counter-argument is his firm conviction, asserted on several occasions, that creative artists should not get married. When Alfredo and Hélène Casella were divorced after eleven years of marriage in 1919, he wrote to commiserate with Mme Casella and drew a moral, 'which I practise and which I am determined to continue: we are not made for marriage, we artists. We are rarely normal and our life is even less so.'

The initial decision never to get married he seems to have taken, for somewhat different reasons, in the critical few days after the outbreak of war in 1914. Having made a firm resolution to enlist in spite of his fear of the effect this would have on his ailing mother, he declared 'a second resolution, in the event that I come back alive. This resolution is just as irrevocable as the other.' He was bargaining with fate and, consciously or not, he was swearing life-long fidelity to his mother. Inevitably, the exceptionally close and adoring relationship that Ravel had with his mother has led to speculation on the nature of his sexuality. If it has led nowhere in particular it is because it has been unreasonable and ill-informed. A composer surely cannot reasonably be classified as homosexual, for example, on the ground of certain perceived similarities between his music and that of a known homo-sexual like Camille Saint-Saëns. In Ravel's case the argument cannot be supported either by postulating an inimical relationship between the composer and his father: it must be clear enough from the evid-ence offered in preceding chapters of this book that this was simply not the case.

Ravel once asserted that 'my only mistress is music.' Everyone who knew him and who said anything about it confirms that he had no long-term relationship with anyone of either sex. Francis Poulenc, who was well placed to observe developments of this kind from about 1914 (when he became a piano pupil of Ricardo Viñes), firmly declared that 'he had no love-affair to be spoken of; no one knows of any Ravel love affair.' If Ravel did have a romantic attachment to anyone – which is not necessarily the same thing as a sexual relation-ship – it was before Poulenc knew him. Of all the men and women in his circle at that time, the most likely candidate is Léon-Paul Fargue, the talented poet and brilliant conversationalist who in his Apache period combined the looks of Rimbaud with the profile of 'a young Roman Emperor'. According to Hélène Jourdan-Morhange, Fargue was 'united to Ravel by a tender friendship of youth' and he remained an object of his admiration, though not a constant companion, for the rest of his life. Although Fargue was later to achieve notoriety for his amorous exploits with women, his intense teenage friendship with Alfred Jarry, youthful author of *Ubu Roi*, was so disturbing to his parents that they took drastic action to separate them. The change in Fargue's sexual orientation coincided, apparently, with his military service and liberation from the attentions of his over-indulgent mother. He did not get married, however, until she died, by which time the mother was ninety-four and the son was sixty.

It is possible to trace a similar development in Ravel's case, even though his sexuality was surely never as potent, in whatever direction, as Fargue's. If he did experience homosexual inclinations in his early maturity – and his work on Verlaine's 'Le Ciel est, pardessus le toit' and 'Un Grand Sommeil noir' suggests that he had a keen interest in at least the consequence of the poet's affair with Rimbaud – they were almost certainly repressed, as his surprisingly revealing setting of Verhæren's 'Si morne!' confirms. Basically, Ravel's problem was not one of sexual identity but the sad belief, formed perhaps during his Montmartre upbringing and confided to Marguerite Long years later, that 'love never rises above licentiousness.' This does not mean that he rose above licentiousness himself: Vaughan Williams, Inghelbrecht and Rosenthal have all, independently, made observations to the effect that he had relations with (female) prostitutes and, difficult though it is to reconcile that kind of evidence with Ravel's fastidiousness in other matters, there is no reason to disbelieve it. In the context of the time and the milieu in which he lived, it is not very significant anyway: even Nijinsky took to 'chasing tarts' when he was in Paris (and when Diaghilev wasn't chasing him). What is significant, and basic to Ravel's life and art, is the other and entirely opposite reaction to his identification of love with licentiousness. His erotic ideal was neither heterosexual nor homosexual, neither bisexual nor asexual, but an ambiguity so evenly balanced that the masculine and the feminine cancel each other out.

In mundane terms it is reflected in his infatuation with the Italian cabaret entertainer Maria Valente, 'a wonderful girl', according to Rosenthal, 'who made her appearance dressed in black and wearing trousers (which was very unusual at the time), very slim, very elegant, very beautifully shaped.' Her acrobatic performance on the xylophone and other instruments was such an exciting display of virtuosity apparently that Ravel actually thought about writing something for her. In artistic terms it is reflected, on the one hand, in his long struggle to remove all trace of licentiousness from the love of Daphnis and Chloe and, on the other hand, by the uniquely inspired recognition of his ideal in 'L'Indifférent' in *Shéhérazade*.

The other side of sublimation is repression. In Ravel's case sexual repression seems to have led to a decline in interest in all but those basic necessities which could be purchased in casual encounters. Together with the loss of the principal object of his affection on the death of his mother, repression was responsible for an emotional void which could not be filled by any amount of jealous affection for his friends, for the much indulged children of his friends, for his pets, his toys and everything he gathered round him at Le Belvédère. The effect on his development as a composer is clearly perceptible. Ravel, who regretted the exchange of his early freshness for his later mastery, was very aware of what was happening to his music. The antithetical contrast between the directly palpable sensuality of the *Shéhérazade* songs (1903) and the intellectual eroticism of the *Chansons madécasses* (1925–6) or between the lyrical inspiration of the String Quartet in F (1902–3) and the structural perfection of the Sonata for violin and cello (1920–22) – the kind of comparison Ravel himself was apt to make – illustrates the point convincingly enough. The turning point was the critical period from the beginning of the war in 1914 to the death of his mother in 1917. The music written after that time is no less exciting, though now more often in anger than in joy, and no less truthful than the music written before it. Sometimes, as in the miraculous symbiosis of Colette's maternal devotion and Ravel's filial devotion in *L'Enfant et les Sortilèges*, youthful freshness was restored. But, in general, the distinction is clear and so pronounced that it cannot be attributed solely to the changing aesthetic around him or an ordinary maturing process in his own personality.

It could even be argued that Ravel never did mature in the ordinary sense, that he was no more grown up emotionally than he was physically. He was one of the most intelligent and, technically, one of the most sophisticated composers of his time and yet his creative vision was limited. So was his stamina. He wrote nothing lasting longer than an hour and it would take you less than a day to listen to every one of his published compositions. He was not a creative figure of the stature of a Debussy or a Messiaen who could command a whole generation of disciples and followers. Certainly, his influence was widespread, not least in Britain where he was an inspiration not only to Vaughan Williams, whom he taught, and Lennox Berkeley, to whom he gave advice, but also to composers as robustly individual as John Ireland and William Walton. Most of his younger French contemporaries – and some of the older ones, including Debussy – were influenced by him in one way or another, although it is notable that the music of his pupils actually has less in common with Ravel's than that of, say, Francis Poulenc, who only briefly rejected him, and Jean Françaix, whom he encouraged at the start of his career. The influence persists, although it is now more a matter of example than imitation. One of his most distinguished successors, Henri Dutilleux, cites Ravel's 'extreme lucidity, the exceptional keenness of his ear, those exemplary qualities which have compelled us to be as demanding of ourselves.'

If Ravel's vision was limited in scope it was all the more penetrative in those areas on which it was focused. It was Ravel who saw clearly into Debussy's impressionism and who in *Jeux d'eau* structured it as Cézanne did Pissarro's impressionism; it was Ravel who in *Rapsodie espagnole* set colour free in the concert hall as Matisse did on the canvas; it was Ravel who in *Histoires naturelles* turned to the café-concert for a new means of expression long before Cocteau was preaching the renewal of art in popular sources. These were all pre-1914 achievements. Later, but for the decline in his health, he might have added other dimensions to French music. After the two piano concertos, which are comparatively broad in conception, he might have expanded his structural ambitions. He had demonstrated in *Daphnis et Chloé* that, with a supreme effort, he could sustain a large-scale dramatically articulated orchestral panorama. Given his increasingly abstract way of thought and a few more years of properly co-ordinated intellectual and physical faculties, there is no reason why he should not have written a symphony as convincing as any by a French composer in the twentieth century. That, however, was not his destiny.

Ravel was destined to concentrate for most of his life, even in his two operatic scores, on the small scale. But his music is not small scale in effect. A precise impression of the unpredictable play of a fountain at Versailles, a finely focused glimpse of an indefinable erotic ideal, a breathtaking close-up of a kingfisher poised to take flight, an atmospheric evocation of a vibrantly tranquil night in Spain, a vivid hallucination of a haunted landscape, a microscopic observation of tiny creatures in concert in an exotic fairy tale, a lucid insight into the evanescent imagery of a Mallarmé poem: these are all minute visions, unique to Ravel and yet realized with such freshness of perception and such perfection of technique that they move the sympathetic listener no less profoundly than anything else in music.

Classified List of Works

Dates in parentheses are those of composition. The abbreviation 'fp' denotes first public performance; details are given where known.

Stage Works

L'Heure espagnole, 'comédie musicale' in one act, libretto by Maurice Ravel after Franc-Nohain (1907–11). fp Paris, 19 May 1911

Ma Mère l'Oye, ballet, scenario by Maurice Ravel (1911–12); orchestral version, with additional *Prélude, Danse du Rouet* and connecting material, of piano-duet original (1908–10)

Adélaïde ou le langage des fleurs, ballet, scenario by Maurice Ravel (1912); orchestral version of *Valses nobles et sentimentales* for piano (1911). fp Paris, 22 April 1912

Daphnis et Chloé, ballet in one act for chorus and orchestra, scenario by Michael Fokin and Maurice Ravel after Longus (1909–12). fp Paris, 8 June 1912

La Valse, 'poème chorégraphique', scenario by Maurice Ravel (1919–20). fp Paris, 23 May 1929

Le Tombeau de Couperin, ballet (1920); 2nd, 3rd and 4th movements of orchestral version of *Le Tombeau de Couperin* for piano (1914–17). fp Paris, 8 November 1920

L'Enfant et les Sortilèges, 'fantaisie lyrique' in two parts, libretto by Colette (1920–25). fp Monte Carlo, 21 March 1925

Fanfare, prelude to a collective ballet, *L'Eventail de Jeanne* (1927). fp Paris, 4 March 1929

Boléro, ballet, scenario by Ida Rubinstein (1928). fp Paris, 22 November 1928

Orchestral

Shéhérazade, 'ouverture de féerie' (1898). fp Paris, 27 May 1899

Une Barque sur l'océan (1906; revised 1926); version of 3rd movement of *Miroirs* for piano (1904–5). fp Paris, 3 February 1907; (revised version) Paris, 30 October 1926

Rapsodie espagnole (*Prélude à la nuit, Malagueña, Habanera, Feria*) (1907–8; *Habanera* is a version of the 1895 two-piano original). fp Paris, 15 March 1908

Pavane pour une Infante défunte (1910); version of piano original (1899). fp Manchester, 27 February 1911; (the first Paris performance, attributed by some authorities to 1910, did not take place until 25 December 1911)

Ma Mère l'Oye, 'cinq pièces enfantines' (*Pavane de la Belle au bois dormant, Petit Poucet, Laideronnette, Impératrice des pagodes, Les Entretiens de la Belle et de la Bête, Le Jardin féerique*) (1911); version of piano-duet original (1908–10). fp Paris, 28 January 1912

Daphnis et Chloé, 'fragments symphoniques'; 1st suite: *Nocturne–Interlude–Danse guerrière,* extract from unfinished ballet score (1909–11). fp Paris, 2 April 1911

Daphnis et Chloé, 'fragments symphoniques' for chorus and orchestra; 2nd suite: *Lever du jour–Pantomime–Danse générale* (1913), extract from ballet score (1909–12)

Valses nobles et sentimentales (1912); version of piano original (1911). fp (as *Adélaïde* ballet) Paris, 22 April 1912

Alborada del gracioso (1918); version of 4th movement of *Miroirs* for piano (1904–5). fp Paris, 17 May 1919

Le Tombeau de Couperin, suite (*Prélude, Forlane, Menuet, Rigaudon*) (1919); version of 1st, 3rd, 5th and 4th movements of piano original (1914–17). fp Paris, 28 February 1920

La Valse, 'poème chorégraphique' (1919–20); same as ballet. fp (concert) Paris, 12 December 1920

Tzigane, 'rhapsodie de concert' for violin and orchestra (1924); version of original for piano and violin (1924). fp Paris, 30 November 1924

Boléro (1928); same as ballet. fp (concert) Paris, 11 January 1930

Menuet antique (1929); version of piano original (1895). fp 11 January 1930

Piano Concerto in D major for the left hand, in one movement (1929–30). fp Vienna, 5 January 1932

Piano Concerto in G major (*Allegramente, Adagio assai, Presto*) (1929–31). fp Paris, 14 January 1932

Songs for Solo Voice
(a) with orchestra

Shéhérazade, 'Trois Poèmes' for voice and orchestra ('Asie', 'La Flûte enchantée', 'L'Indifférent'), text by Tristan Klingsor (1903). fp Paris, 17 May 1904

'Manteau de fleurs', text by Paul Gravollet (1903?); version of voice and piano original (1903)

Cinq Mélodies populaires grecques, text traditional (1906); version of Nos. 1 and 5 of voice and piano original (1904–6), remaining songs orchestrated by Manuel Rosenthal in 1935

Deux Mélodies hébraïques ('Kaddisch', 'L'Énigme éternelle'), text traditional (1919); version of voice and piano original (1914). fp Paris, 17 April 1920

Chanson hébraïque ('Mejerke mein Suhn'), text traditional (1923–4); version of voice and piano original (No. 4 of *Chants populaires*) (1910)

Don Quichotte à Dulcinée, for baritone and orchestra ('Chanson romanesque', 'Chanson épique', 'Chanson à boire'), text by Paul Morand (1932–3); orchestrated in collaboration with Manuel Rosenthal. fp Paris, 1 December 1934

'Ronsard à son âme', text by Pierre de Ronsard (1934); version in collaboration with Manuel Rosenthal of voice and piano original (1924). fp Paris, 17 February 1935

Songs for Solo Voice
(b) with chamber ensemble

Trois Poèmes de Stéphane Mallarmé ('Soupir', 'Placet futile', 'Surgi de la croupe et du bond'), text by Stéphane Mallarmé (1913). fp Paris, 14 January 1914

Chansons madécasses ('Nahandove', 'Aoua!', 'Il est doux'), text by Évariste-Désiré Parny de Forges (1925–6). fp Paris, 13 June 1926

Songs for Solo Voice
(c) with piano

'Ballade de la reine morte d'aimer', text by Roland de Marès (1893)

'Un Grand Sommeil noir', text by Paul Verlaine (1895)

'Sainte', text by Stéphane Mallarmé (1896). fp Paris, 8 June 1907

'Chanson du Rouet', text by Leconte de Lisle (1898). fp New York, 23 February 1975

'Si morne!', text by Emile de Verhæren (1898). fp New York, 23 February 1975

Deux Epigrammes de Clément Marot ('D'Anne jouant de l'espinette', 'D'Anne qui me jecta de la neige'), text by Clément Marot (1896–9). fp Paris, 27 January 1900

Shéhérazade, 'Trois Poèmes' ('Asie', 'La Flûte enchantée', 'L'Indifférent'), text by Tristan Klingsor (1903); version of voice and orchestra original

'Noël des Jouets', text by Maurice Ravel (1905). fp Paris, 24 March 1906

Cinq Mélodies populaires grecques ('Chanson de la mariée', 'Là-bas, vers l'église', 'Quel galant m'est comparable', 'Chansons des cueilleuses de lentisques', 'Tout gai!'), text traditional (Nos. 3 and 4: 1904; Nos. 1, 2 and 5: 1906). Three other Greek folk-song settings made in 1904 are lost. fp Paris, 1906

'Les Grands Vents venus d'outre-mer', text by Henri de Régnier (1906). fp Paris, 8 June 1907

Histoires naturelles ('Le Paon', 'Le Grillon', 'Le Cygne', 'Le Martin-pêcheur', 'La Pintade'), text by Jules Renard (1906). fp Paris, 12 January 1907

'Vocalise-étude', 'en forme de habanera', wordless (1907)

'Sur l'herbe', text by Paul Verlaine (1907). fp Paris, 12 December 1907

'Tripatos', Greek traditional text (1909)

Chants populaires ('Chanson espagnole', 'Chanson française', 'Chanson italienne', 'Chanson hébraïque'), text traditional (1910). fp 19 December 1910

Chanson écossaise, text by Robert Burns (1910). fp New York, 23 February 1975

Trois Poèmes de Stéphane Mallarmé ('Soupir', 'Placet futile', 'Surgi de la croupe et du bond'), text by Stéphane Mallarmé (1913); version of voice and chamber ensemble original

Deux Mélodies hébraïques ('Kaddisch', 'L'Énigme éternelle'), text traditional (1914). fp Paris, 3 June 1914

'Ronsard à son âme', text by Pierre de Ronsard (1924). fp London, 26 April 1924

Chansons madécasses ('Nahandove', 'Aoua!', 'Il est doux'), text by Évariste-Désiré Parny de Forges (1926); version of voice and chamber ensemble original

'Rêves', text by Léon-Paul Fargue (1927). fp Paris, 19 March 1927

Don Quichotte à Dulcinée ('Chanson romanesque', 'Chanson épique', 'Chanson à boire'), text by Paul Morand (1933); version of baritone and orchestra original

Choral

Trois Chansons for mixed voices, unaccompanied ('Nicolette', 'Trois Beaux Oiseaux du paradis', 'Ronde'), text by Maurice Ravel (1914–15). fp Paris, 11 October 1917

Chamber/Instrumental

Sonata for violin and piano in A minor, in one movement (1897). fp Paris, 1897?

String Quartet in F major (1902–3). fp Paris, 5 March 1904

Introduction and Allegro, for harp, flute, clarinet and string quartet (1905). fp Paris, 22 February 1907

Trio, for violin, cello and piano (1914). fp Paris, 28 January 1915

Sonata, for violin and cello (1920–22). fp Paris, 6 April 1922

Tzigane, 'rhapsodie de concert', for violin and piano (1924). fp London, 26 April 1924

Berçeuse sur le nom de Gabriel Fauré, for violin and piano (1922). fp Paris, 13 December 1922

Sonata in G major, for violin and piano (1923–7). fp Paris, 30 May 1927

Piano

Sérénade grotesque (1893). fp Paris, 13 April 1901

Menuet antique (1895). fp Paris, 18 April 1898

La Parade (1896?); unpublished

Sites Auriculaires, for two pianos (*Habanera, Entre Cloches*) (1895, 1897). fp Paris, 5 March 1898

Shéhérazade, 'ouverture de féerie', for two pianos (1898); version of orchestral score

Valse (1898?); unpublished

Pavane pour une Infante défunte (1899). fp Paris, 5 April 1902

Jeux d'eau (1901). fp Paris, 5 April 1902

Menuet (1904); unpublished

Introduction and Allegro, for two pianos 1905; version of chamber ensemble original

Sonatine (1903–5). fp Lyon, 10 March 1906

Miroirs (*Noctuelles, Oiseaux tristes, Une Barque sur l'océan, Alborada del gracioso, La Vallée des cloches*) (1904–5). fp Paris, 6 January 1906

Rapsodie espagnole, for two pianos (1 *Prélude à la nuit*; 2 *Malagueña*; 3 *Habanera* (from *Sites auriculaires*); 4 *Feria*) (3: 1895; 1, 2, 4 simultaneously with orchestral version)

Gaspard de la nuit (*Ondine, Le Gibet, Scarbo*) (1908). fp Paris, 9 January 1909

Menuet sur le nom de Haydn (1909). fp Paris, 11 March 1911

Ma Mère l'Oye, 'cinq pièces enfantines' for four hands (*Pavane de la Belle au bois dormant, Petit Poucet, Laideronnette, Impératrice des pagodes, Les Entretiens de la Belle et de la Bête, Le Jardin féerique*) (1908–10). fp Paris, 20 April 1910

Valses nobles et sentimentales (1911). fp Paris, 9 May 1911

À la manière de … (1 Borodine, 2 Chabrier) (1912). fp Paris, 10 December 1913

Prélude (1913). fp Paris, June 1913

Le Tombeau de Couperin (1914–17). fp Paris, 11 April 1919

Frontispice, for two pianos, five hands (1918)

La Valse, 'poème choréographique', versions for piano and for two pianos (1919–20); simultaneous with orchestral version. fp (two-piano version) Vienna, 23 October 1920

Boléro, arrangements for piano and piano duet of 1928 orchestral original (1929)

Selected Juvenilia and Academic

(a) voices and orchestra

Myrrha, cantata for soprano, tenor, baritone and orchestra; for Prix de Rome (1901)

Alcyone, cantata for soprano, alto tenor and orchestra; for Prix de Rome (1902)

Alyssa, cantata for soprano, tenor, baritone and orchestra; for Prix de Rome (1903)

L'Aurore, for tenor, chorus and orchestra; for Prix de Rome (1905)

Selected Juvenilia and Academic
(b) for piano

Variations on a theme by Grieg, for piano (after 1887);
unpublished

Variations on a theme by Schumann, for piano
(after 1887); unpublished

Significant Fragments and Sketches

Le Ciel est pardessus le toit (three pages)
Prelude to *Intérieur* (one page)
part of a symphony (one page)
Zazpiac Bat (three pages)
La Cloche engloutie (fifteen pages)
La Nonne maudite (three pages)
Morgiane (one page)

Arrangements of Works by Other Composers

Debussy: *Sirènes* (from *Nocturnes*), for female chorus
and orchestra, arranged for two pianos (1902). fp Paris,
20 April 1903

Delius: *Margot la Rouge*, opera in one act, arranged for
voices and piano (1902)

Debussy: *Trois Nocturnes*, for female chorus and
orchestra, arranged for two pianos (1908). fp Paris,
24 April 1911

Debussy: *Prélude à l'après-midi d'un faune* for orchestra,
arranged for piano duet (1910)

Satie: *Prélude pour le fils des étoiles* for piano, arranged
for orchestra (1911); lost

Chopin: *Nocturnes, Etudes, Valses* for piano, arranged
for orchestra as *Les Sylphides* (1914); all but one piece
lost. fp London, 2 March 1914

Schumann: *Carnaval* for piano, arranged for orchestra
(1914); all but four movements lost. fp London,
2 March 1914

Chabrier: *Menuet pompeux* for piano, arranged for
orchestra (1917–18). fp London, 18 July 1918

Mussorgsky: *Pictures at an Exhibition* for piano,
arranged for orchestra (1922). fp Paris, 19 October 1922

Debussy: *Sarabande* (from *Pour le piano*), arranged for
orchestra (1922). fp Paris, 18 March 1923

Debussy: *Tarantelle styrienne* for piano, arranged for
orchestra as *Danse* (1922). fp Paris, 18 March 1923

Further Reading

Many more books and periodicals than listed here were of use in the preparation of this biography. The following selection is intended for the general reader and is restricted (with one exception) to works devoted exclusively to Ravel. Books in French, of which there are many more of course, are listed separately.

In English

All but a few publications in this category are either seriously outdated or ill-informed and are best avoided.

Hopkins, G. W. 'Ravel' in **Sadie, S.** (ed.) *The New Grove Dictionary of Music and Musicians* (London, Macmillan, 1980). Although not as authoritative as it ought to be, this Grove entry is useful for quick reference.

Jourdan-Morhange, H. and Perlemuter, V. *Ravel according to Ravel* (New York/London, 1988/1991). Transcriptions of broadcast conversations with Vlado Perlemuter who studied Ravel's piano works with the composer and who recalls here the (largely technical) advice he was given (translated by F. Tanner).

Long, M. *At the Piano with Ravel* (London, 1973). English translation of observations by a pianist who knew Ravel well and whose variably illuminating comments are by no means restricted to his music.

Nichols, R. *Ravel* (London, Dent, 1977). Though written before the Orenstein publications listed below, this biography retains much of its original value, particularly in musical commentaries more technically analytical than the format of the present book allows.

Nichols, R. (ed.) *Ravel remembered* (London, Faber, 1987). A fascinating anthology of memories of the composer from many contemporary sources. (Roger Nichols has also edited and interestingly annotated authentic texts of most of Ravel's piano music for Peters Edition.)

Orenstein, A. (ed.) *A Ravel Reader* (New York and Oxford, Columbia University Press, 1990). First published in French (see below), this comprehensively annotated collection of correspondence, articles and interviews is an invaluable source of information on the composer. Unfortunately, not all his letters are published here and, while some of those previously edited by R. Chalupt (in French; see below) are included, others are omitted.

Orenstein, A. *Ravel: Man and Musician* (New York, Dover, 1991). An updated version of a text originally published in 1968 and revised in 1975, this is a useful and commendably thorough study by a scholar and musician who has considerably amplified our knowledge of Ravel's life and music in recent years.

Roland-Manuel *Ravel* (London, Dobson, 1947). As a long-term pupil of Ravel, one of his best friends and his first biographer, Roland-Manuel still has authority in spite of his blind spots and his translator's inadequacy.

In French

Chalupt, R., and Gerar, M. *Ravel au miroir de ses lettres* (Paris, Laffont, 1956). The first published selection from Ravel's correspondence, though faulty in several respects, has the virtue of containing letters unobtainable elsewhere.

Colette (et al.) *Maurice Ravel par quelques-uns de ses familiers* (Paris, Tambourinaire, 1939). Memories of Ravel by several of his closest friends and colleagues, including Delage, Fargue, Vuillermoz and Klingsor.

Jankélévitch, V. *Ravel* (Paris, Seuil, 1995). Previously published in 1956, this short and provocative study, as newly edited and supplemented by J.-M. Nectoux, is particularly valuable for its illustrations.

Jourdan-Morhange, H. *Ravel et nous* (Geneva, Milieu du Monde, 1945). Close to Ravel as both a friend and a musician, Hélène Jourdan-Morhange has drawn an authentic and touchingly affectionate portrait of the composer and his music.

Jourdan-Morhange, H. and Perlemuter, V. *Ravel d'après Ravel* (Aix-en-Provence, Alinéa, 1989). Transcriptions of broadcast conversations with Vlado Perlemuter who studied Ravel's piano works with the composer and who recalls here the (largely technical) advice he was given (first published 1953).

Lesure, F., and Nectoux, J.-M. *Maurice Ravel* (Paris, Bibliothèque Nationale, 1975). A generally reliable and well illustrated catalogue of a Ravel exhibition presented at the Bibliothèque Nationale on the centenary of the composer's birth.

Long, M. *Au piano avec Maurice Ravel* (Paris, Billaudot, 1971). French original of Long's *At the Piano with Ravel* (see above).

Marnat, M. Maurice Ravel (Paris, Fayard, 1986). A vast, ill-organized and detailed study which contains valuable items of information among the speculations and cultural divagations.

Marnat, M. (ed.) *Ravel: Souvenirs de Manuel Rosenthal* (Paris, Hazan, 1995). Rosenthal's indispensable but unreliable memories of Ravel need more careful editing than Marnat has provided.

Narbaïtz, P. *Maurice Ravel, un orfèvre basque* (St-Jean-de-Luz, 1975). A frequently overlooked and yet unique insight into Ravel in his Basque background

Orenstein, A. (ed.) *Maurice Ravel: lettres, écrits, entretiens* (Paris, Flammarion, 1989). The French version of Orenstein's *Ravel Reader* (see above) is even more valuable to French readers in that the letters are published as Ravel wrote them, in his own style and without the intervention of (occasionally dubious) translation.

'Hommage à Maurice Ravel', *Revue Musicale*, December 1938. Dedicated to the memory of the composer a year after his death and containing a hundred more or less formal studies, commentaries, memories and homages of all kinds, this special number of a distinguished periodical is mostly still relevant today. An earlier Ravel number of the *Revue Musicale*, published on his fiftieth birthday in 1925, is less useful.

Roland-Manuel *À la gloire de Ravel* (Paris, Nouvelle Revue Critique, 1938). The French original is more convincing than the English version (see above).

Selective Discography

There are more than a hundred recordings of *Boléro* in the current catalogue and, taking both the orchestral and piano versions into account, even more of the *Pavane pour une Infante défunte*. The modest and until recently obscure piano *Prélude* is available in no fewer than twenty different versions. Clearly, in these circumstances it is impossible to prevent a reasoned and comprehensive review of the Ravel discography, work by work and recording by recording: a survey like that would fill a book at least the size of this one.

The suggestions offered here – all of them CDs – are under two main headings, historical and modern. The first lists all the recordings made by Ravel either as pianist or conductor, together with some of those made by others but supervised or explicitly approved by him; the comparatively recent recordings appended to this category – Ansermet's of *La Valse*, Monteux's of *Daphnis et Chloé*, Perlemuter's piano collections – are included because Ravel worked with those musicians in those particular areas at early stages in their careers. The CDs listed in the modern category are of three main kinds: standard recommendations like Maazel's recordings of the operas and Boulez's of the orchestral works; personal favourites like the CBSO/Rattle interpretations which I have come to know and admire in the concert hall; interesting alternatives, like Tortelier's discreet use of orchestral strings in the *Introduction and Allegro* (as authorized by the composer at one time), and thoughtful programmes like the Britten Quartet's association of the Quartet in F with Vaughan Williams in what he described as 'an attack of French fever'. Paul Crossley's recording of the complete piano music is the first to use the Urtext edition recently established by Roger Nichols.

The one area of the Ravel work list which is under-represented in the catalogue is the songs, one or two of which are still not recorded. Taken together, however, the Souzay and Fischer-Dieskau discs offer – in their very different ways – an extensive insight into Ravel's genius as a song composer.

Historical

Boléro (1)
Piano Concerto in G (2)
(1) Lamoureux Orchestra conducted by Ravel (1930), (2) Marguerite Long (piano); Symphonic Orchestra conducted by Pedro de Freitas-Branco, supervised by Ravel (1932); with works by Debussy and Fauré
PEARL GEMM CD 9927

Boléro (1)
Introduction and Allegro (2)
String Quartet in F (3)
Pavane pour une Infante défunte (4)
La Valse (5)
(1) Lamoureux Orchestra conducted by Ravel (1930), (2) ensemble conducted by Ravel (1923), (3) International String Quartet supervised by Ravel (1927), (4) Colonne Orchestra conducted by Gabriel Pierné (1929), (5) Lamoureux Orchestra conducted by Albert Wolff, approved by Ravel (1931)
MUSIC & ARTS CD 703

Gaspard de la nuit – Le Gibet (1)
Miroirs (2a) *Oiseaux tristes* (2b) *Vallée des cloches*
Pavane pour une Infante défunte (3)
Sonatine, 1st and 2nd movements (4)
Le Tombeau de Couperin – Toccata (5)
Valses nobles et sentimentales (6)
(1), (5) Robert Casadesus (piano) approved by Ravel (1922); (2a), (3) Maurice Ravel (piano) (1922); (2b) Maurice Ravel (piano)(1929); (4), (6) Maurice Ravel (piano) (1913); with other Ravel piano pieces performed by contemporaries
BELLAPHON 690–07–005

Daphnis et Chloé; suites 1 and 2 (1)
Ma Mère l'Oye, suite (2)
Shéhérazade (3)
La Valse (4)
(1) Paris Conservatoire Orchestra conducted by Charles Munch (1946), (2) National Symphony Orchestra conducted by Sidney Beer (1945) (3) Suzanne Danco (soprano); Paris Conservatoire Orchestra conducted by Ernest Ansermet (1948), (4) Paris Conservatoire Orchestra conducted by Ansermet (1947)
DUTTON CDK 1201

Daphnis et Chloé (complete)
Rapsodie espagnole
Pavane pour une Infante défunte
Chorus of the Royal Opera House; London Symphony
Orchestra conducted by Pierre Monteux
DECCA 425 956–2

Complete Piano Music (apart from *Sérénade grotesque*)
Vlado Perlemuter (piano)
NIMBUS 5005, 5011 (2 CDs)

Modern

Stage Works

Boléro
Daphnis et Chloé (complete)
City of Birmingham Symphony Orchestra and Chorus
conducted by Sir Simon Rattle
EMI CDC7 54303-2

L'Enfant et les Sortilèges
Françoise Ogéas, Jeanine Collard, Jane Berbié, Sylvaine
Gilma, Colette Herzog, Heinz Rehfuss, Camille
Maurane, Michel Sénéchal; Chorus and Children's
Voices of French Radio; French Radio National
Orchestra conducted by Lorin Maazel
DG 423 718–2GH

L'Heure espagnole
Jane Berbié, Michel Sénéchal, Jean Giraudeau, Gabriel
Bacquier, José Van Dam; Paris Opera Orchestra
conducted by Lorin Maazel
DG 423 719–2
[for *Ma Mère l'Oye*, *La Valse* and *Fanfare* see Orchestral]

Orchestral

Alborada del gracioso
Une Barque sur l'océan
Boléro
Piano Concerto in D for the left hand
Daphnis et Chloé (complete)
Fanfare pour l'Éventail de Jeanne
Menuet antique
Ma Mère l'Oye (complete ballet version)
Pavane pour une Infante défunte

Rapsodie espagnole
Shéhérazade; overture
Le Tombeau de Couperin
La Valse
Valses nobles et sentimentales
Philippe Entremont (piano); Camerata Singers
Cleveland Orchestra, New York Philharmonic
conducted by Pierre Boulez
SONY SM3K 4582 (3 CDs)

Piano Concerto in G
Piano Concerto in D for the left hand
Le Tombeau de Couperin (piano version)
Cécile Ousset (piano); City of Birmingham Symphony
Orchestra conducted by Sir Simon Rattle
EMI CDC7 54158–2

Alborada del gracioso
Fanfare (L'Éventail de Jeanne)
Ma Mère l'Oye (ballet)
Shéhérazade; songs
La Vallée des cloches (arr. Grainger)
La Valse
Maria Ewing (soprano); City of Birmingham
Symphony Orchestra conducted by Sir Simon Rattle
EMI CDC7 54204–2

Introduction and Allegro
Don Quichotte à Dulcinée
Tzigane
Stephen Roberts (baritone); Rachel Masters (harp), Yan
Pascal Tortelier (violin); Ulster Orchestra conducted by
Yan Pascal Tortelier; with orchestral works by Debussy
CHANDOS 8972

Songs

Chansons madécasses (1)
Cinq Mélodies populaires grecques (2)
Don Quichotte à Dulcinée (3)
Trois Poèmes de Stéphane Mallarmé (4)
(1) Jessye Norman (soprano), (2) & (3) José van Dam
(baritone), (4) Jill Gomez (soprano), (1) members of
Ensemble InterContemporain, (2) & (3) BBC
Symphony Orchestra, (4) members of the BBC SO
conducted by Pierre Boulez; with a work by Roussel
SONY SMK 64 107

Un Grand Sommeil noir
Deux Epigrammes de Clément Marot
Histoires naturelles
Cinq Mélodies populaires grecques
Chants populaires
Ronsard à son âme
Rêves
Don Quichotte à Dulcinée
Dietrich Fischer-Dieskau (baritone); Hartmut Höll
(piano)
ORFEO C 061–831 A

Chansons madécasses
Don Quichotte à Dulcinée
Deux Epigrammes de Clément Marot
Les Grands Vents venus d'outre-mer
Histoires naturelles
Deux Mélodies hébraïques
Cinq Mélodies populaires grecques
Sainte
Sur l'herbe
Gérard Souzay (baritone); Dalton Baldwin (piano)
PHILIPS 438 964–2PM4
[for *Shéhérazade* songs see Orchestral]

Choral

Trois Chansons
Chœur de Chambre Accentus conducted by Laurence
Equilbey; with choral works by Poulenc
PIERRE VERANY, PV 794042

Chamber/Instrumental

Pièce en forme de habanera (1)
Violin Sonata in A minor (2)
Violin Sonata in G (3)
Violin and Cello Sonata (4)
Tzigane (5)
(1), (2) & (4) Josef Suk, (3) & (5) David Oistrakh
(violin), (4) André Navarra (cello), (1) & (2) Josef Hála
(piano), (3) Frida Bauer (piano), (5) Vladimir
Yampolsky (piano)
PRAGA PR 254016

String Quartet in F
Britten Quartet; with works by Vaughan Williams
EMI CDC7 54346–2

Trio, for violin, cello and piano
Joshua Bell (violin), Steven Isserlis (cello), Jean-Yves
Thibaudet (piano); with Chausson's Concert
DECCA 425 860–2
[for *Introduction and Allegro* see Historical & Orchestral]

Piano

Complete Works for Solo Piano (with *Habanera*)
Paul Crossley
SONY SRCR 1593–4 (2CDs)

Ma Mère l'Oye (piano duet)
Katia and Marielle Labèque; with works by Bizet and
Fauré
PHILIPS 420 159–2

Entre Cloches
Frontispice
Introduction and Allegro (two-piano version)
Rapsodie espagnole (two-piano version)
Shéhérazade, overture (two-piano version)
La Valse (two-piano version)
Stephen Coombs and Christopher Scott
GAMUT CD 517

Arrangements of Works by Other Composers

Chabrier: *Menuet pompeux*
Debussy: *Danse, Sarabande*
Mussorgsky: *Pictures at an Exhibition*
Schumann: *Carnaval*
Orchestre National de Lyon conducted by Emmanuel
Krivine
DENON CO–78929

Index

Photographic Acknowledgements

Bridgeman Art Library,
    London: 85
Bibliothèque Nationale, Paris: 13,
    14, 17, 31, 61, 70, 94, 96, 98,
    123, 129, 144–5, 147, 157, 159,
    162, 166, 182, 191, 202, 206, 210,
    212, 214, 216
Jean-Loup Charmet, Paris: 2, 19,
    25, 27, 47, 53, 93, 99, 171
Generalitat de Catalunya,
    Barcelona/Bridgeman Art
    Library: 39
Hulton Getty, London: 22, 51, 140,
    167, 198
Kunst Historisches Museum,
    Vienna: 59
The Lebrecht Collection: 26, 29,
    37, 63, 65, 81, 83, 91, 105, 112,
    127, 129, 136, 153, 155, 172,
    175, 200
Mary Evans Picture Library,
    London: 37, 44, 67, 77, 111, 115,
    118, 129, 133, 148
Musée d'Art Moderne, Paris: 68,
    106
Roger-Viollet Collection, Paris: 9,
    19, 43, 49, 55, 56, 64, 66, 73, 92,
    97, 108, 112, 185, 194, 204